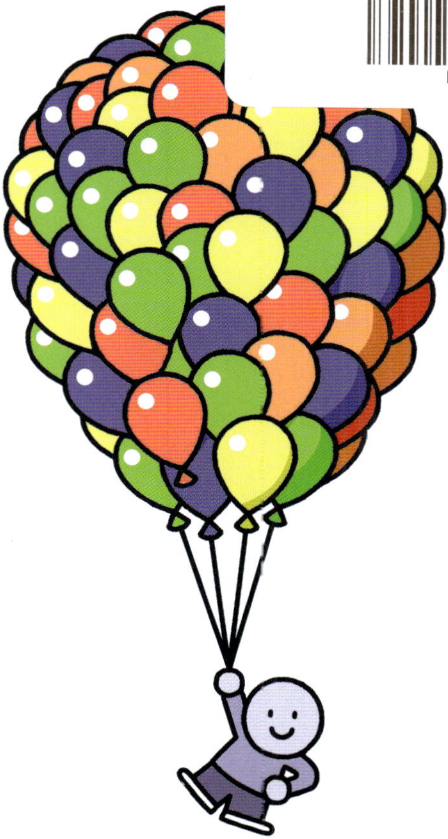

How Not to Get into Heaven

How Not to Get into Heaven © 2021 by Ben Zaehringer. All rights reserved. Printed in China. No part of this book may be used or reproduced in any manner whatsoever without written permission except in the case of reprints in the context of reviews.

Andrews McMeel Publishing
a division of Andrews McMeel Universal
1130 Walnut Street, Kansas City, Missouri 64106

www.andrewsmcmeel.com

21 22 23 24 25 TEN 10 9 8 7 6 5 4 3 2 1

ISBN: 978-1-5248-6983-0

Library of Congress Control Number: 2021937224

Editor: Lucas Wetzel
Art Director: Spencer Williams
Production Editor: Amy Strassner
Production Manager: Tamara Haus

ATTENTION: SCHOOLS AND BUSINESSES
Andrews McMeel books are available at quantity discounts with bulk purchase for educational, business, or sales promotional use. For information, please e-mail the Andrews McMeel Publishing Special Sales Department: specialsales@amuniversal.com.

How Not to Get into Heaven

Berkeley Mews Comics

Ben Zaehringer

Andrews McMeel
PUBLISHING®

For Edith

How Not to . . .

Defuse a Bomb 8
Release Tension 9
Slow Clap 10
Steal the Jewels 11
Worship Idols 12
Upset a Clown 13
Beware of Dog 14
Hunt a Vampire 15
Land on the Moon 16
Run an Ant Farm 17
Delay Gratification 18
Fertilize an Egg 19
Fix the VCR 20
Feed the Squirrels 21
Get into Heaven 22
Fall in Love 24
Run for Office 25
Initiate Contact 26
Keep a Diary 27
Make Progress 28
Win a Spelling Bee 29
Date a Dog Person 30
Outsource Homework 31
Live the Disney Life 32
Deliver the Mail 33
Say Your Last Goodbyes 34
Speak French 35
Give Flowers 36
Keep an Advent Calendar 37
Poop 38
Avoid Distractions 39
Tour the Chocolate Factory ... 40

Pass an Eye Exam 41
Play Russian Roulette 42
Go to the Ball 43
Say Your Prayers 44
Leave a Rose Petal Trail 45
Buy a Used Car 46
Walk the Dog 47
Overcome Paranoia 48
High-Five God 49
Flush 50
Do Time 51
Scream in Space 52
Crush Someone 53
Control Pests 54
Win a Science Fair 55
Believe in Yourself 56
Do Magic Tricks 57
Save a Castaway 58
Return a Crush 59
Play with Legos 60
Be Convicted 61
Inspire Your Child 62
Post a Warning 63
Have the Talk 64
Draw First 65
Win a Duel 66
Cheer Up a Clown 67
Take a Survey 68
Play Internet 69
Inflate a Blimp 70
Greet the Earthlings 72
Spoil a Film 73

Free the Big Cats 74	Hit the Target 99
Hire Movers 75	Marry a Mermaid 100
Conduct an Orchestra 76	Deliver Presents 101
Come in Peace 77	Cheer Up a Kid 102
Abduct a Cow 78	Breakdance 104
Visit the Future 79	Vote 105
Compliment the Chef 80	Kiss a Frog 106
Make a Budget 81	Shop for Superman 107
Solve a Rubik's Cube 82	Ask for Guidance 108
Prostheticize 83	Get Caught 109
Be an Autodidact 84	Play Nietzschémon 110
Get Abducted 85	Tie Knots 111
Steal a Ship 86	Make Man in Your Image 112
Call Your Parents 87	Break Up 113
Serve Zombies 88	Visit the Doc 114
egasseM a evaeL 89	Make a Chart 115
Open a Present 90	Get Your Wish 116
Invent the Wheel 91	Fulfill Your Dreams 117
Face Your Father 92	Time Travel 118
Explore the Multiverse 93	Be Funny 119
Find the Real Dave 94	Quench Your Thirst 120
Scratch and Win 95	Save Christmas 121
Keep Secrets 96	Avoid Paying Rent 126
Be Embarrassed 97	Say Goodbye 128
Commit Regicide 98	

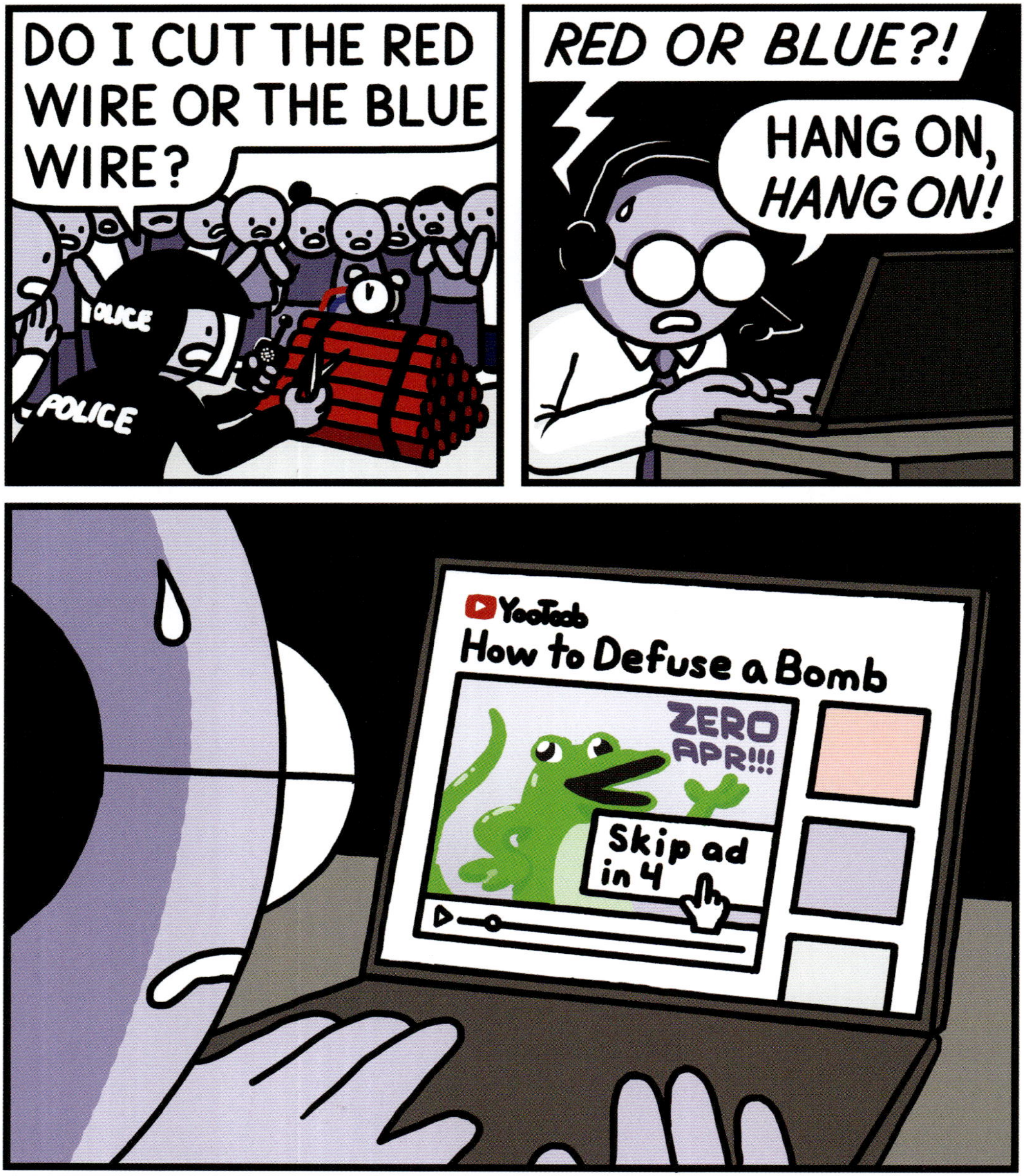
DO I CUT THE RED WIRE OR THE BLUE WIRE?
POLICE
POLICE
RED OR BLUE?!
HANG ON, HANG ON!
YooToob
How to Defuse a Bomb
ZERO APR!!!
Skip ad in 4

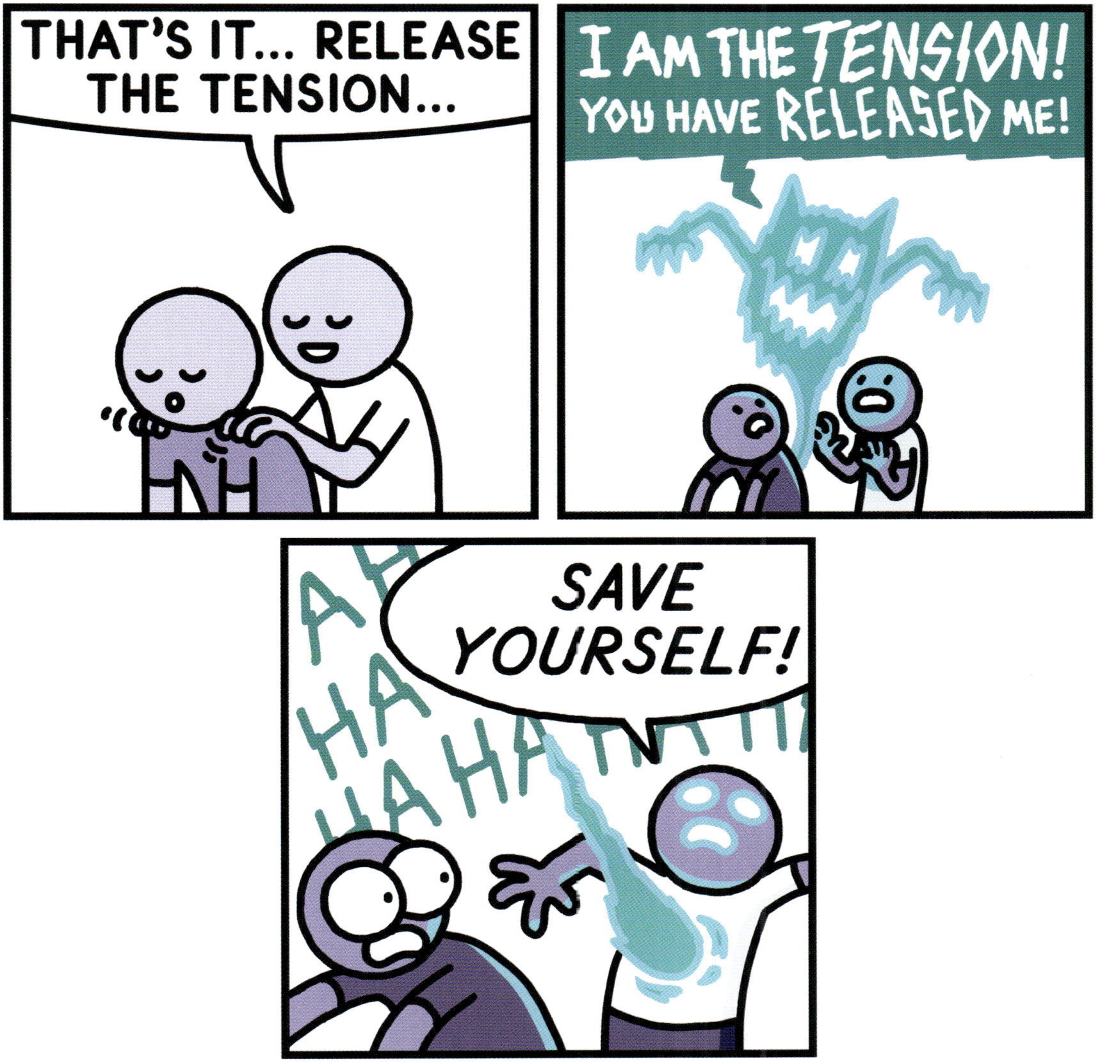
THAT'S IT... RELEASE THE TENSION...
I AM THE TENSION! YOU HAVE RELEASED ME!
SAVE YOURSELF!

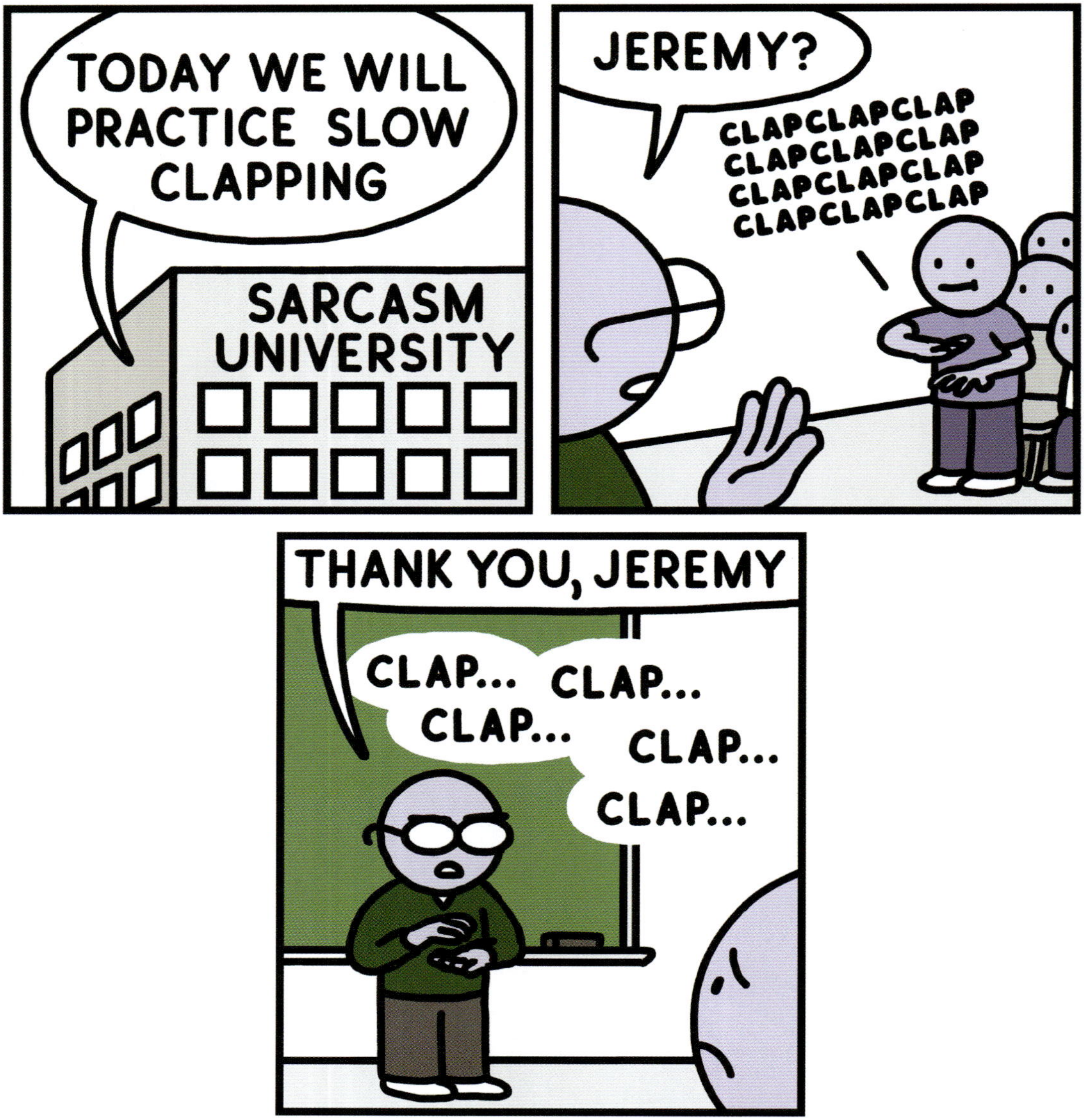
TODAY WE WILL PRACTICE SLOW CLAPPING
SARCASM UNIVERSITY
JEREMY?
CLAPCLAPCLAP CLAPCLAPCLAP CLAPCLAPCLAP CLAPCLAPCLAP
THANK YOU, JEREMY
CLAP... CLAP... CLAP... CLAP... CLAP...

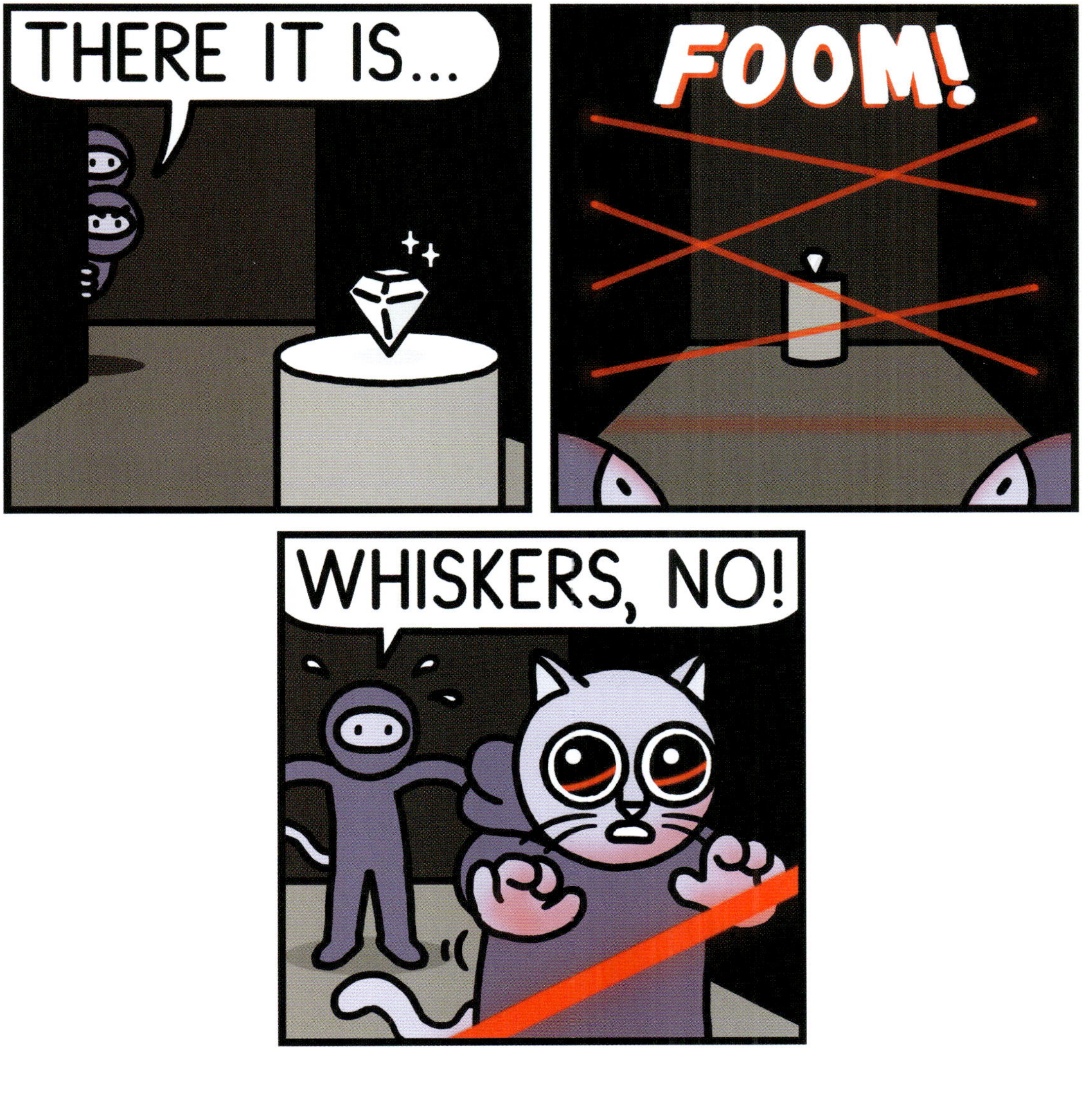
THERE IT IS...
FOOM!
WHISKERS, NO!

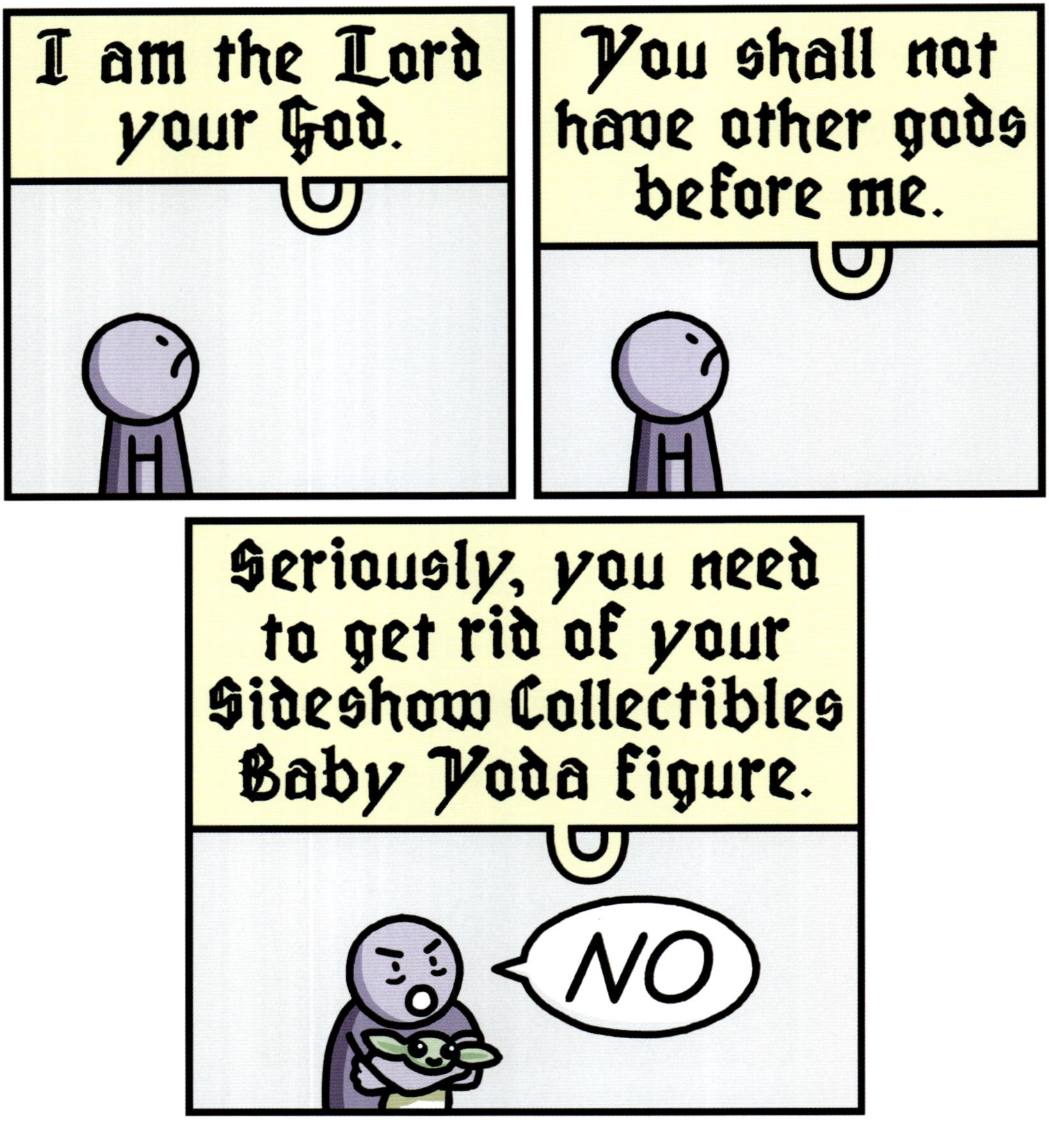
I am the Lord your God.
You shall not have other gods before me.
Seriously, you need to get rid of your Sideshow Collectibles Baby Yoda figure.
NO

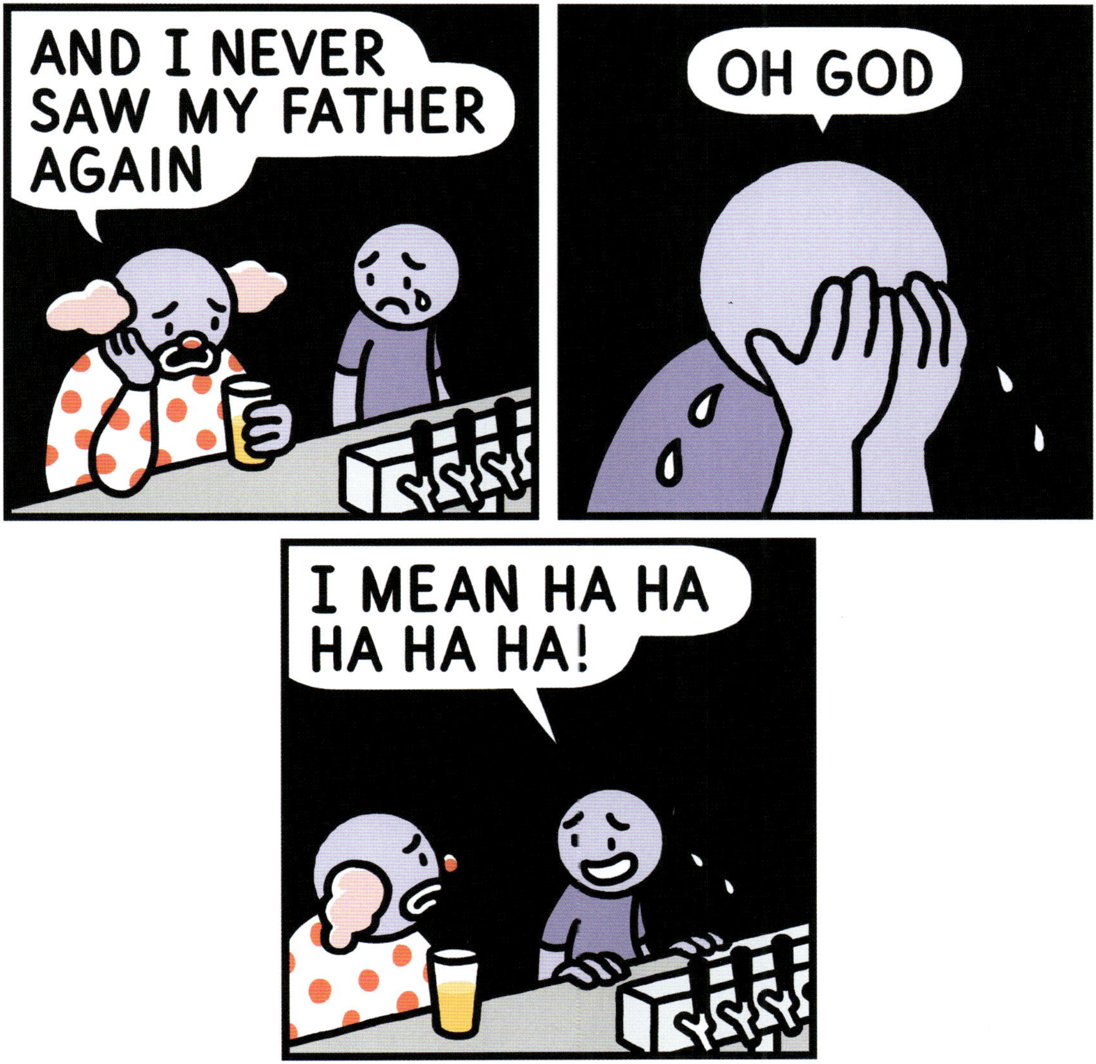
AND I NEVER SAW MY FATHER AGAIN
OH GOD
I MEAN HA HA HA HA HA!

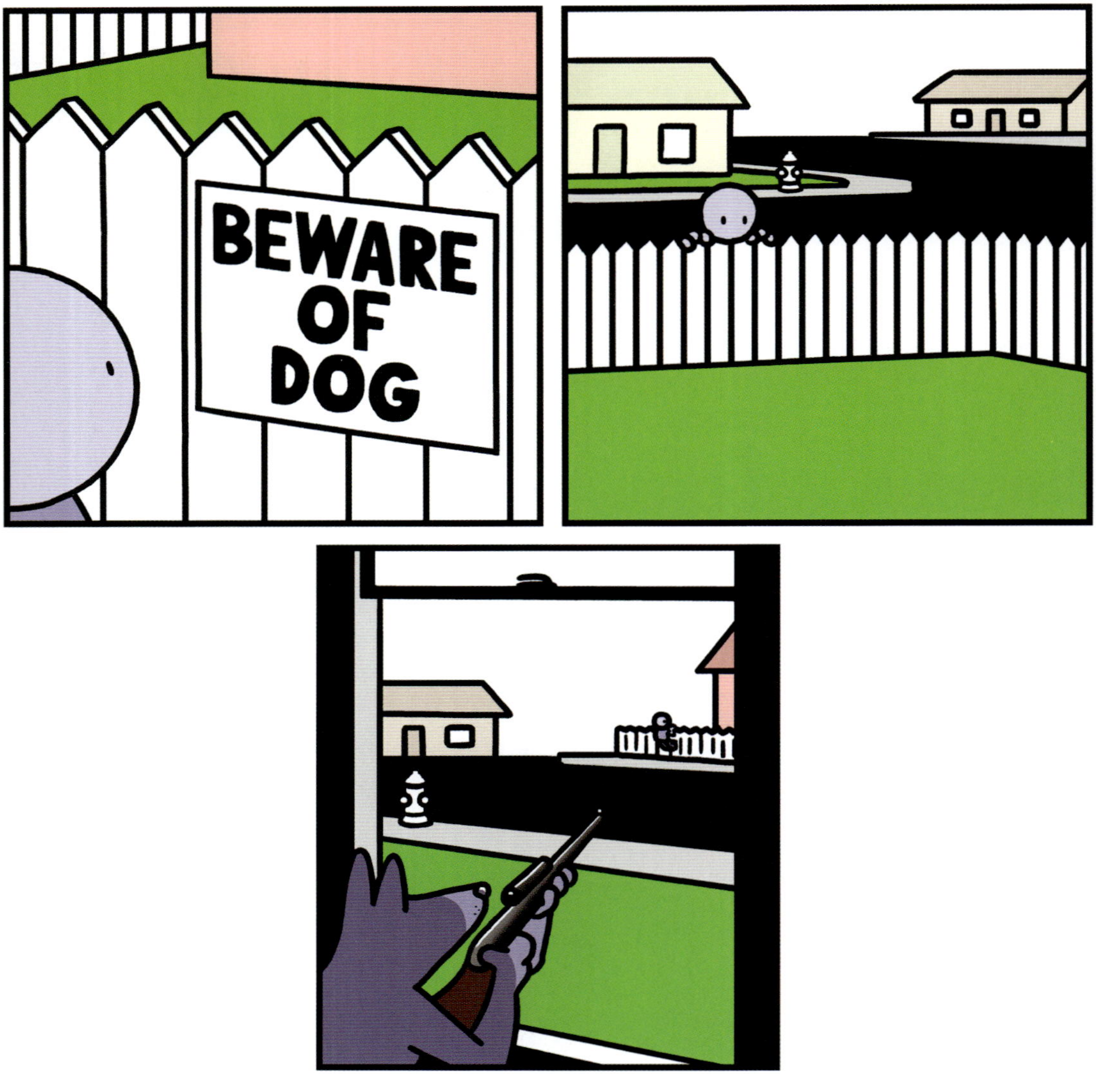
BEWARE OF DOG

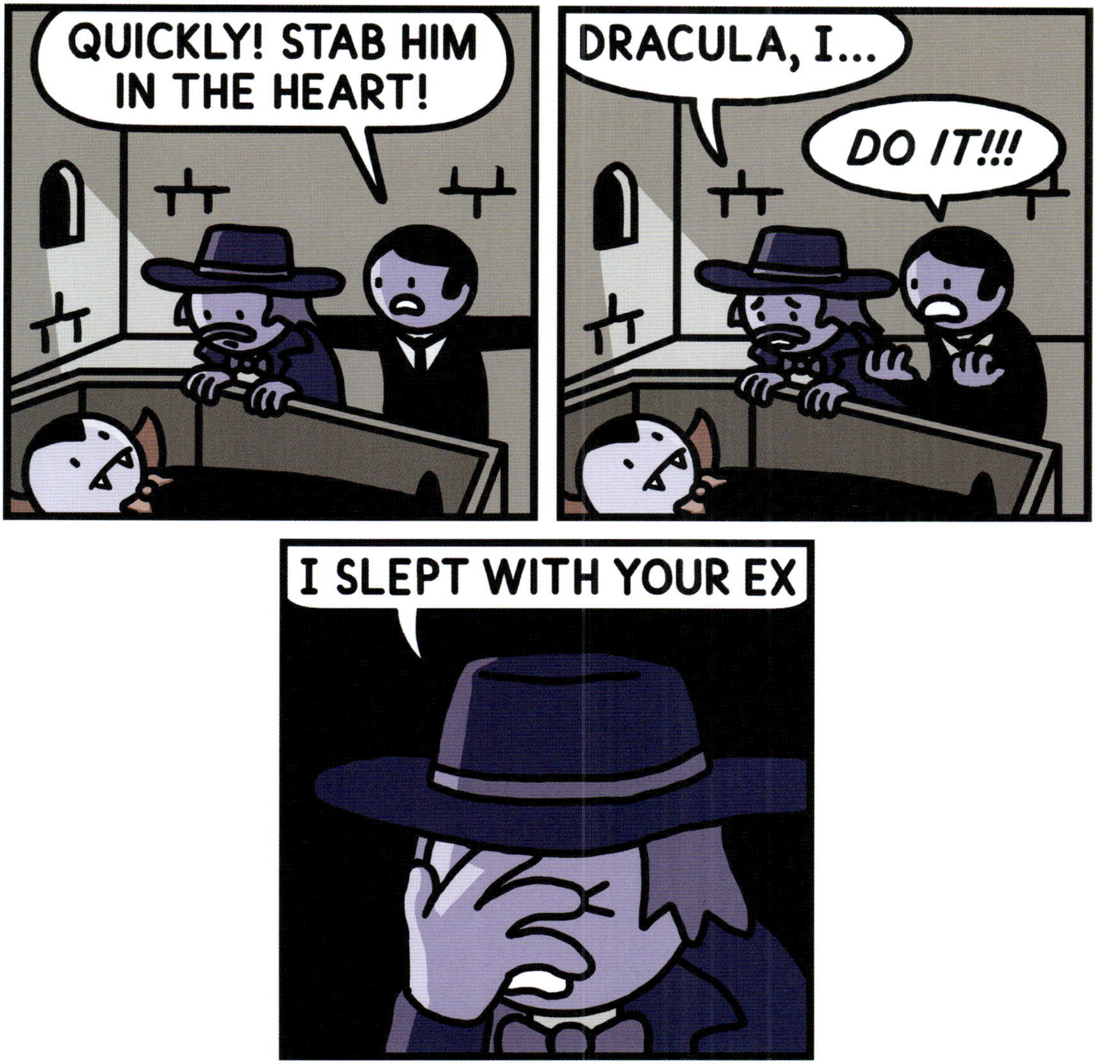
QUICKLY! STAB HIM IN THE HEART!
DRACULA, I...
DO IT!!!
I SLEPT WITH YOUR EX

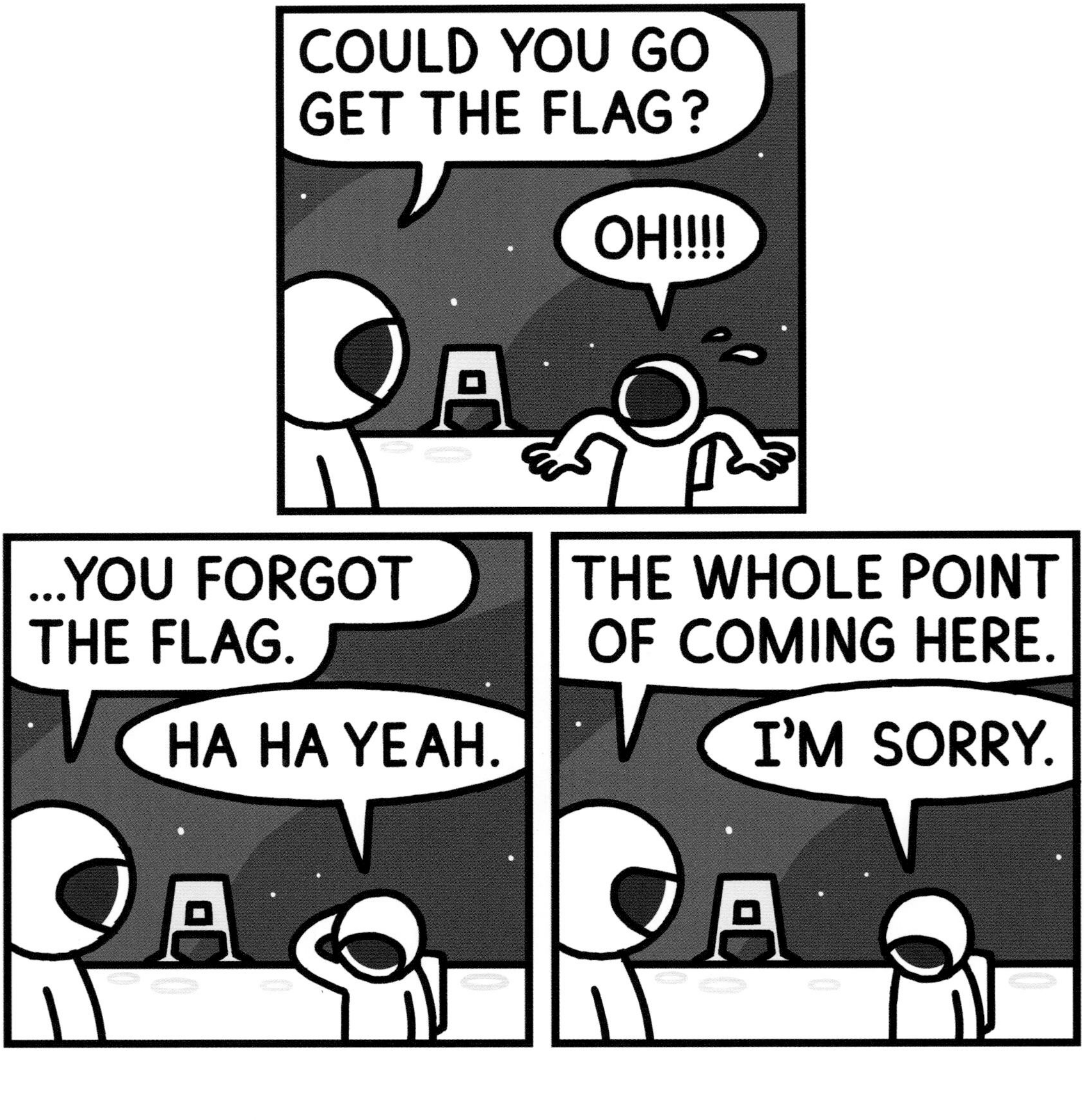
COULD YOU GO GET THE FLAG?
OH!!!!
...YOU FORGOT THE FLAG.
HA HA YEAH.
THE WHOLE POINT OF COMING HERE.
I'M SORRY.

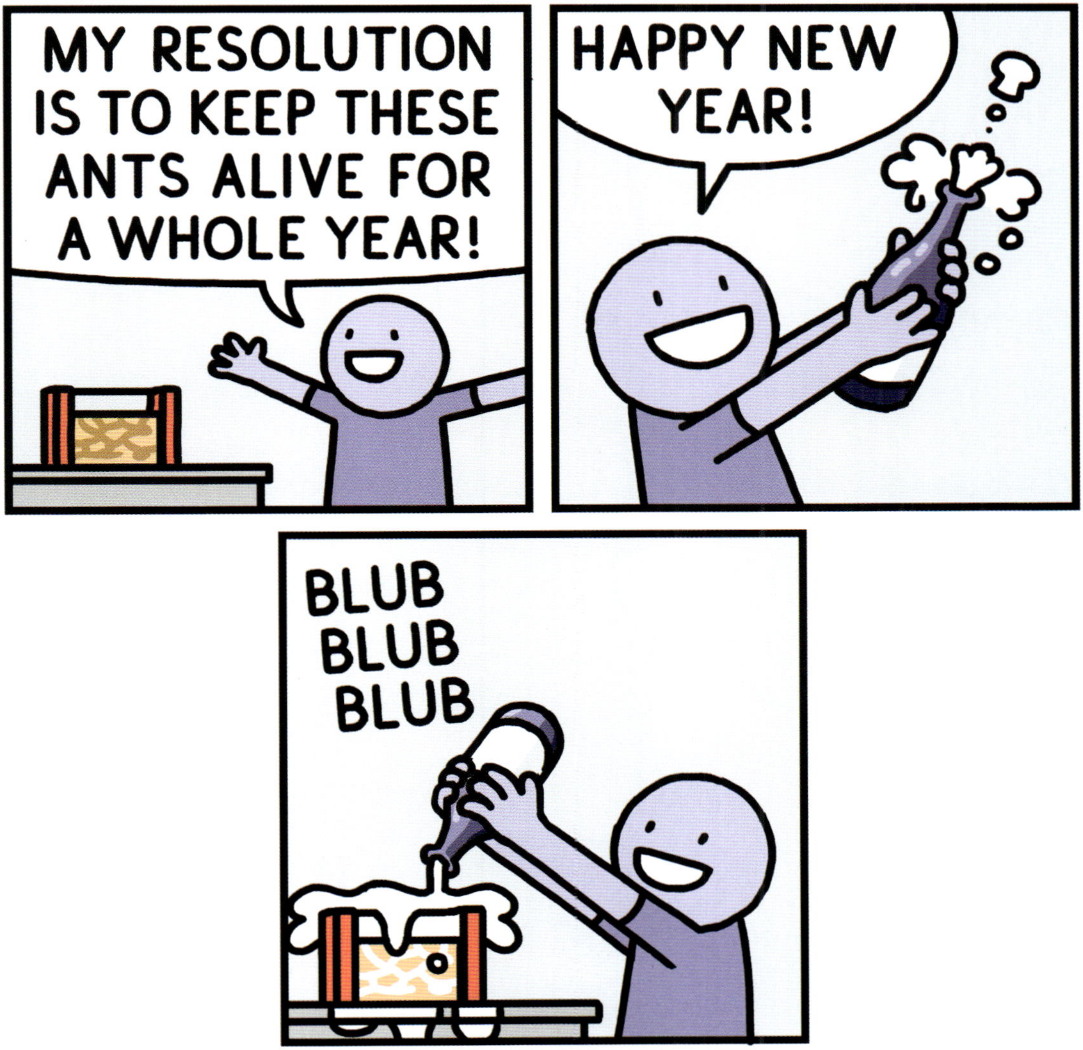
MY RESOLUTION IS TO KEEP THESE ANTS ALIVE FOR A WHOLE YEAR!
HAPPY NEW YEAR!
BLUB BLUB BLUB

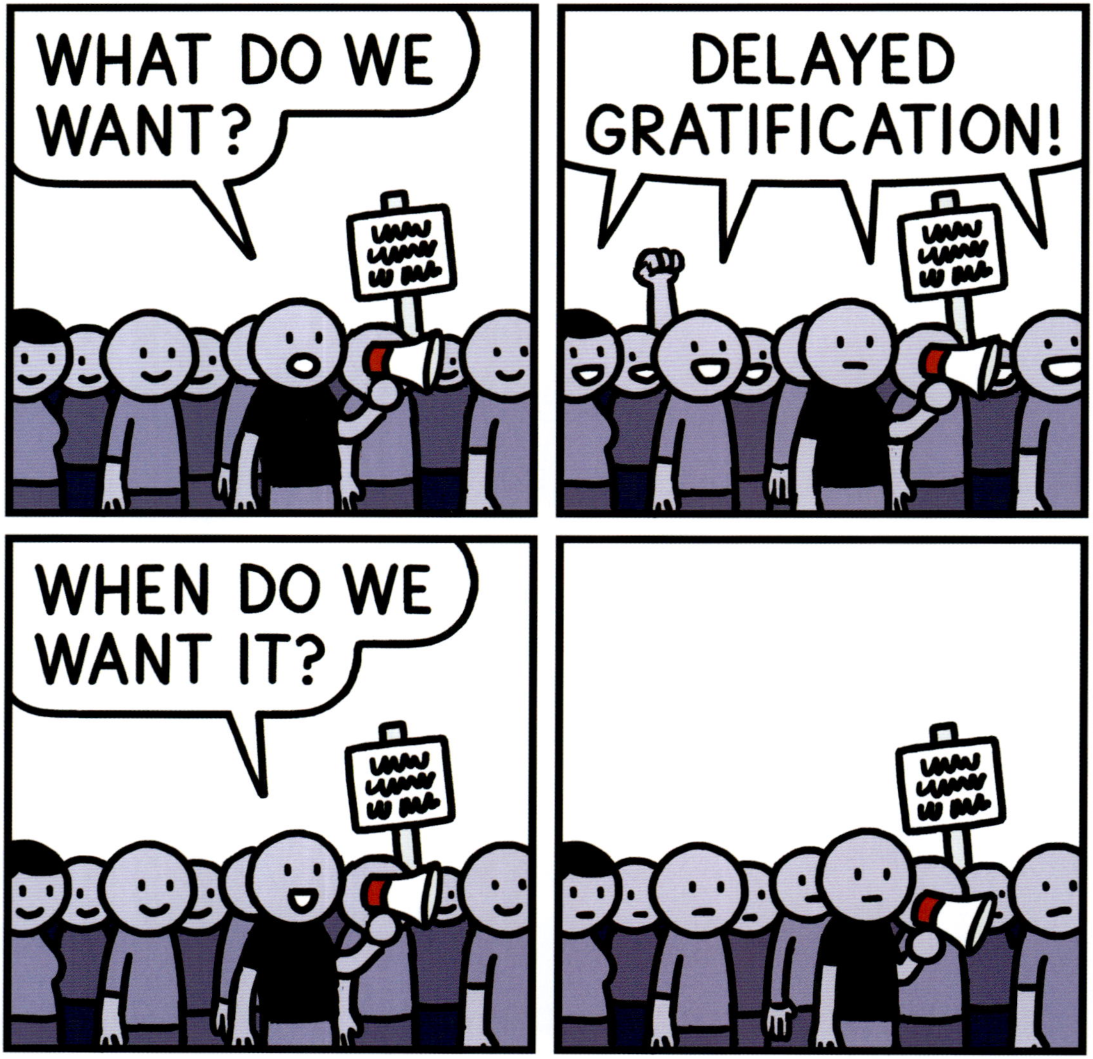
WHAT DO WE WANT?
DELAYED GRATIFICATION!
WHEN DO WE WANT IT?

LET'S GO SOMEWHERE ELSE

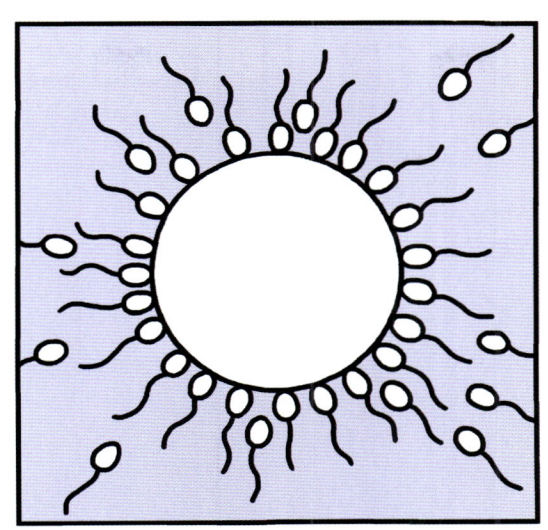

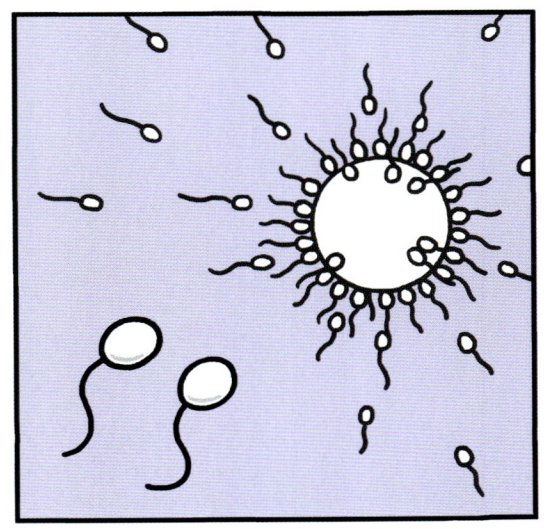

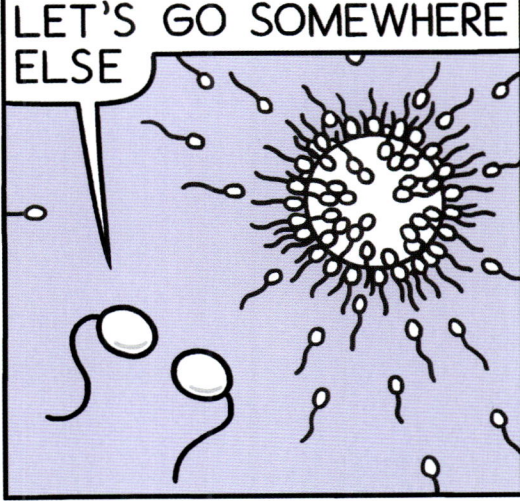

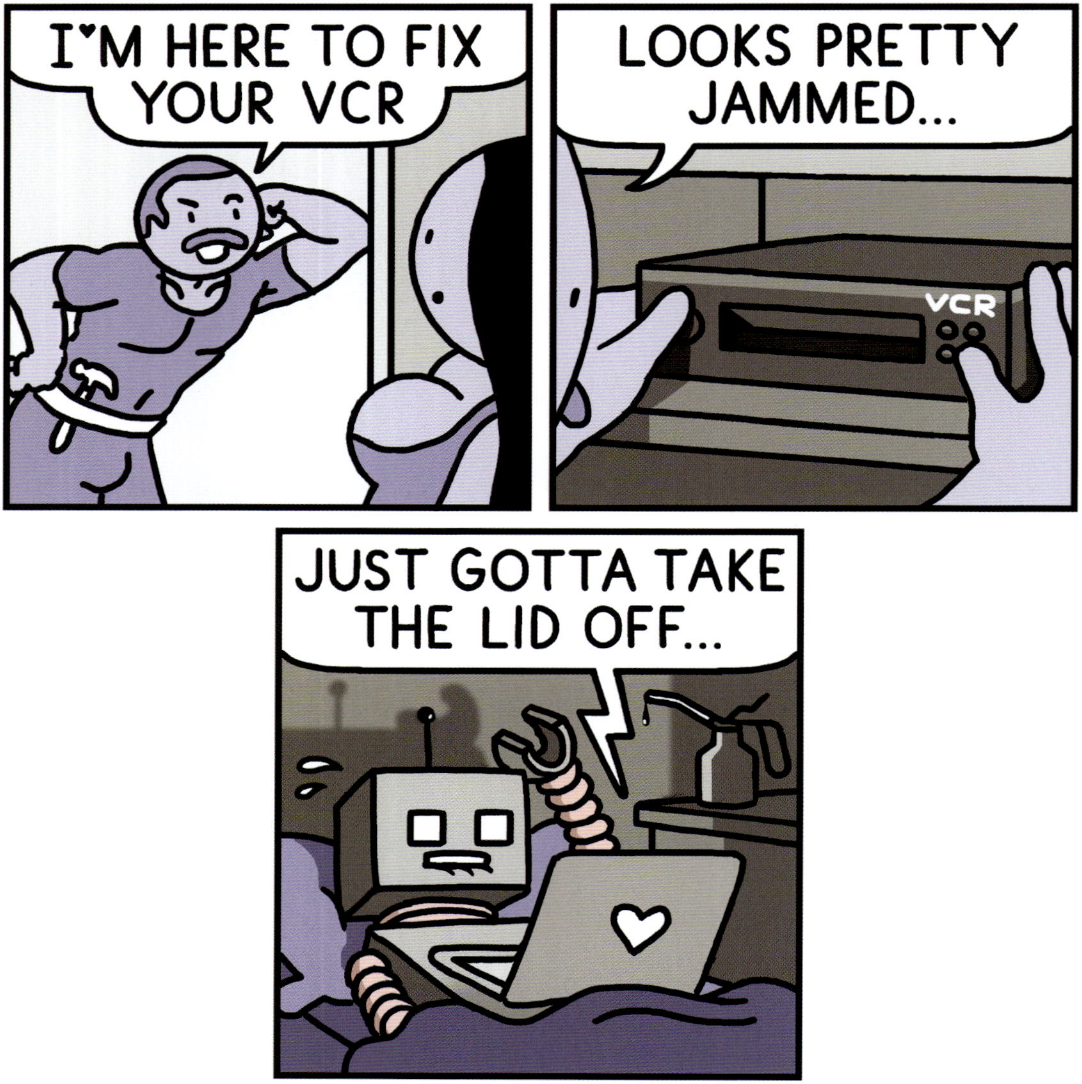
I'M HERE TO FIX YOUR VCR
LOOKS PRETTY JAMMED...
VCR
JUST GOTTA TAKE THE LID OFF...

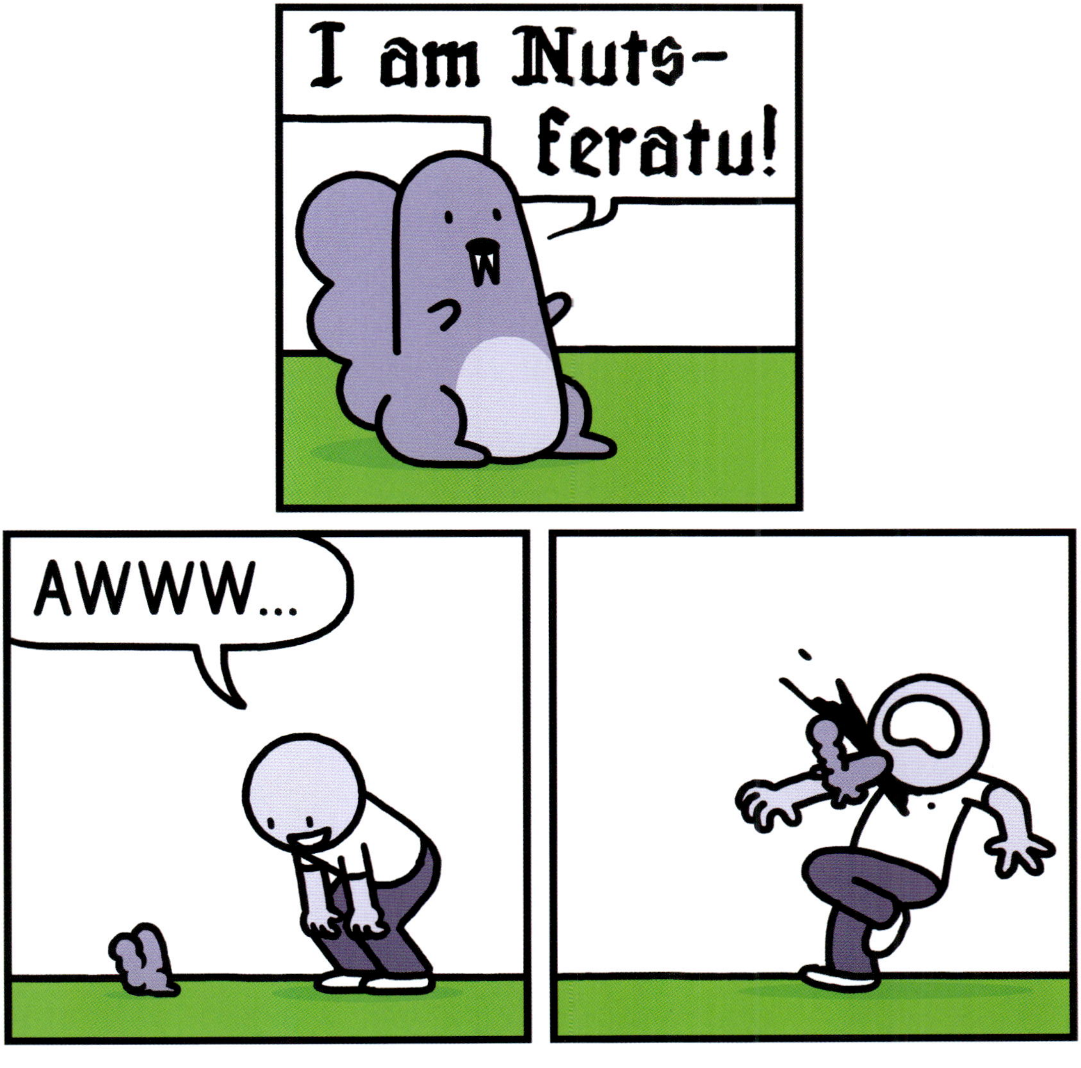
I am Nuts-
feratu!
AWWW...

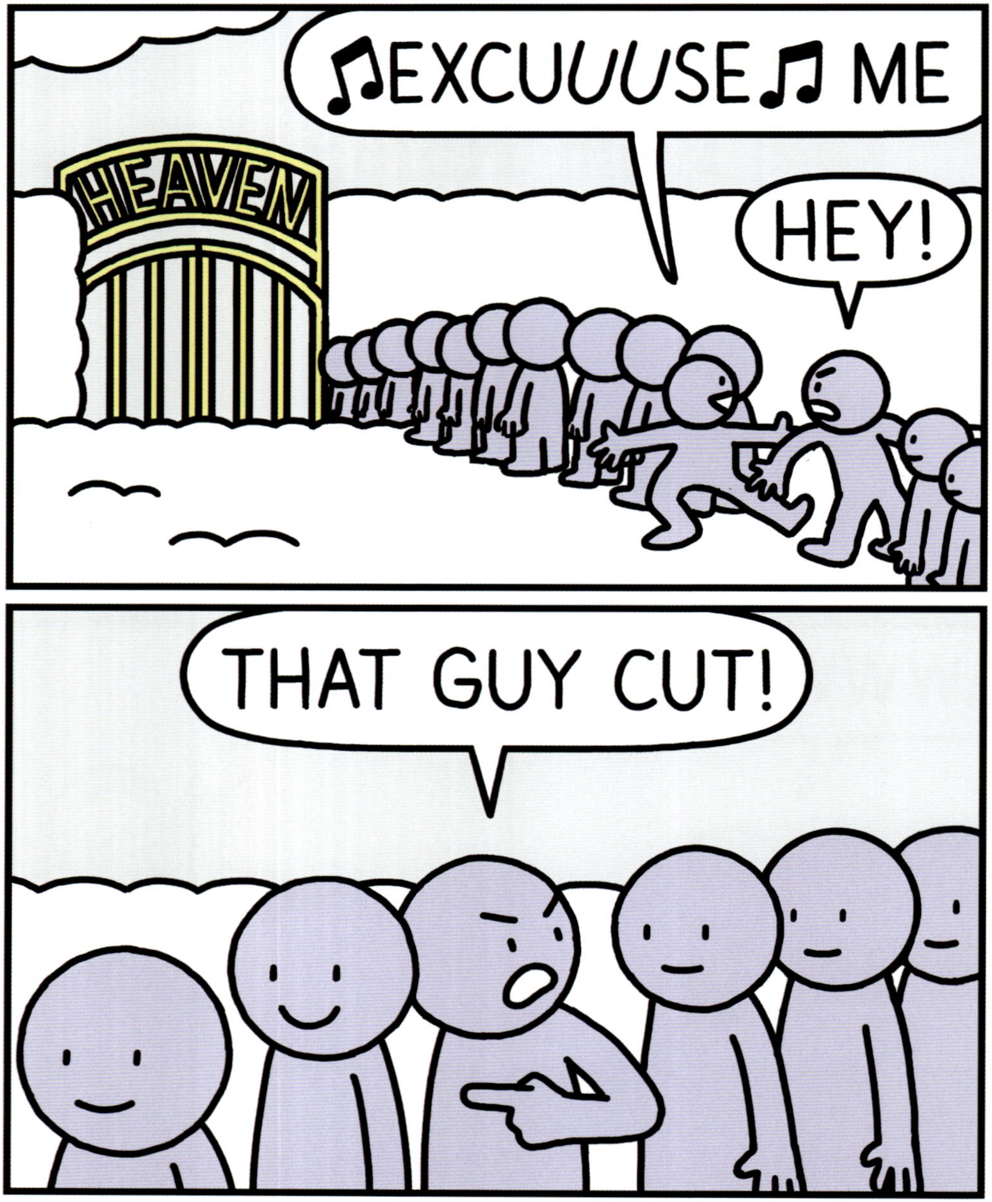
♫EXCUUUSE♫ ME
HEAVEN
HEY!
THAT GUY CUT!

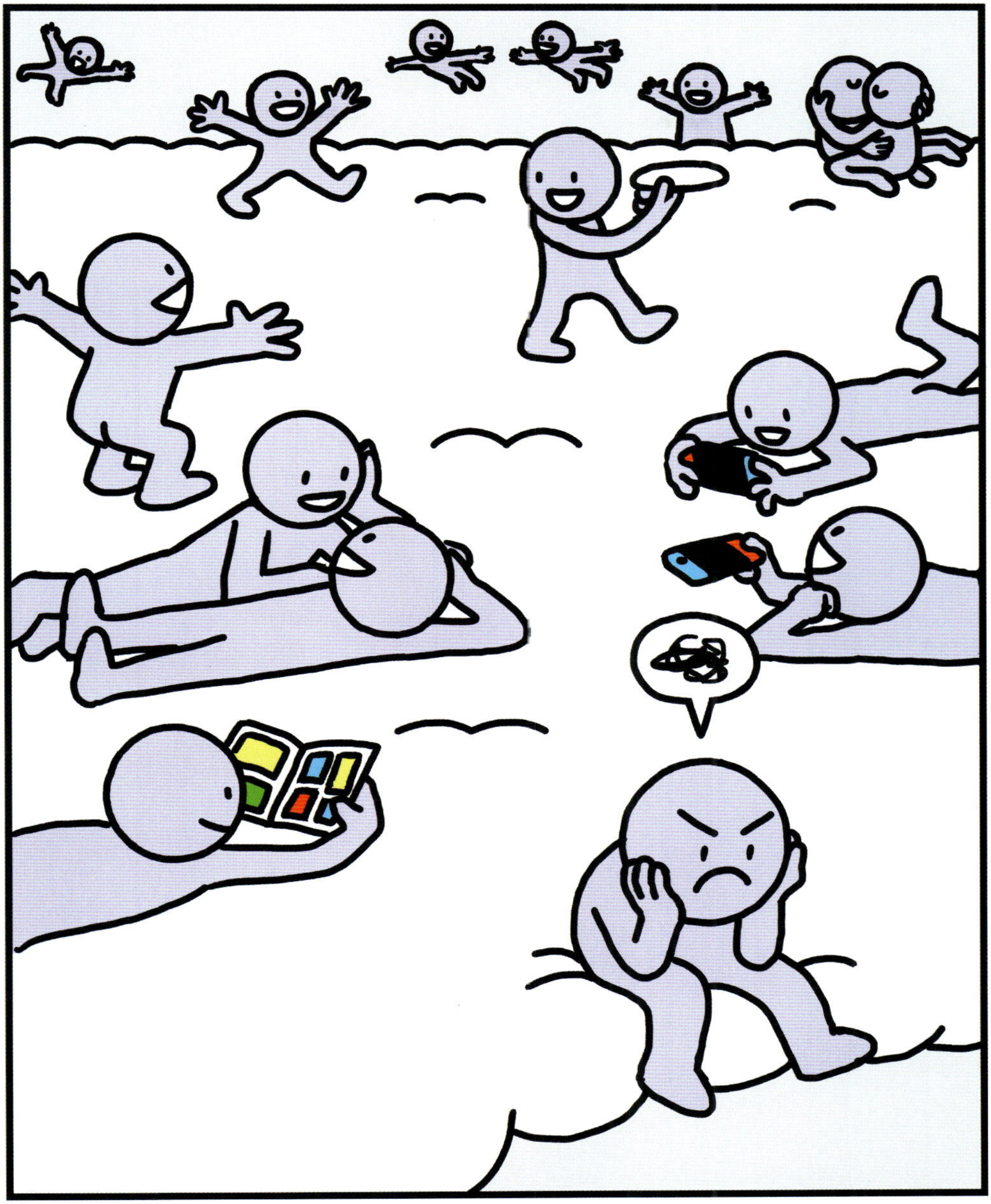

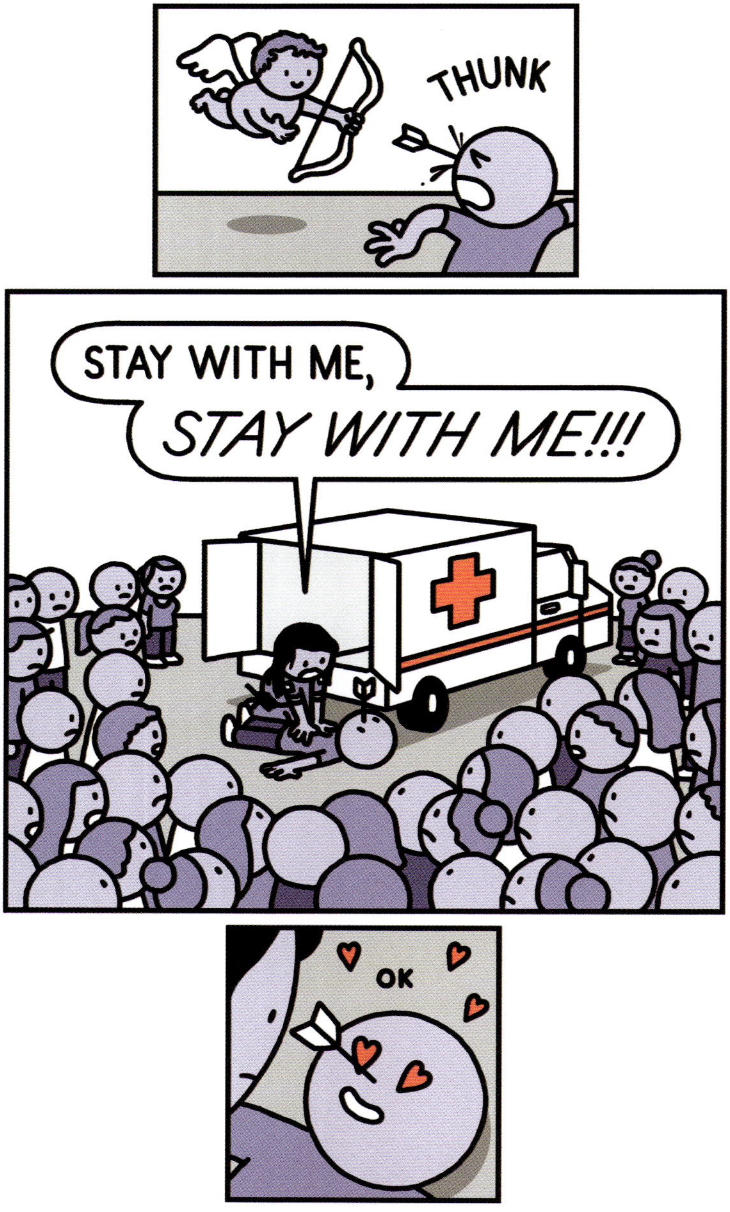
THUNK
STAY WITH ME,
STAY WITH ME!!!
OK

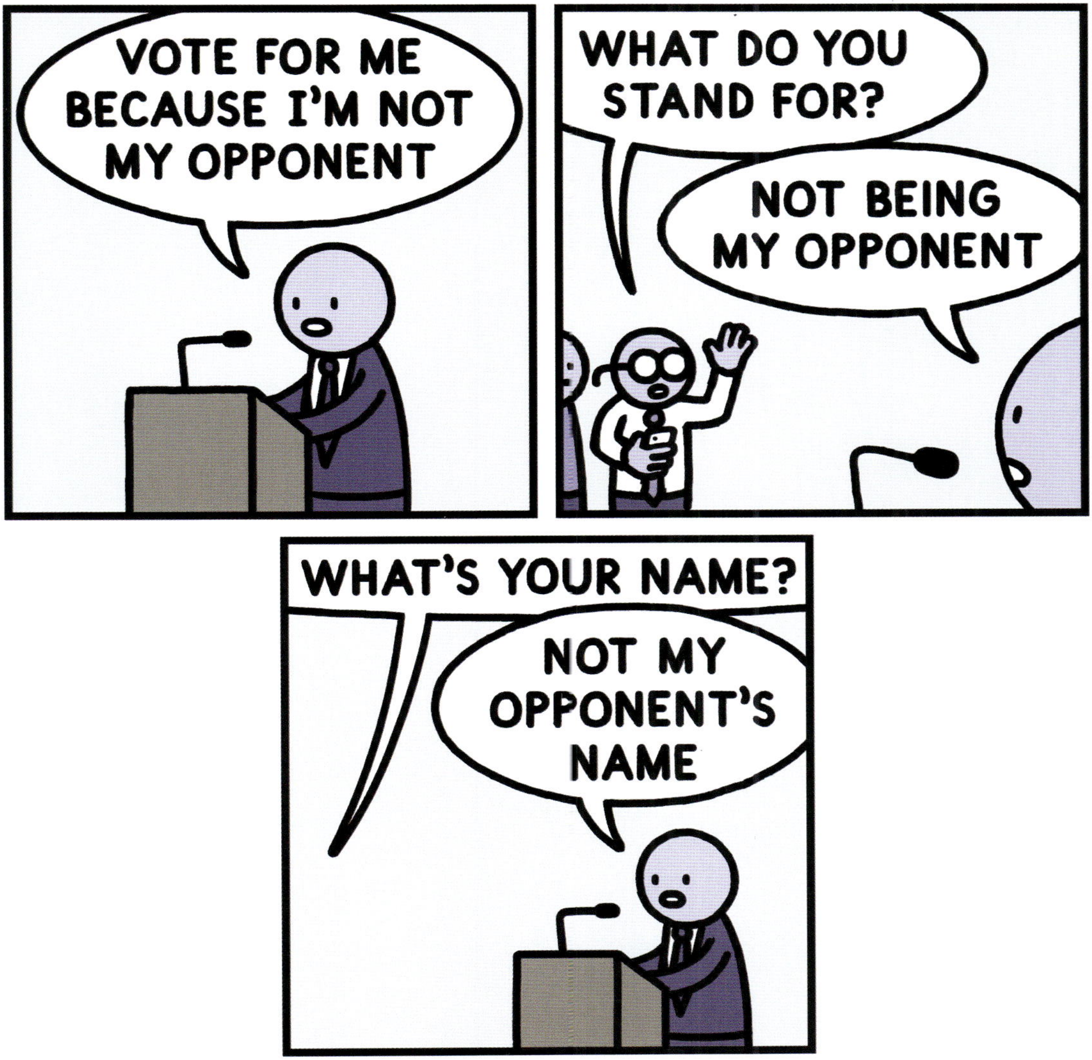
VOTE FOR ME BECAUSE I'M NOT MY OPPONENT
WHAT DO YOU STAND FOR?
NOT BEING MY OPPONENT
WHAT'S YOUR NAME?
NOT MY OPPONENT'S NAME

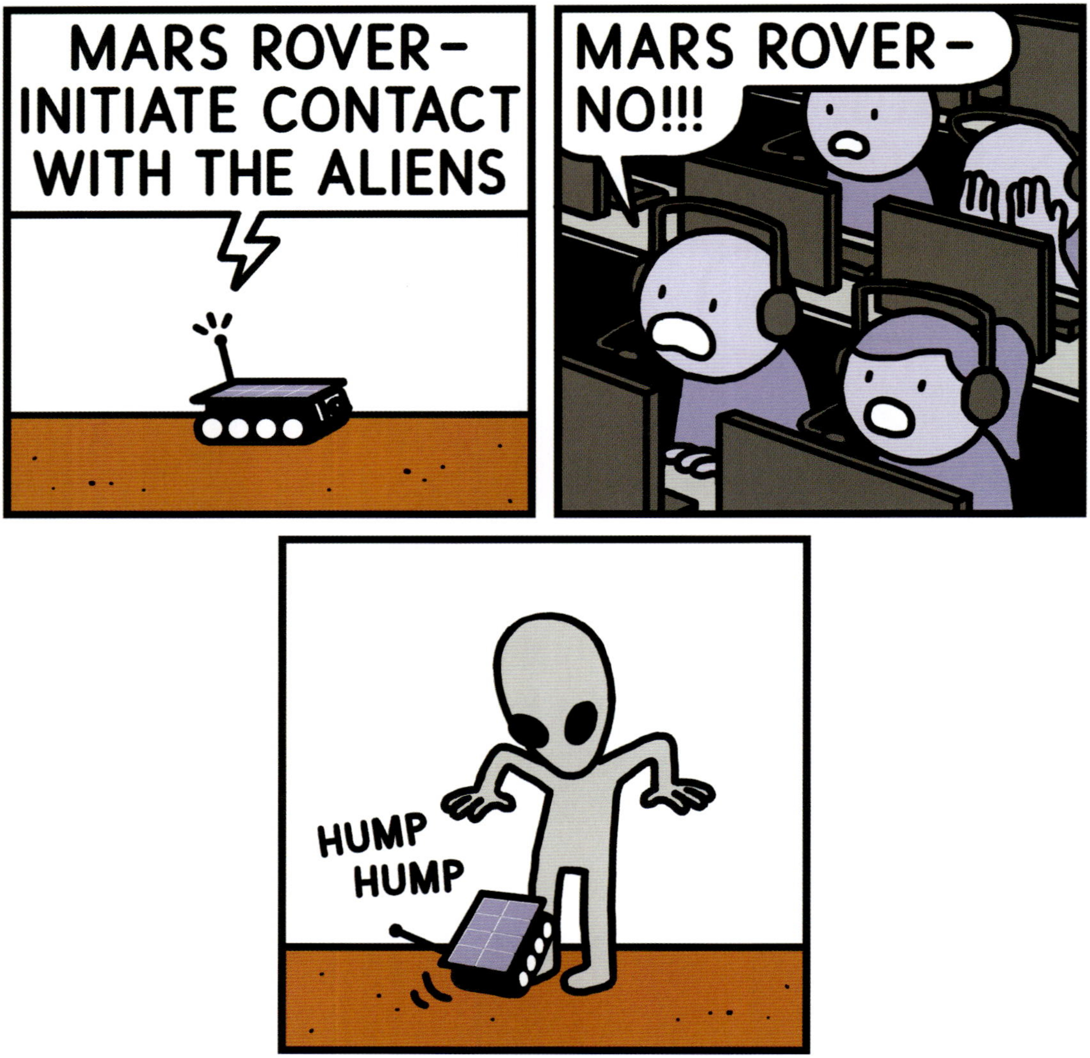
MARS ROVER- INITIATE CONTACT WITH THE ALIENS
MARS ROVER- NO!!!
HUMP HUMP

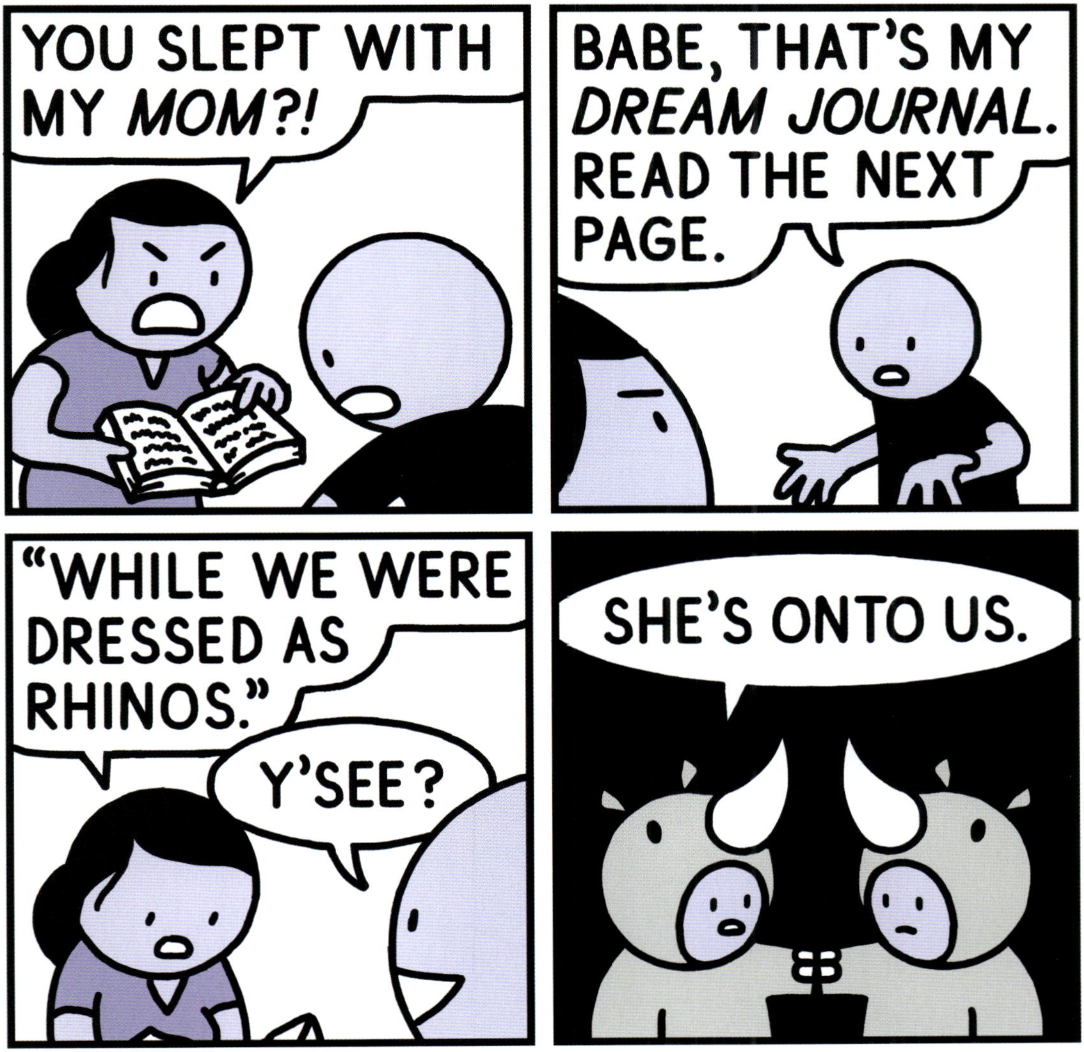
YOU SLEPT WITH MY *MOM*?!
BABE, THAT'S MY *DREAM JOURNAL*. READ THE NEXT PAGE.
"WHILE WE WERE DRESSED AS RHINOS."
Y'SEE?
SHE'S ONTO US.

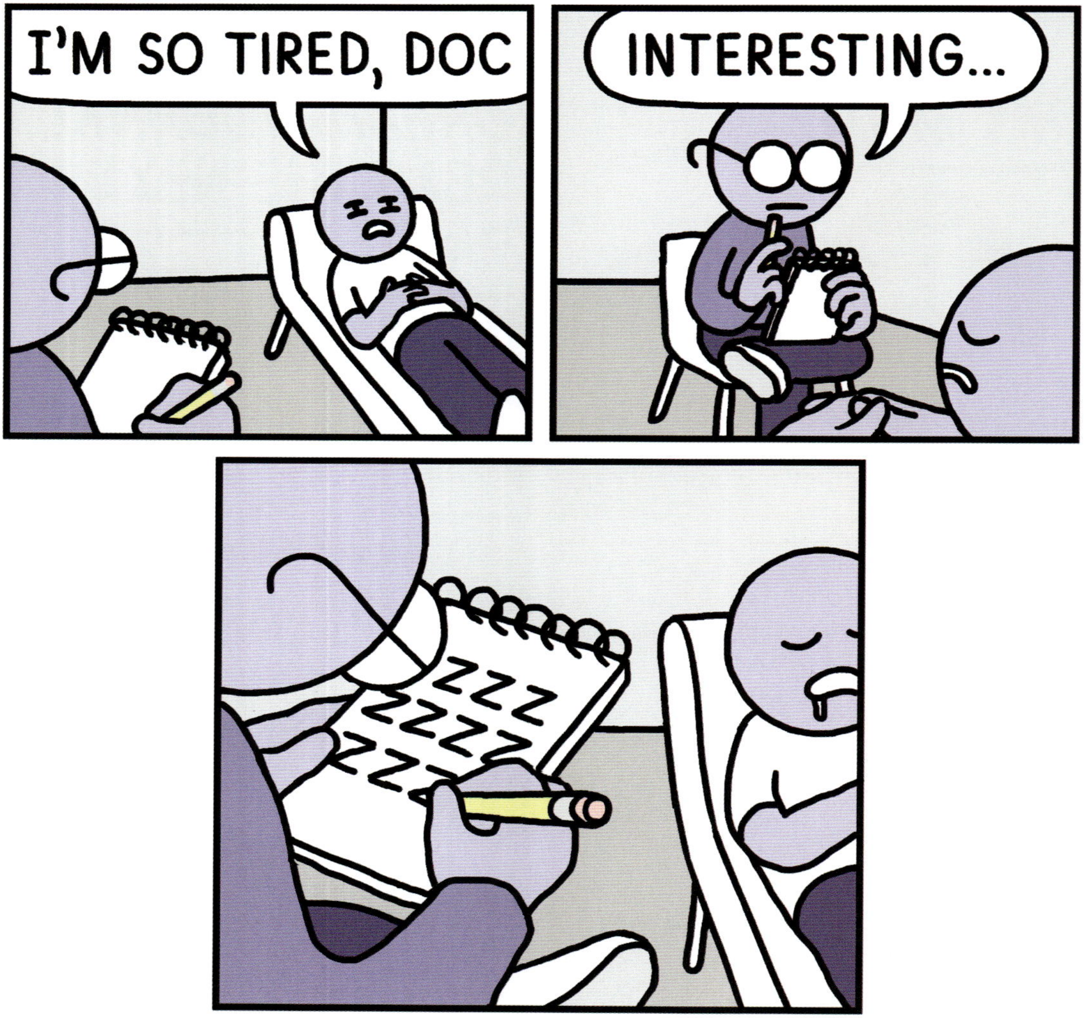
I'M SO TIRED, DOC
INTERESTING...

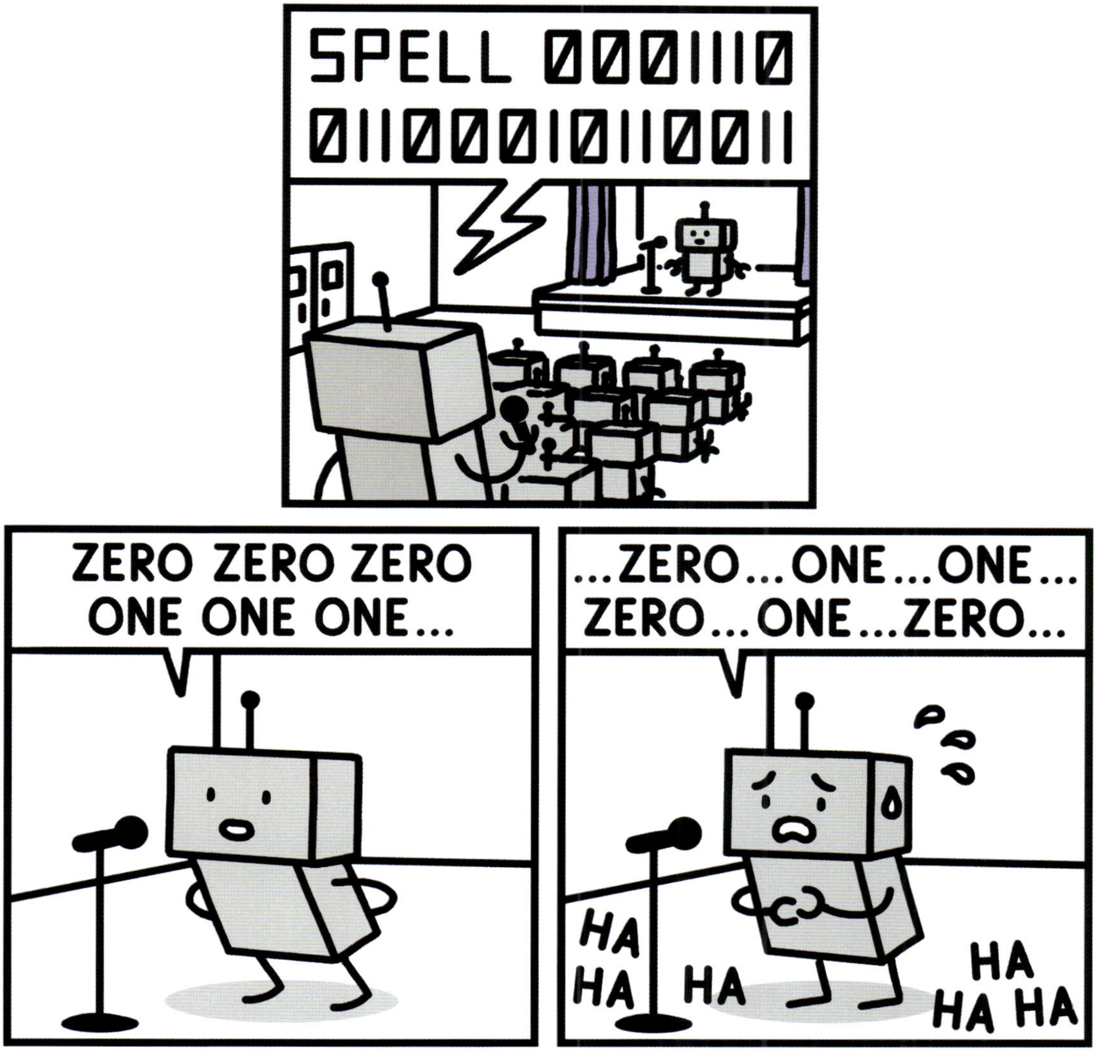
SPELL 0001110
01100010110011
ZERO ZERO ZERO
ONE ONE ONE...
...ZERO...ONE...ONE...
ZERO...ONE...ZERO...
HA HA
HA
HA HA HA

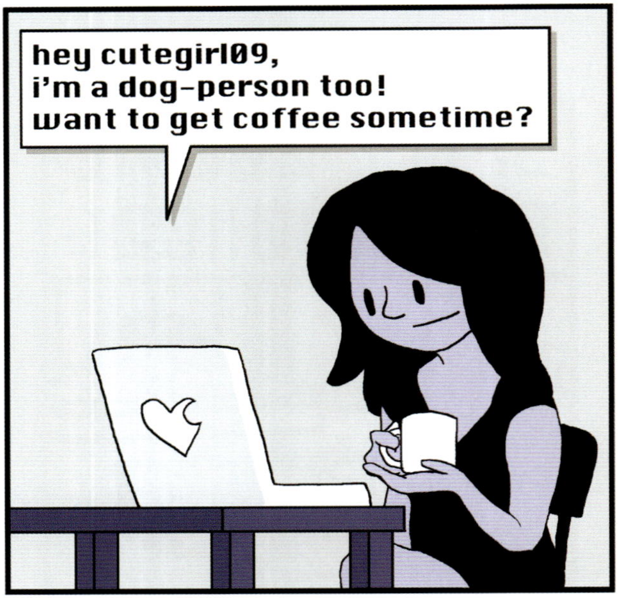
hey cutegirl09,
i'm a dog-person too!
want to get coffee sometime?

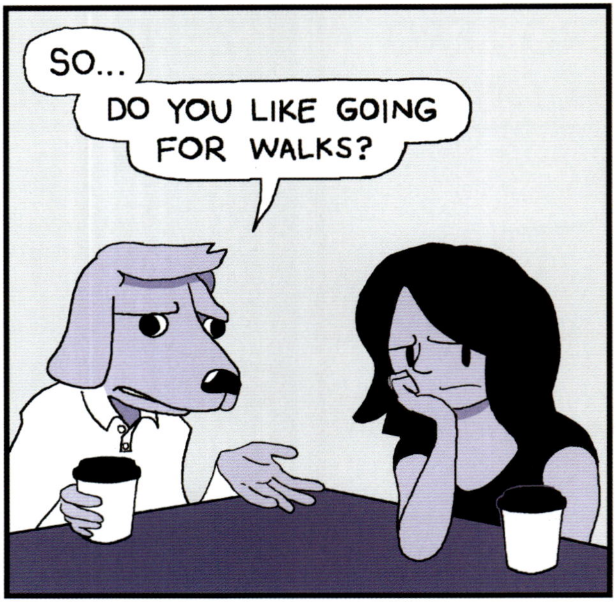
SO...
DO YOU LIKE GOING FOR WALKS?

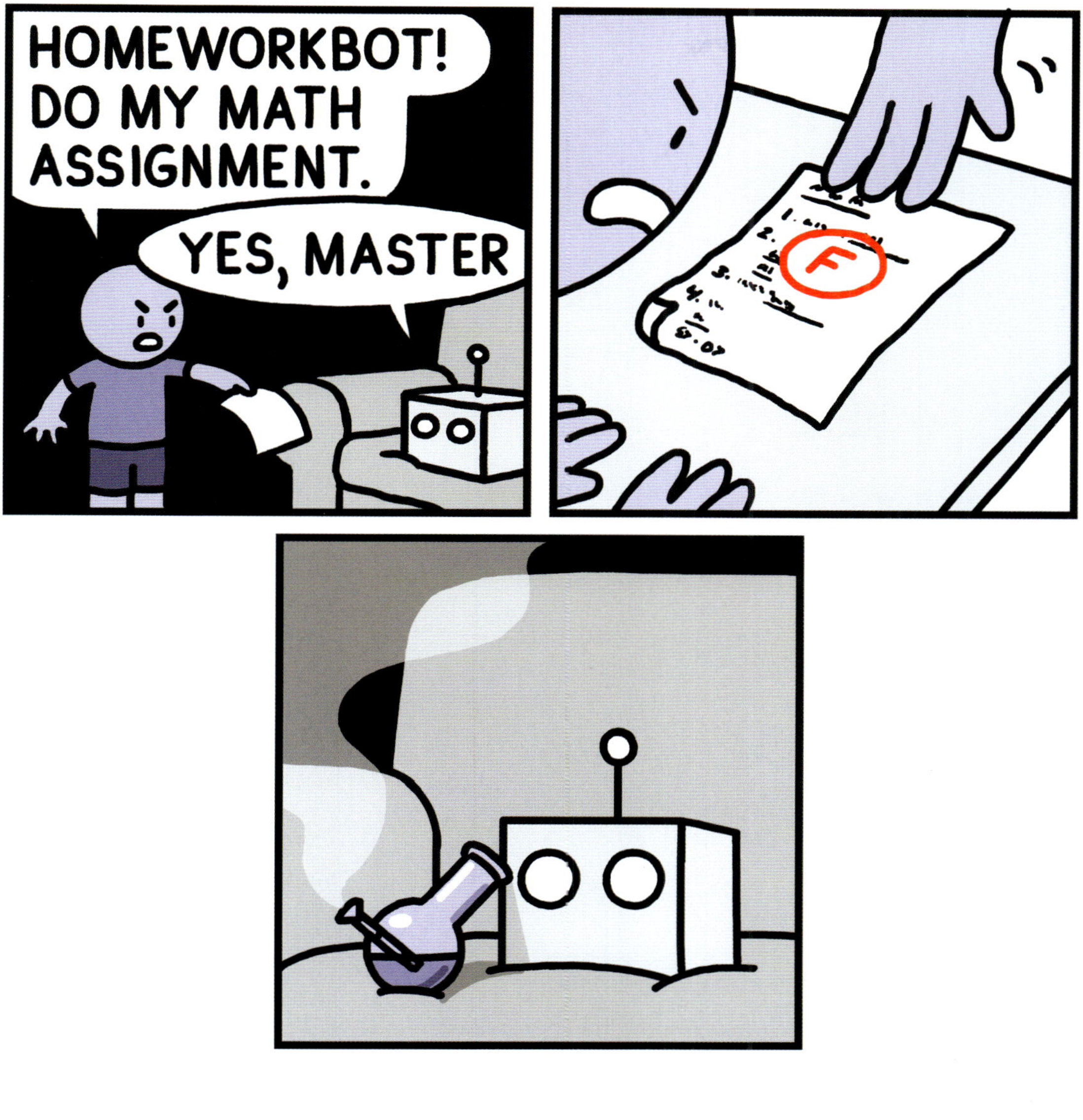
HOMEWORKBOT! DO MY MATH ASSIGNMENT.
YES, MASTER
F

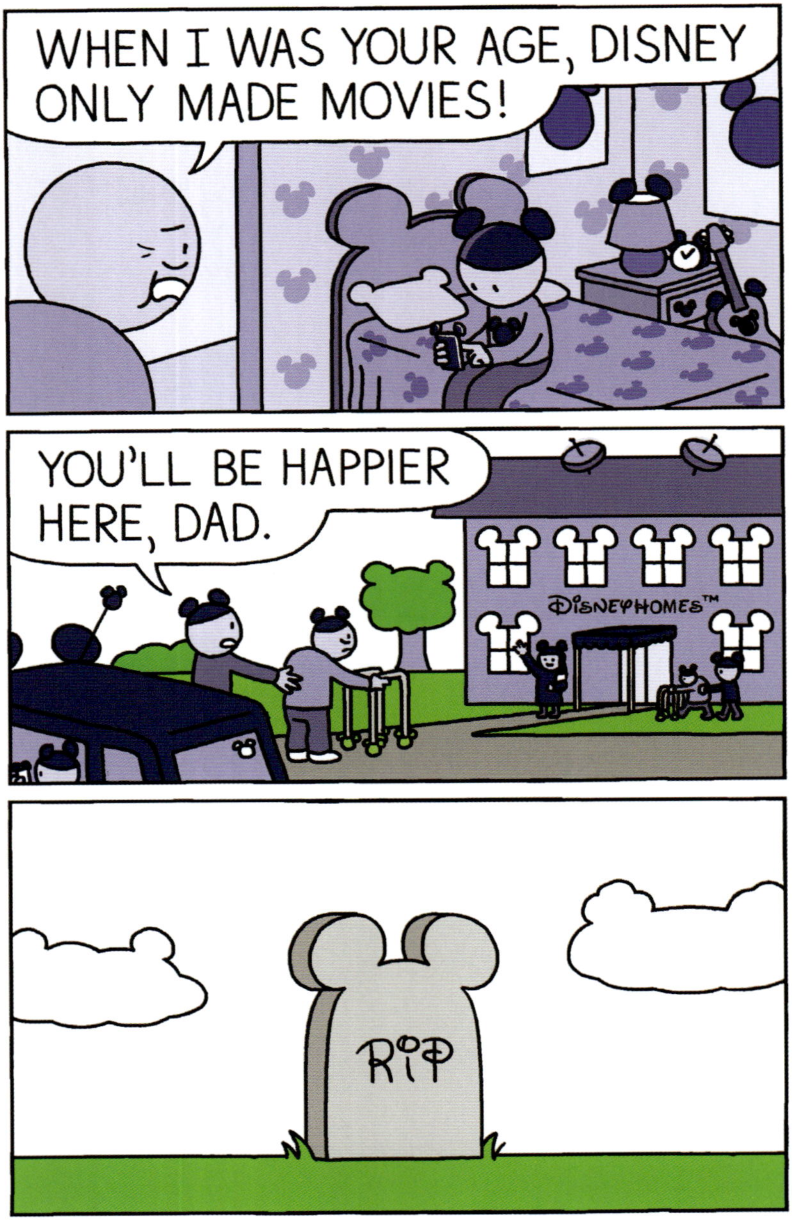
WHEN I WAS YOUR AGE, DISNEY ONLY MADE MOVIES!
YOU'LL BE HAPPIER HERE, DAD.
DISNEYHOMES™
RIP

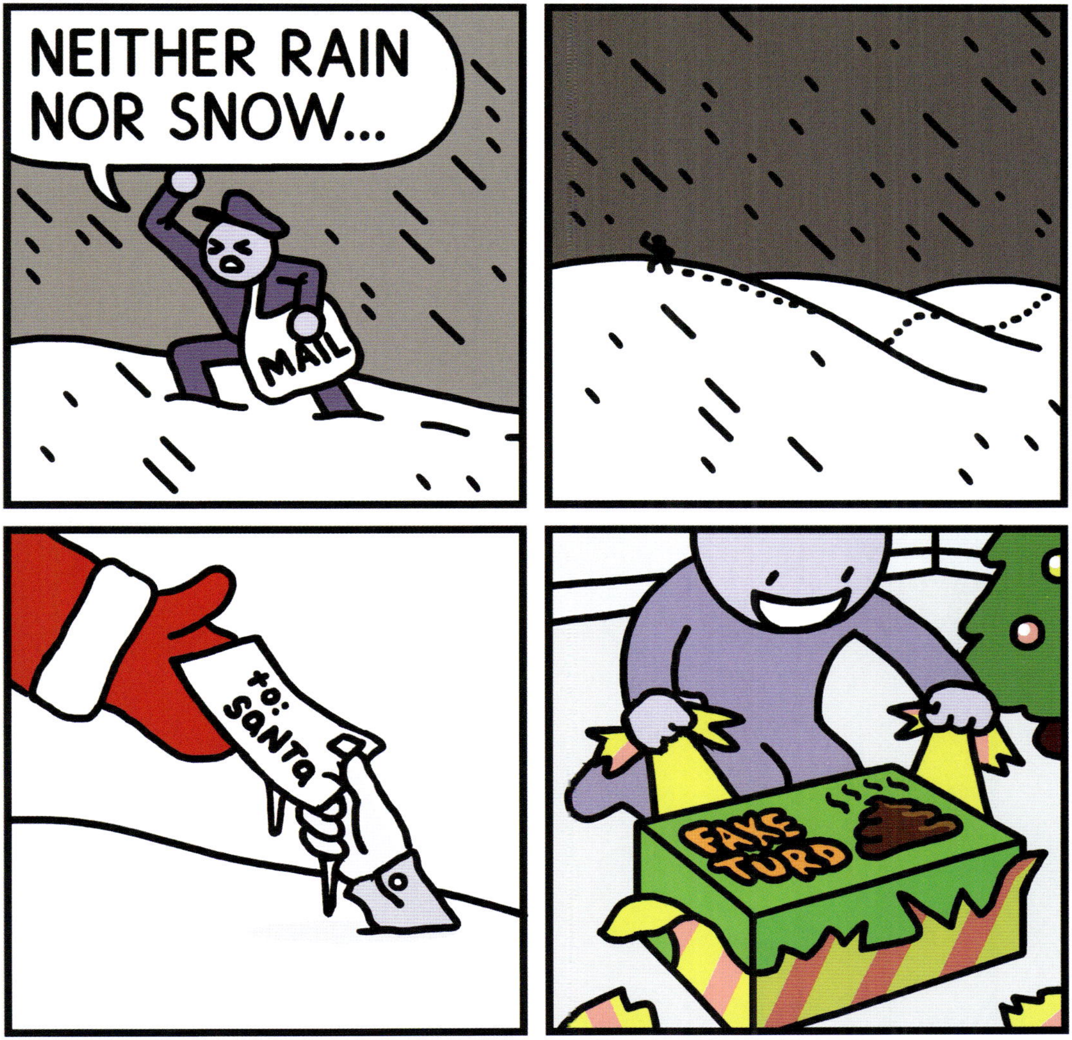
NEITHER RAIN NOR SNOW...
MAIL
to: santa
FAKE TURD

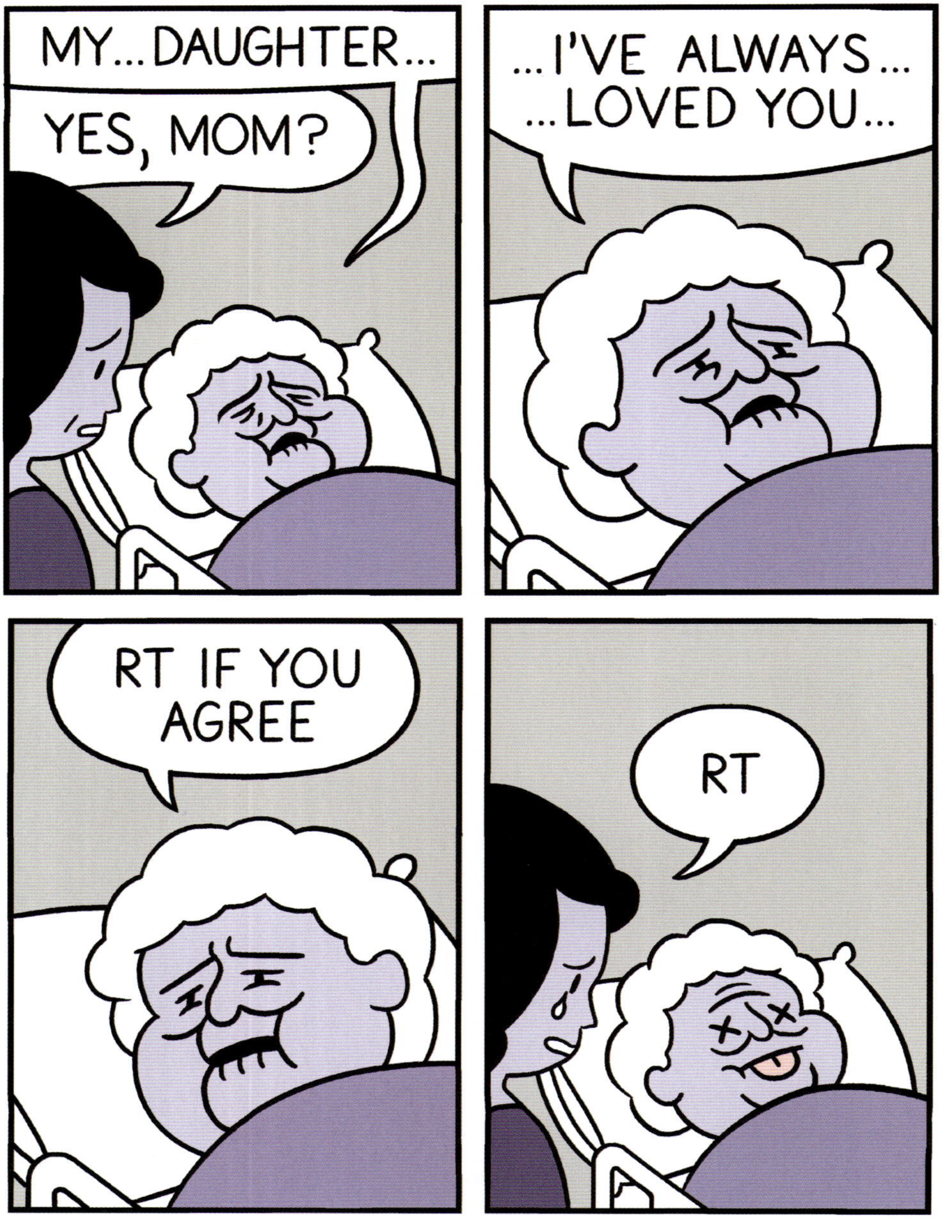
MY...DAUGHTER...
YES, MOM?
...I'VE ALWAYS...
...LOVED YOU...
RT IF YOU AGREE
RT

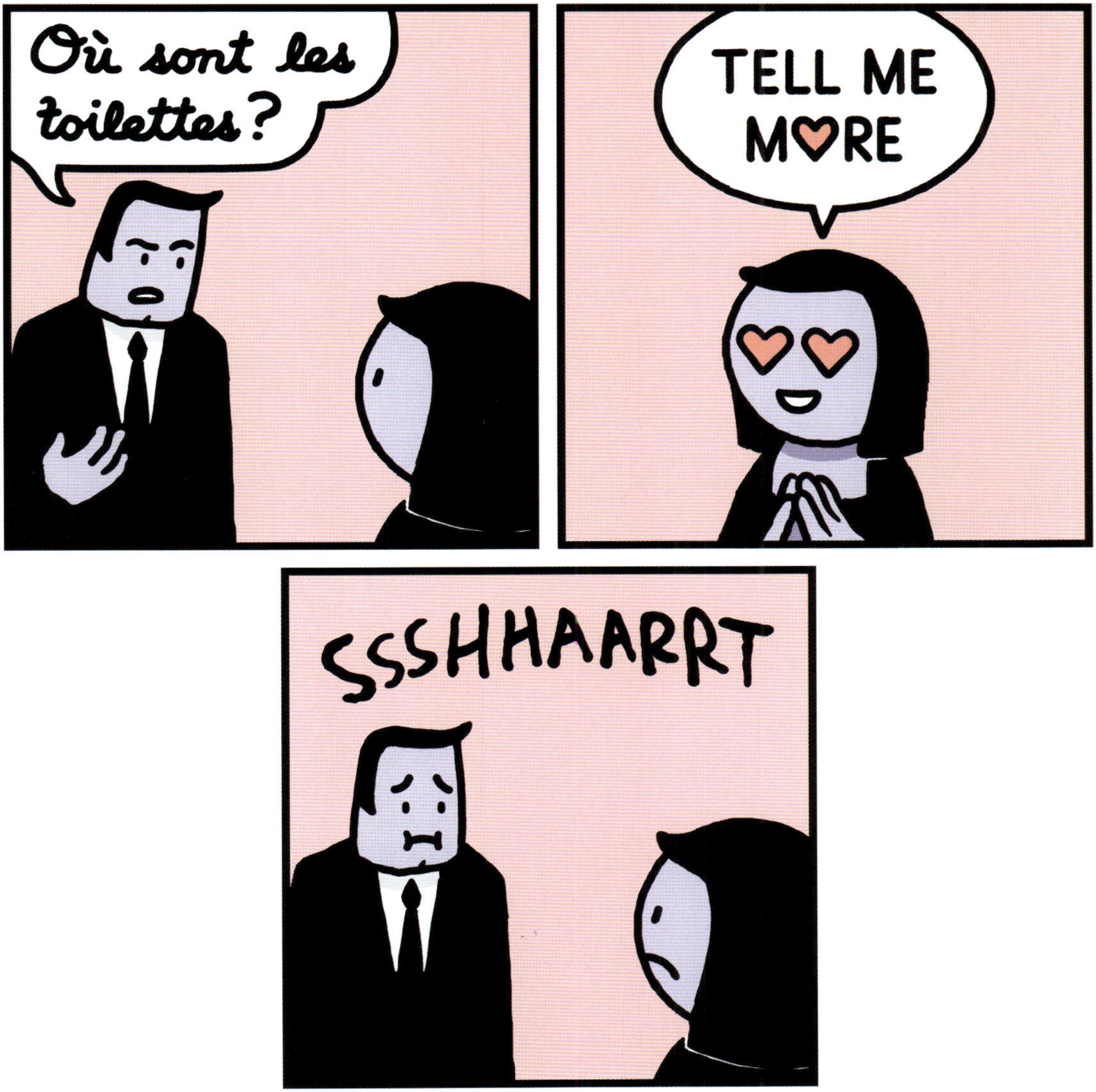
Où sont les toilettes?
TELL ME MORE
SSSHHAARRT

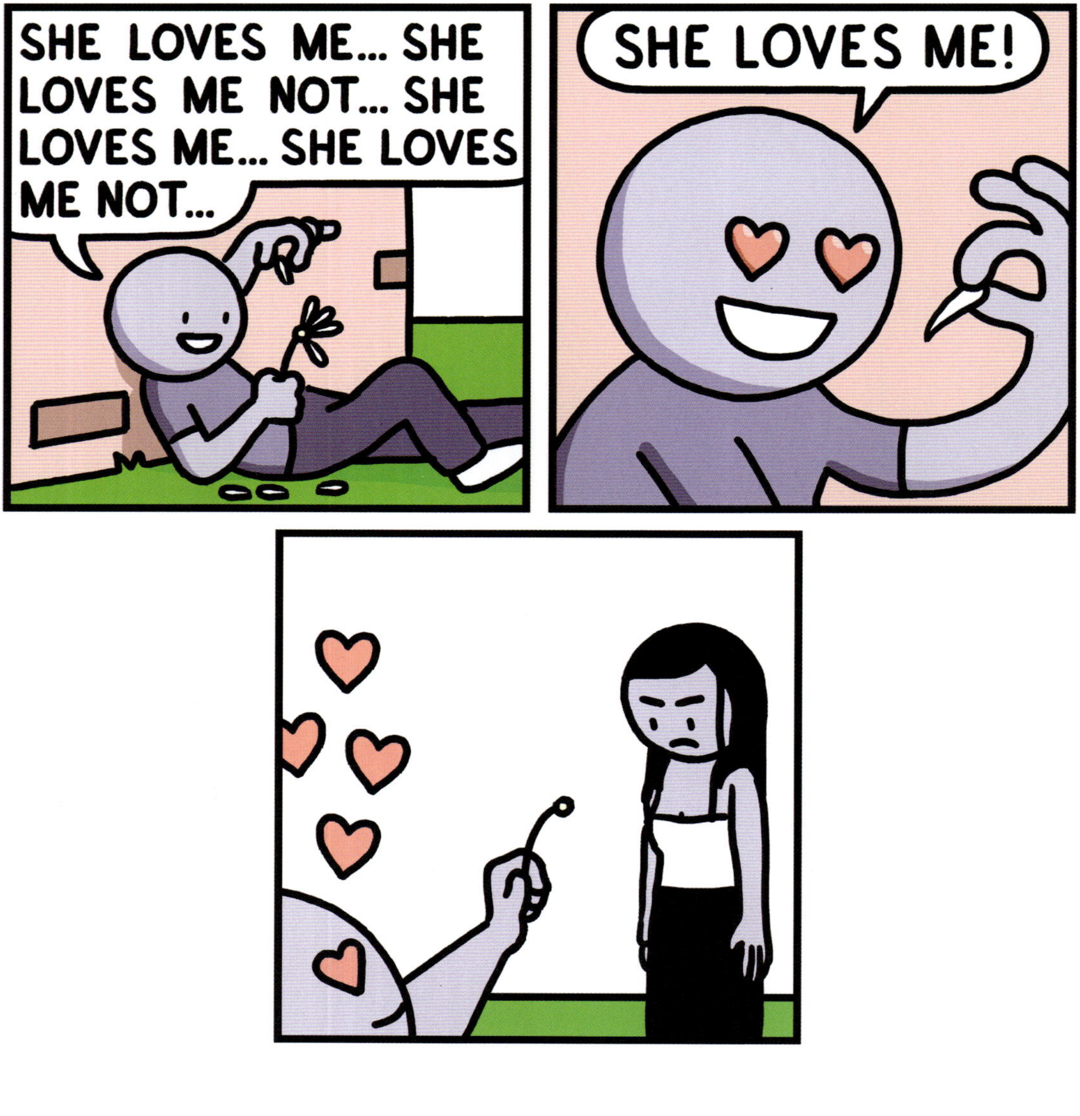
SHE LOVES ME... SHE LOVES ME NOT... SHE LOVES ME... SHE LOVES ME NOT...
SHE LOVES ME!

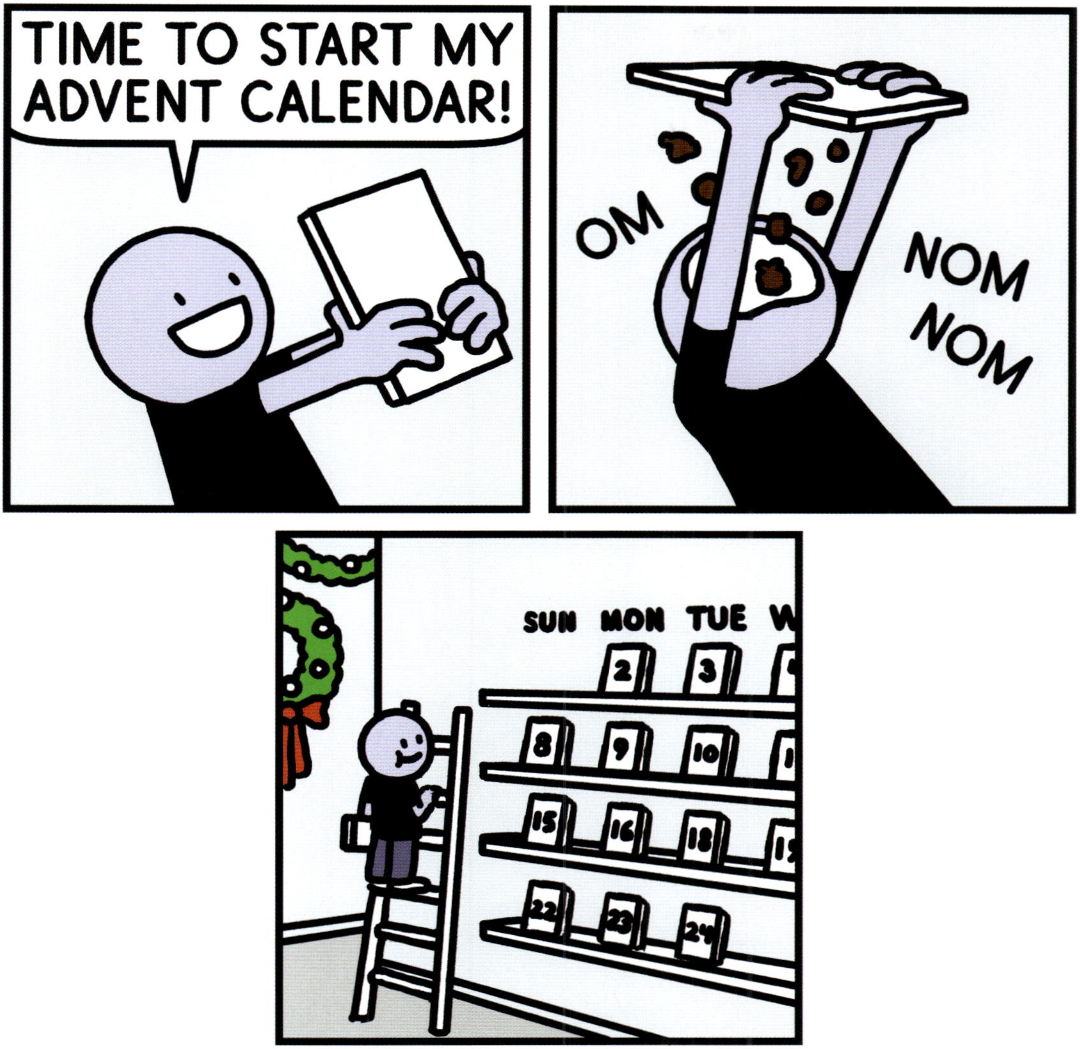
TIME TO START MY ADVENT CALENDAR!
OM
NOM NOM
SUN MON TUE

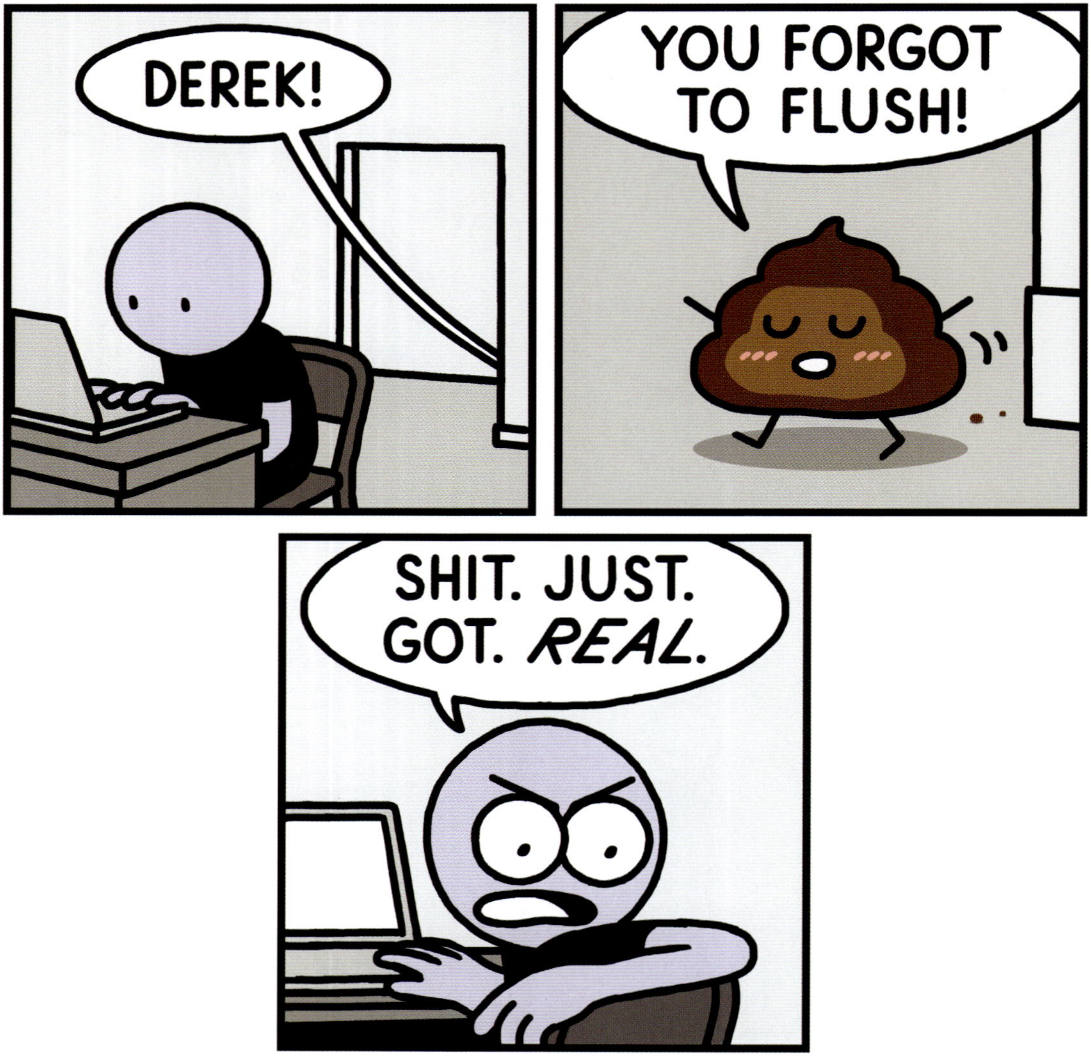
DEREK!
YOU FORGOT TO FLUSH!
SHIT. JUST. GOT. *REAL*.

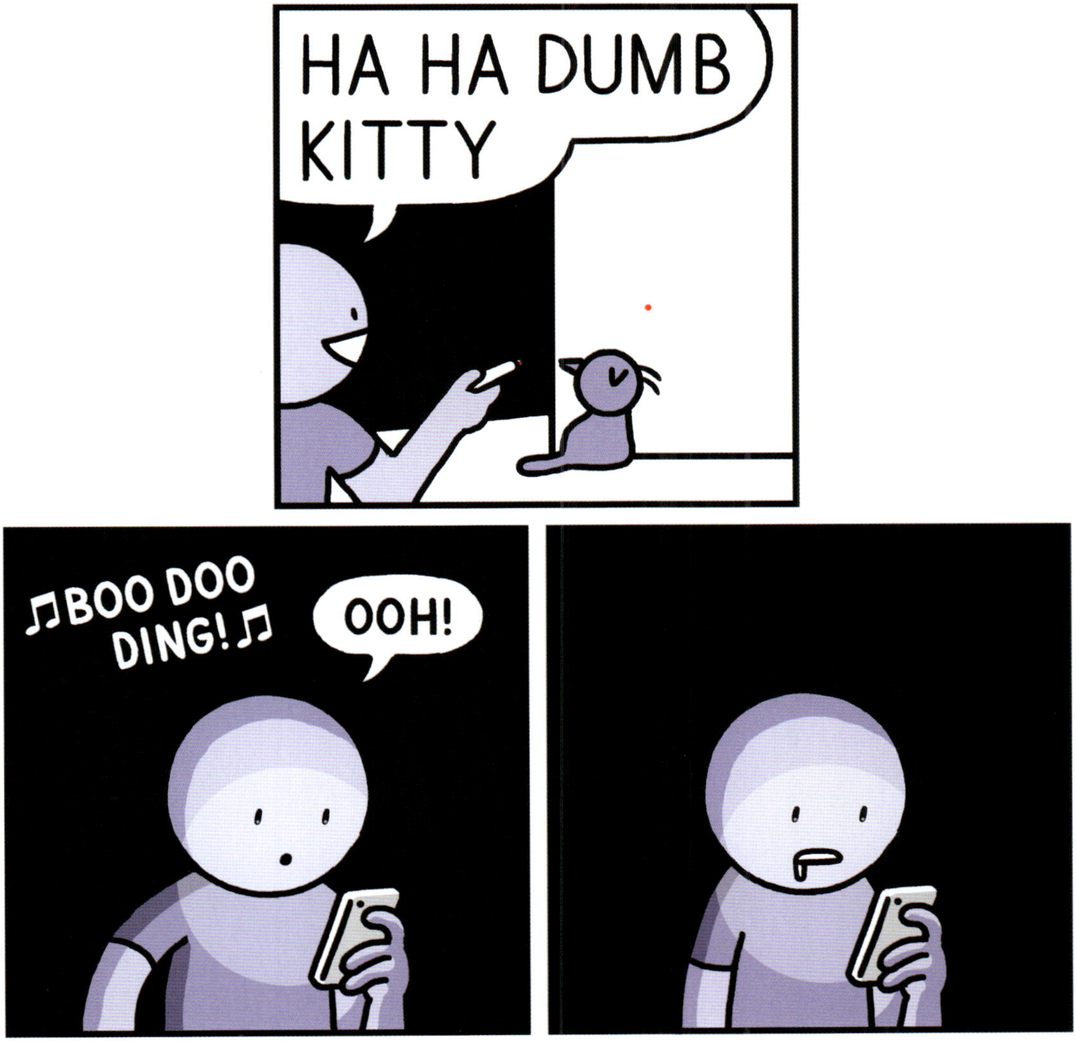
HA HA DUMB KITTY
♫BOO DOO DING!♫
OOH!

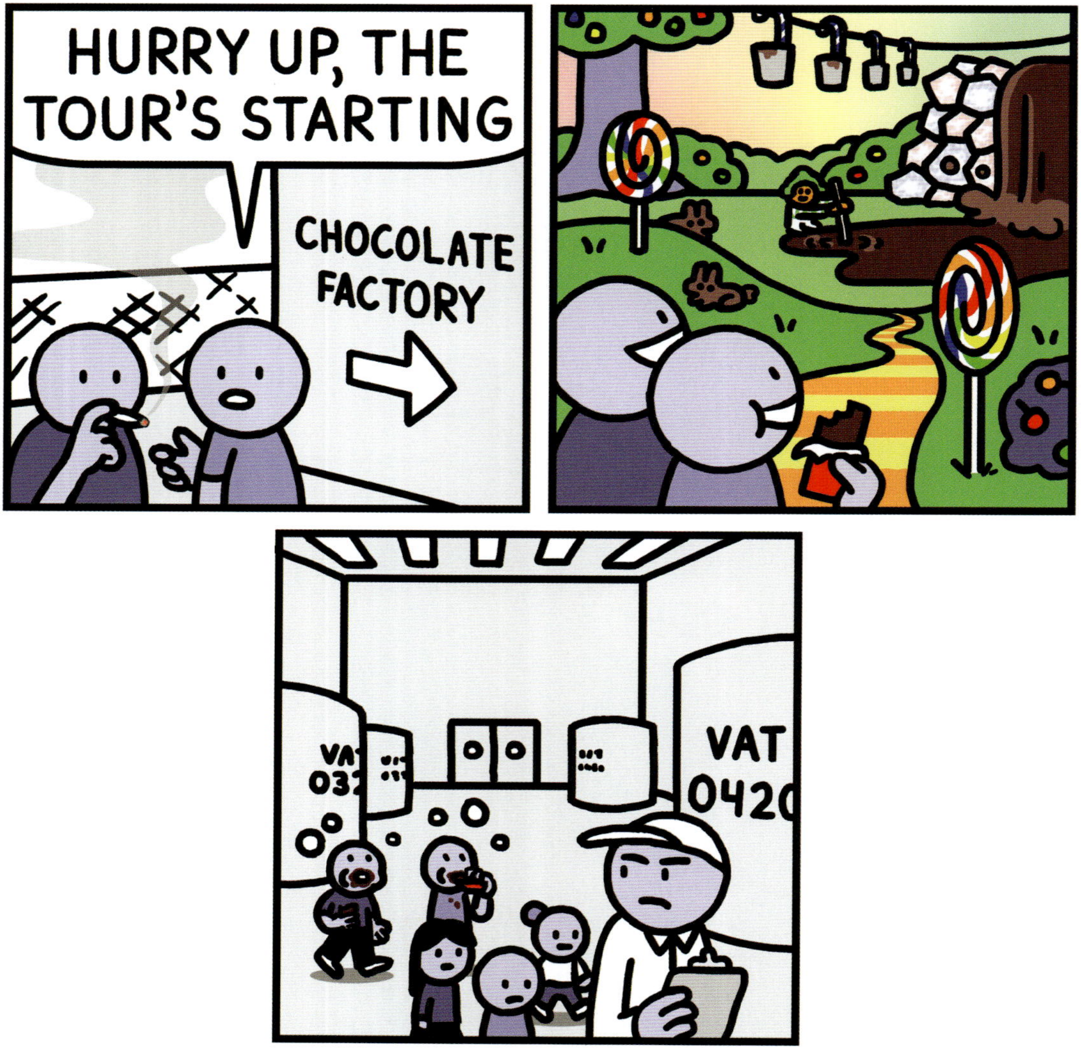
HURRY UP, THE TOUR'S STARTING
CHOCOLATE FACTORY
VAT
042

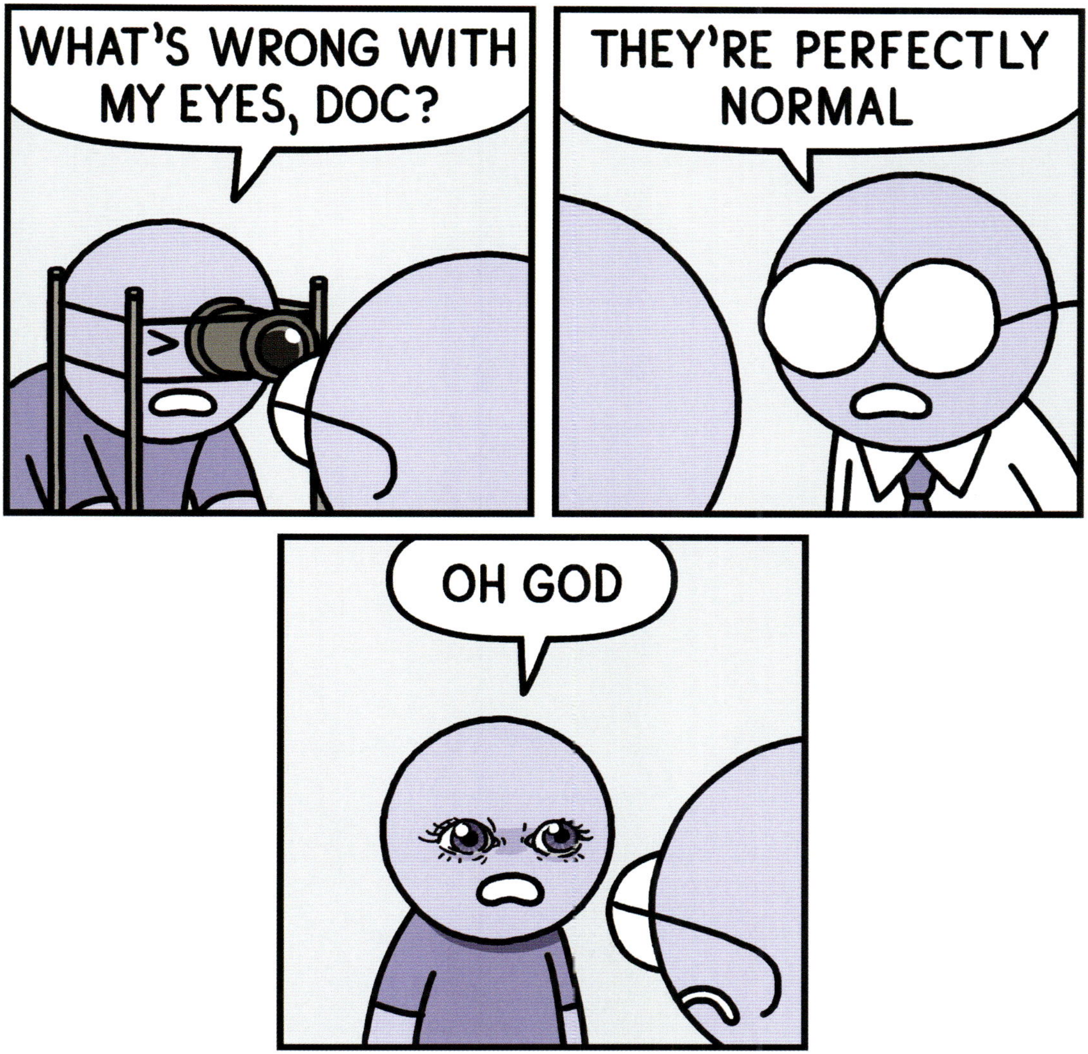
WHAT'S WRONG WITH MY EYES, DOC?
THEY'RE PERFECTLY NORMAL
OH GOD

LET'S PLAY *RUSSIAN ROULETTE*
РУЛЕТКА
SPIN
SPIN
SPIN

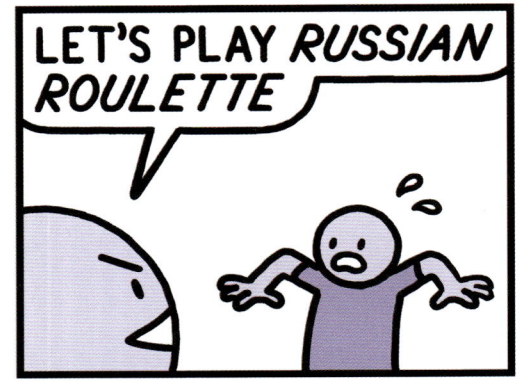

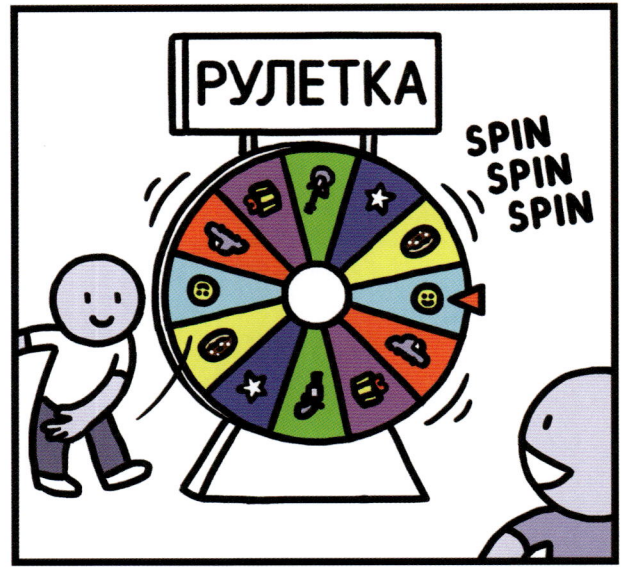

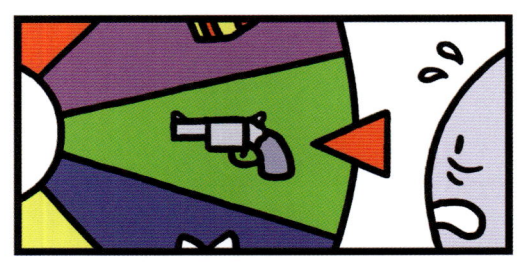

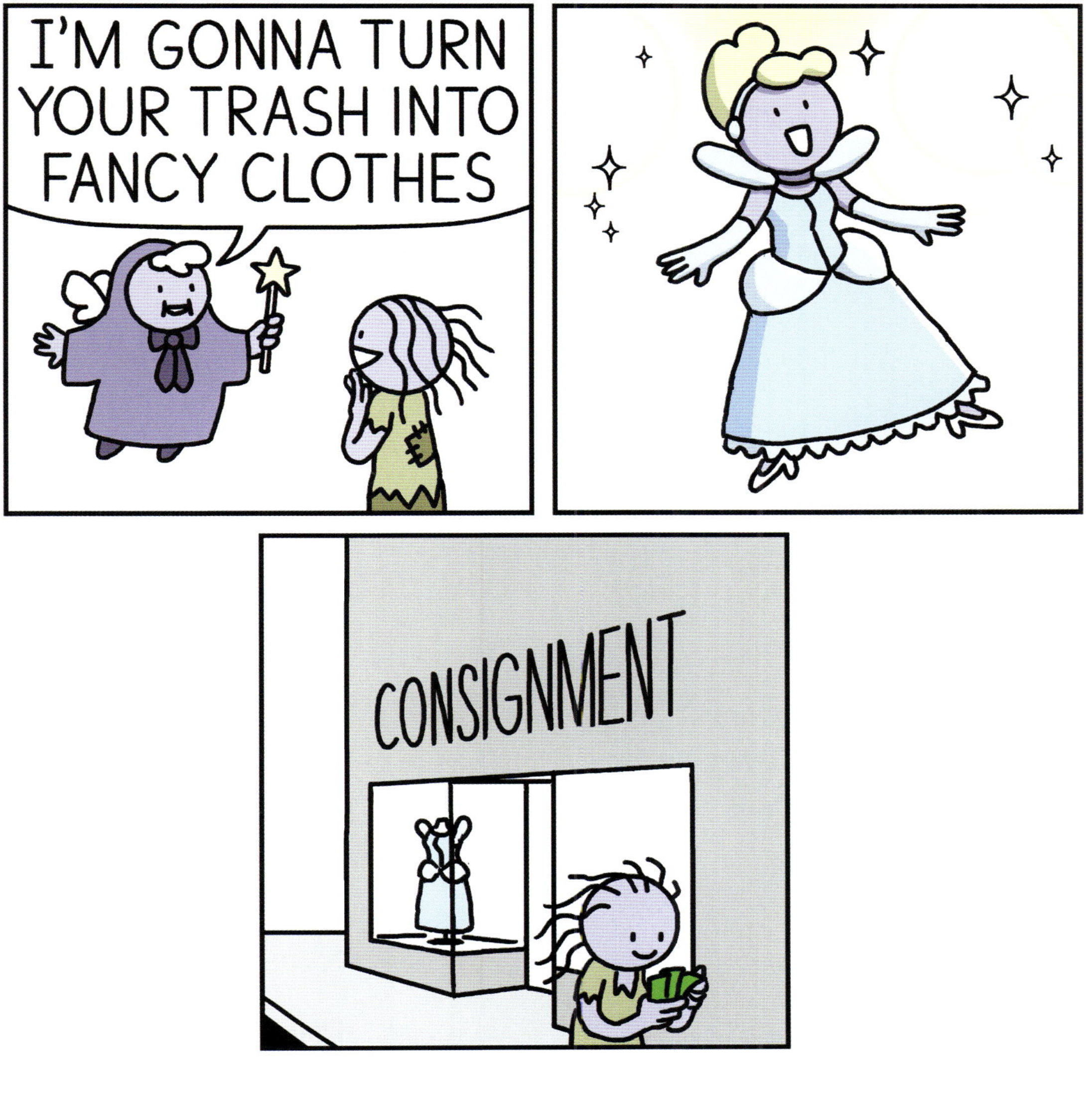
I'M GONNA TURN YOUR TRASH INTO FANCY CLOTHES
CONSIGNMENT

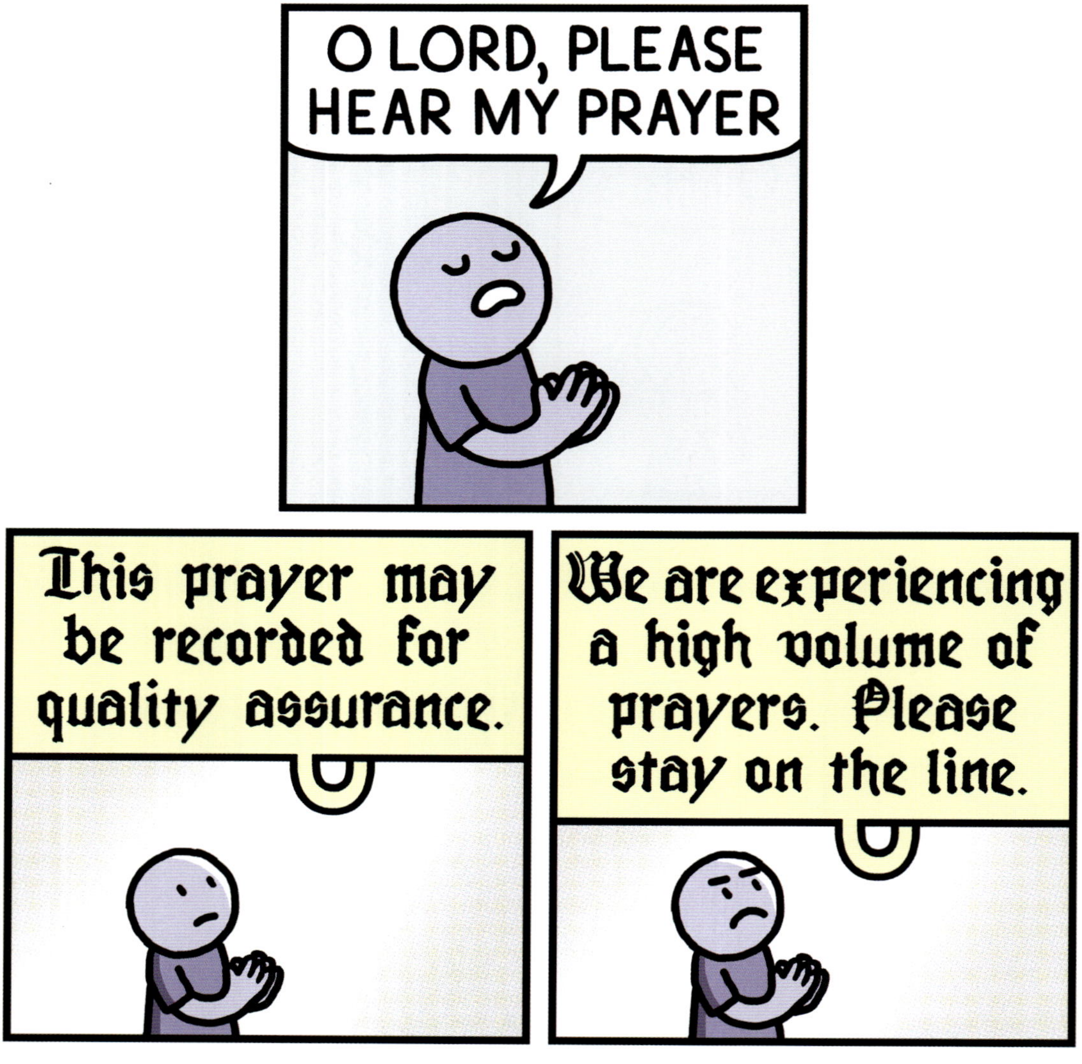

O LORD, PLEASE HEAR MY PRAYER
This prayer may be recorded for quality assurance.
We are experiencing a high volume of prayers. Please stay on the line.

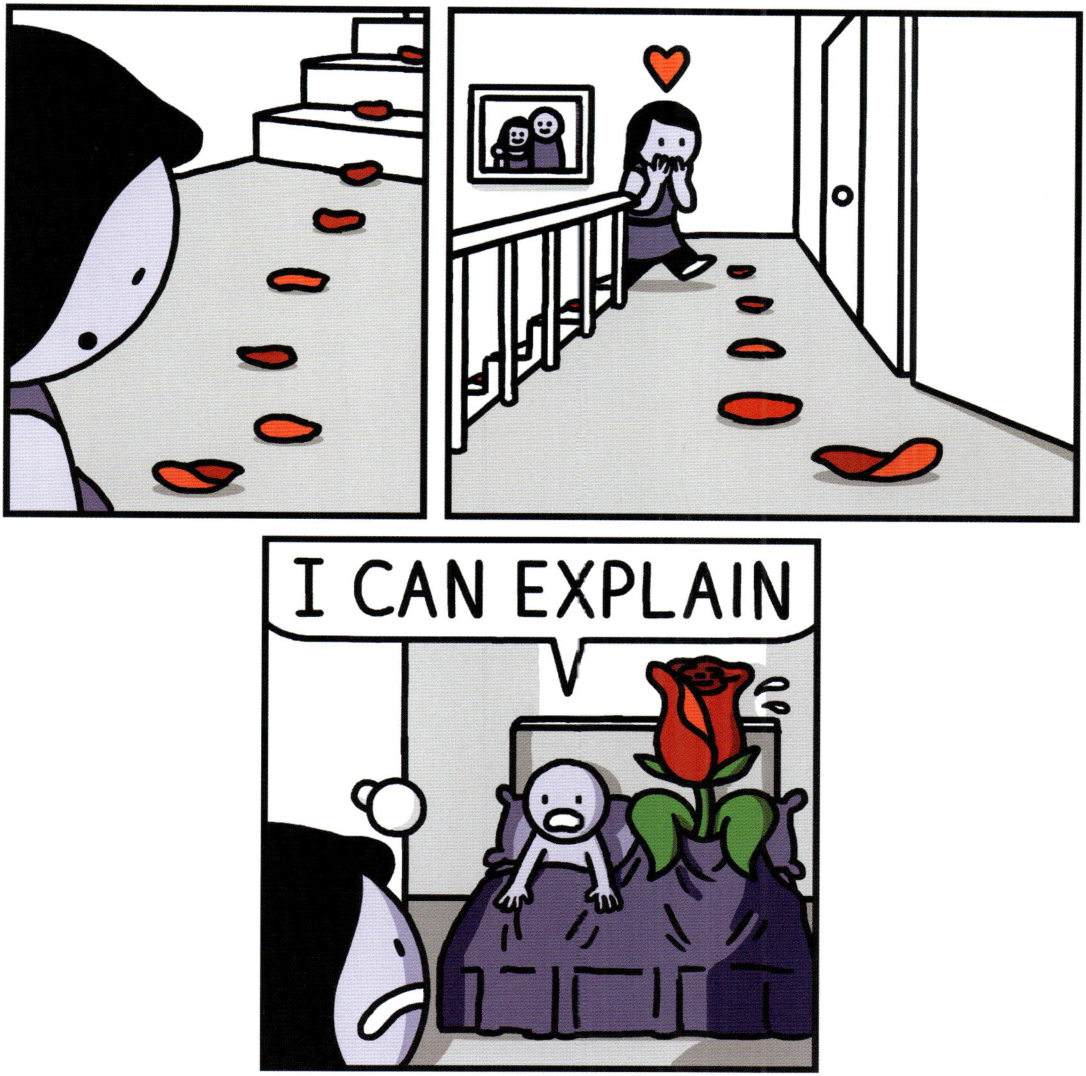
I CAN EXPLAIN

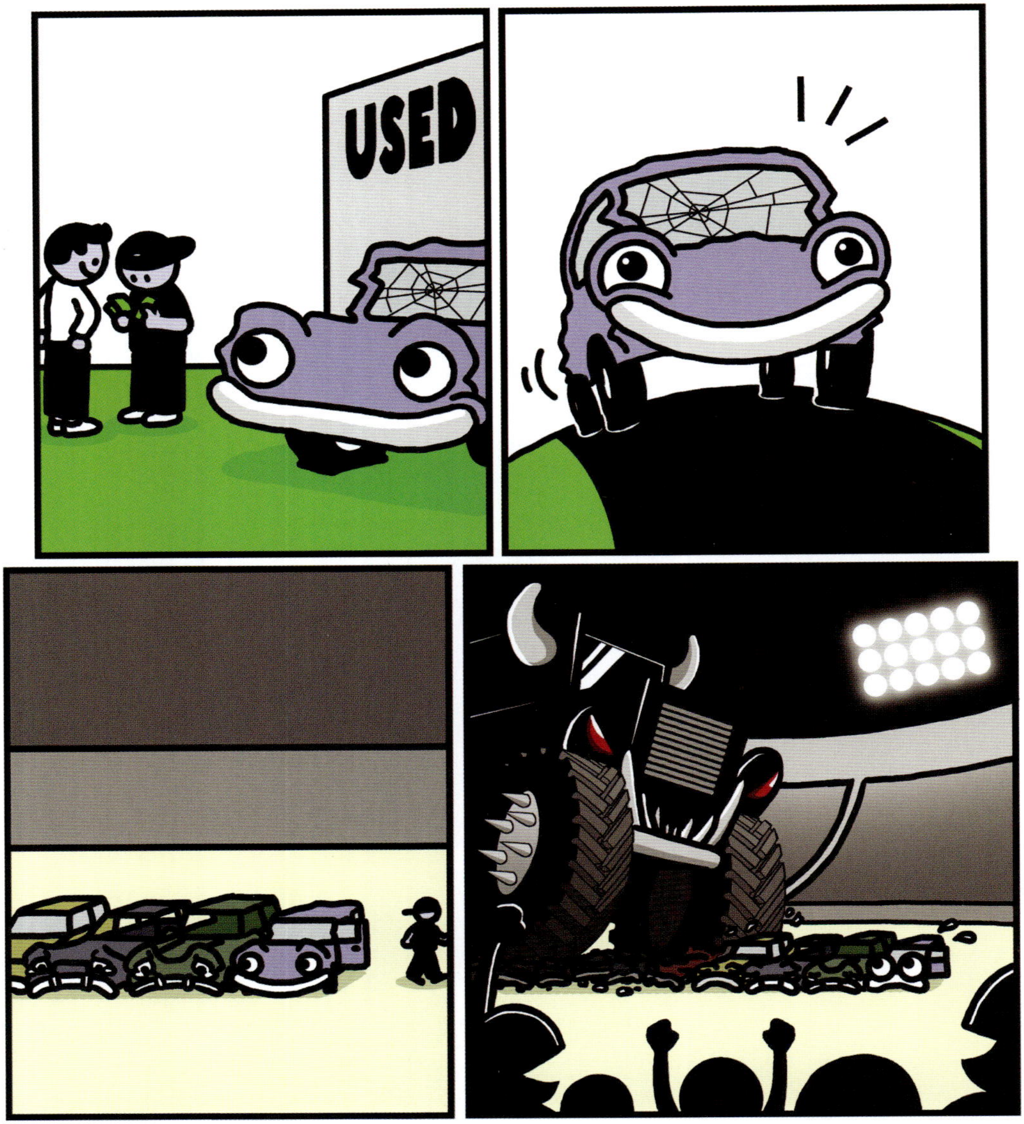
USED

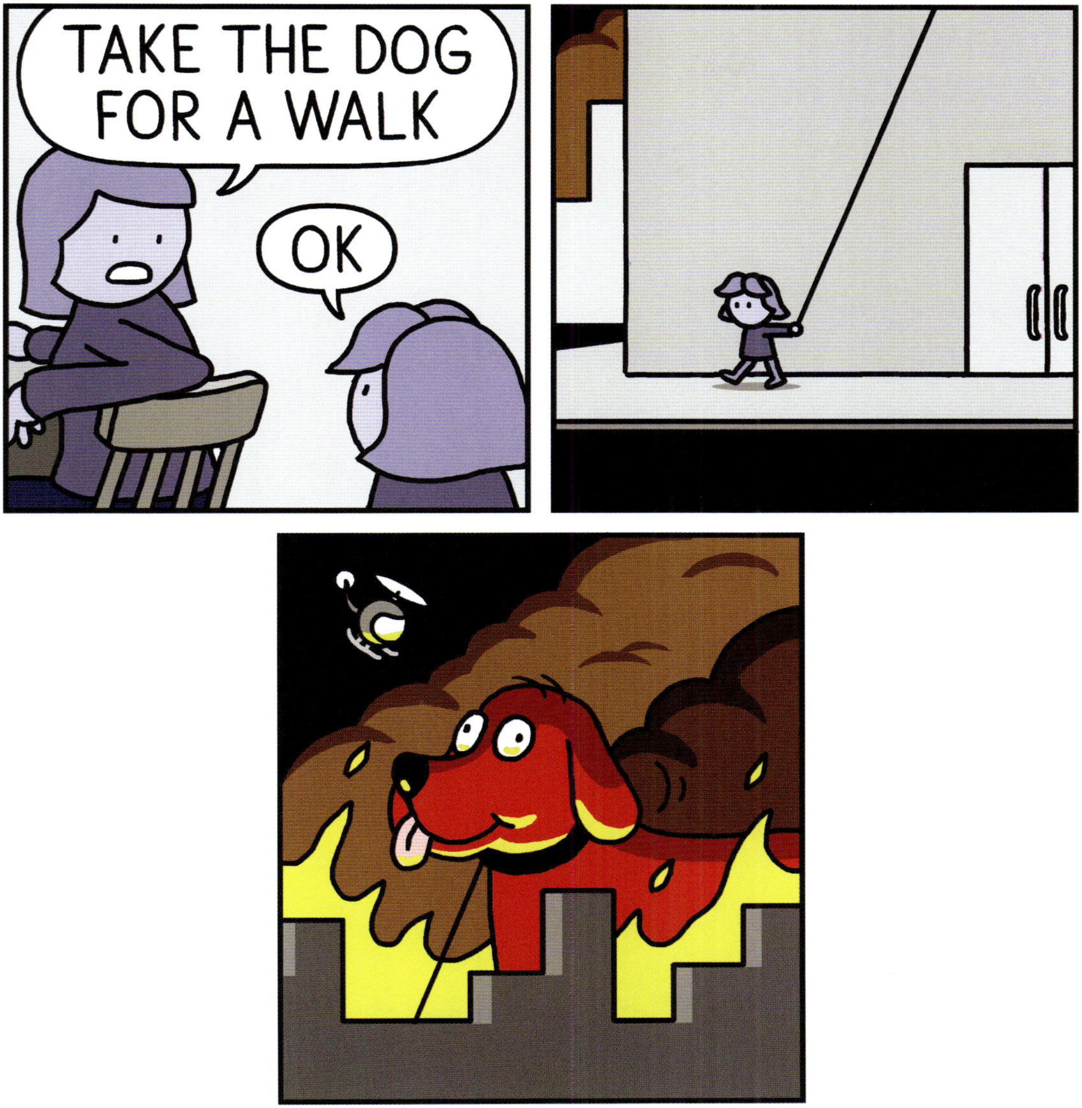
TAKE THE DOG FOR A WALK
OK

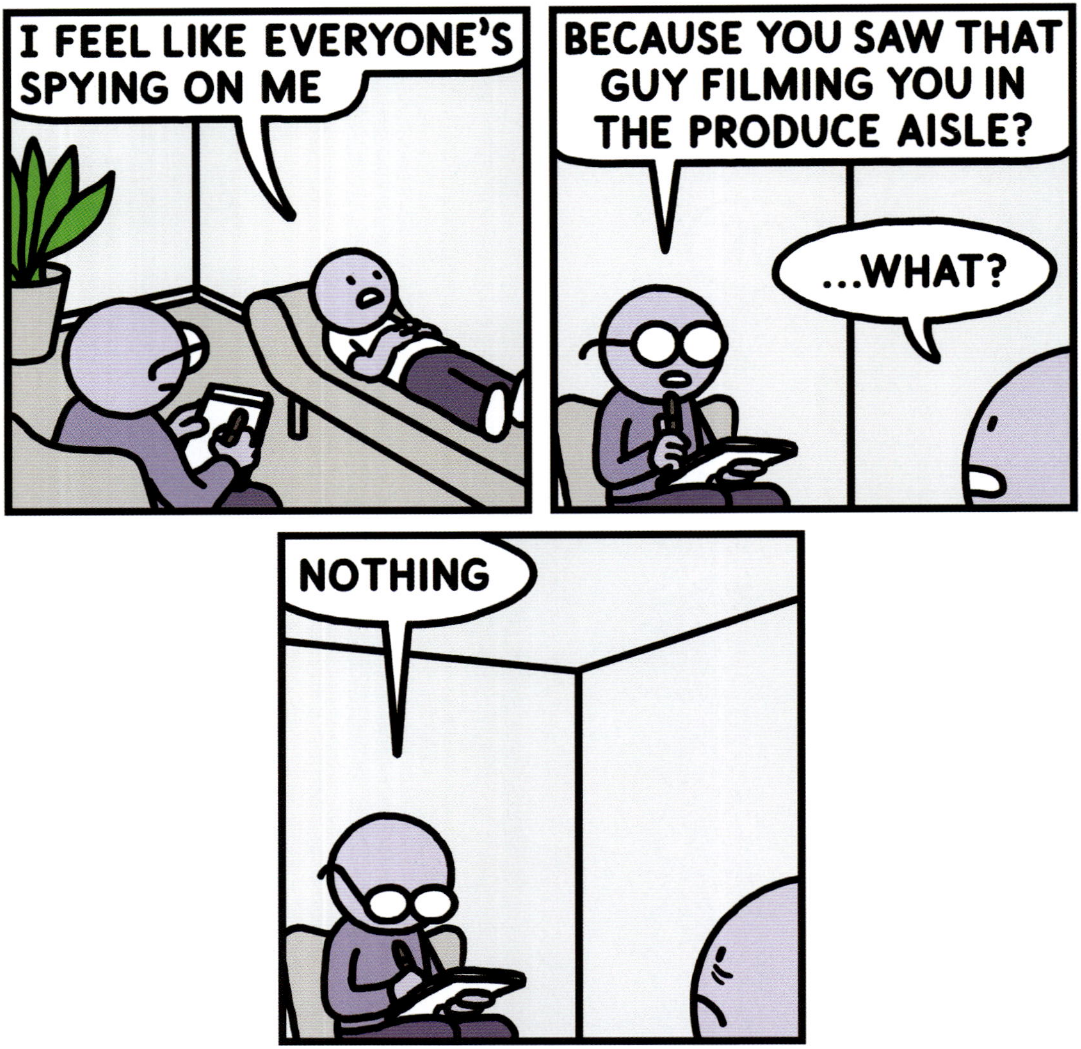
I FEEL LIKE EVERYONE'S SPYING ON ME
BECAUSE YOU SAW THAT GUY FILMING YOU IN THE PRODUCE AISLE?
...WHAT?
NOTHING

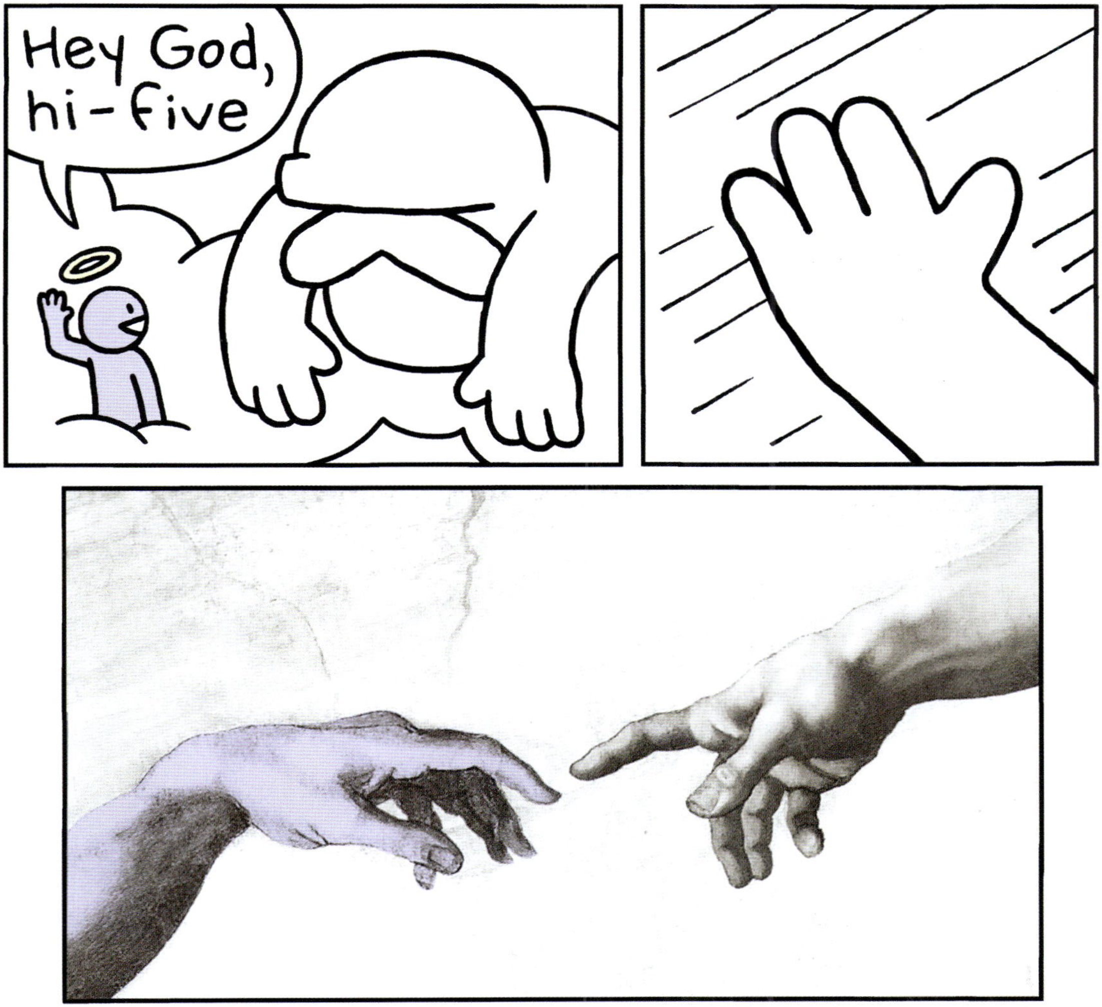
Hey God,
hi-five

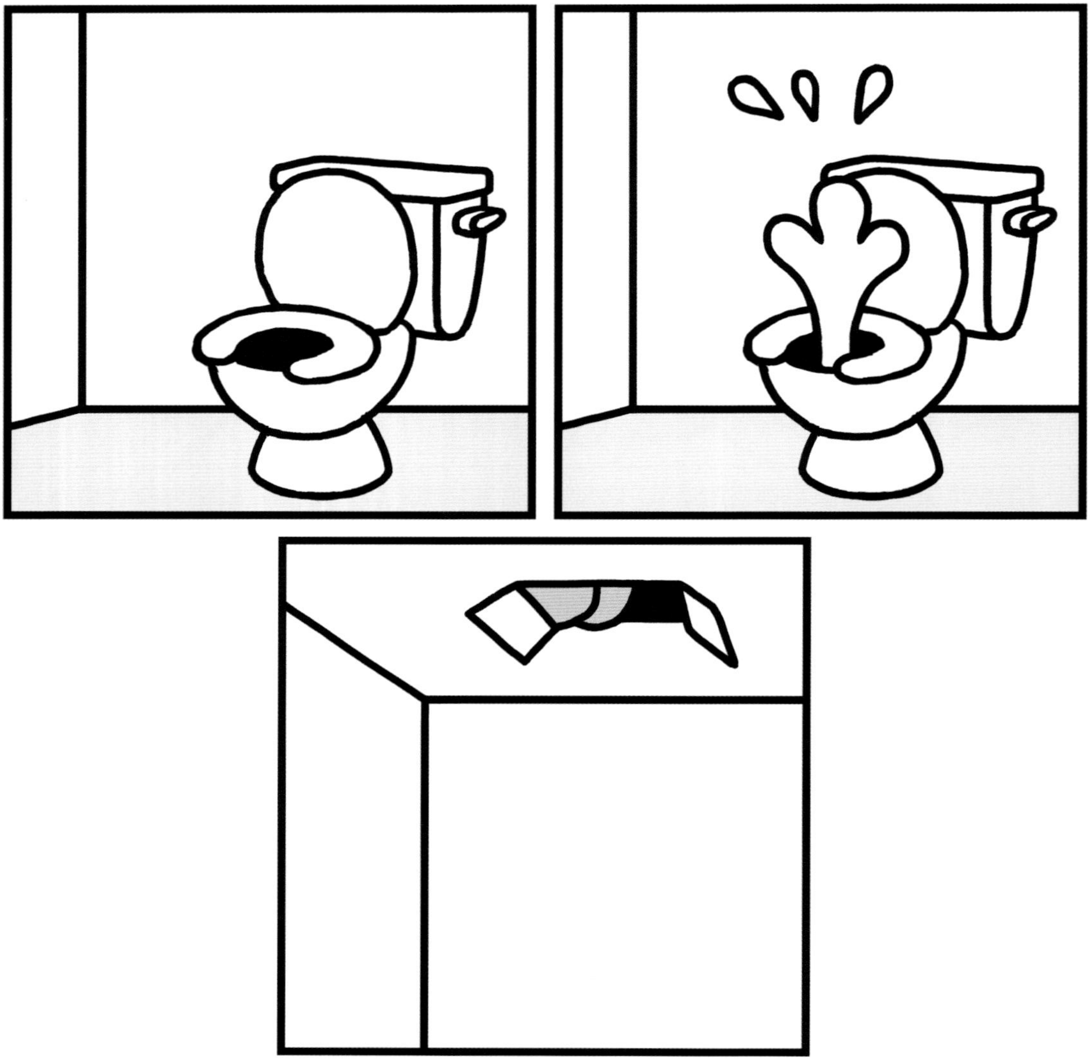

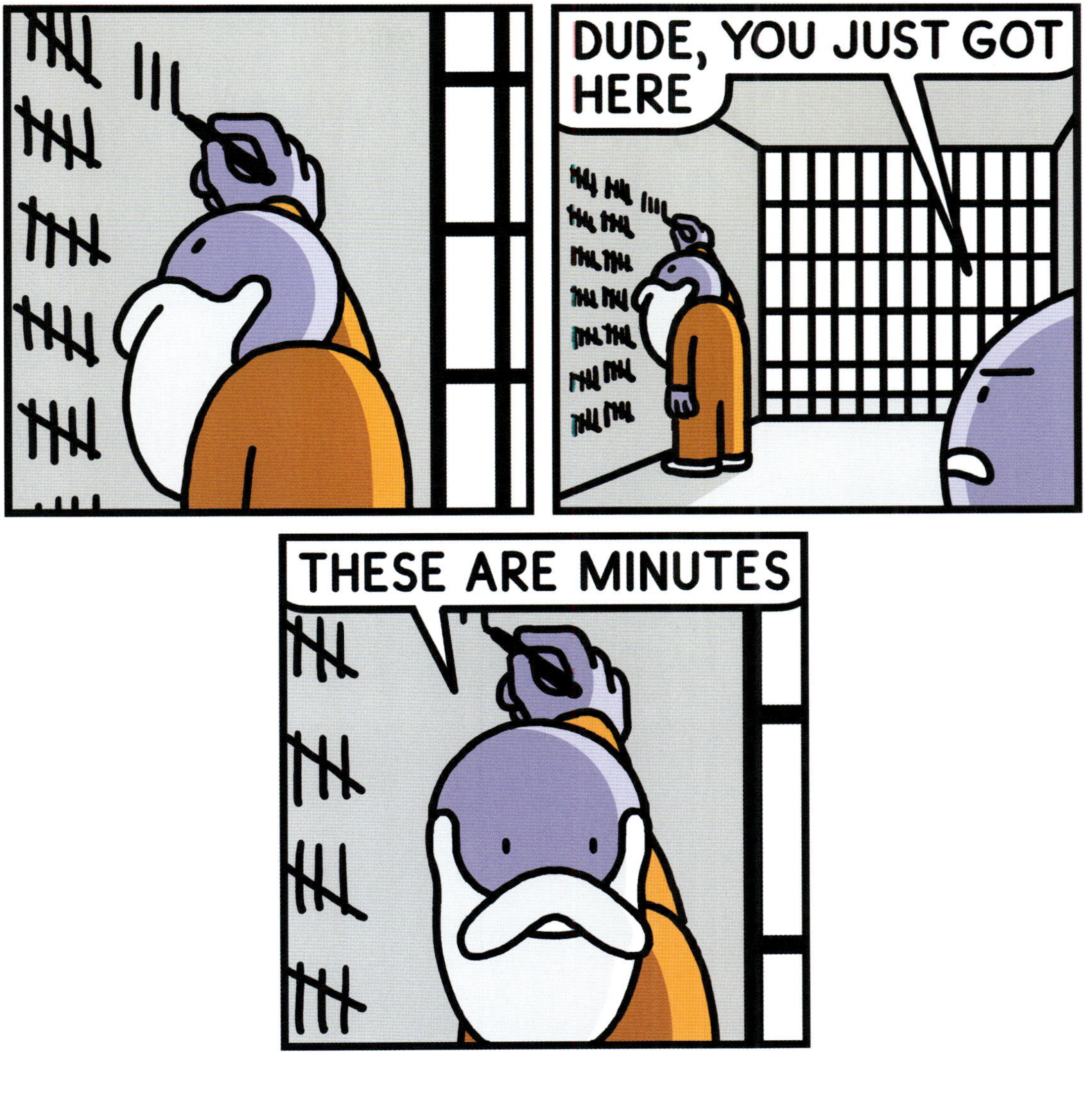
DUDE, YOU JUST GOT HERE
THESE ARE MINUTES

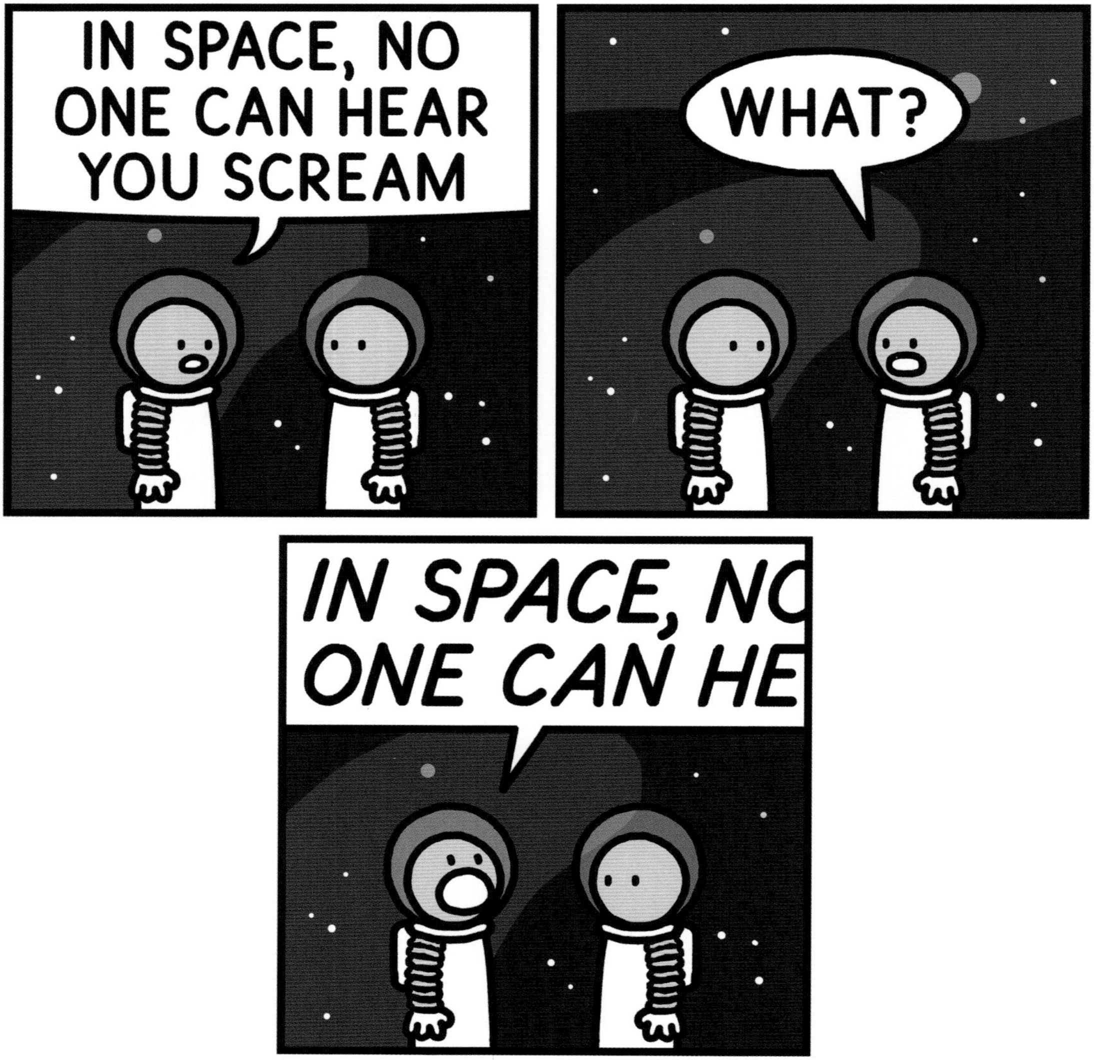
IN SPACE, NO ONE CAN HEAR YOU SCREAM
WHAT?
IN SPACE, NO
ONE CAN HE

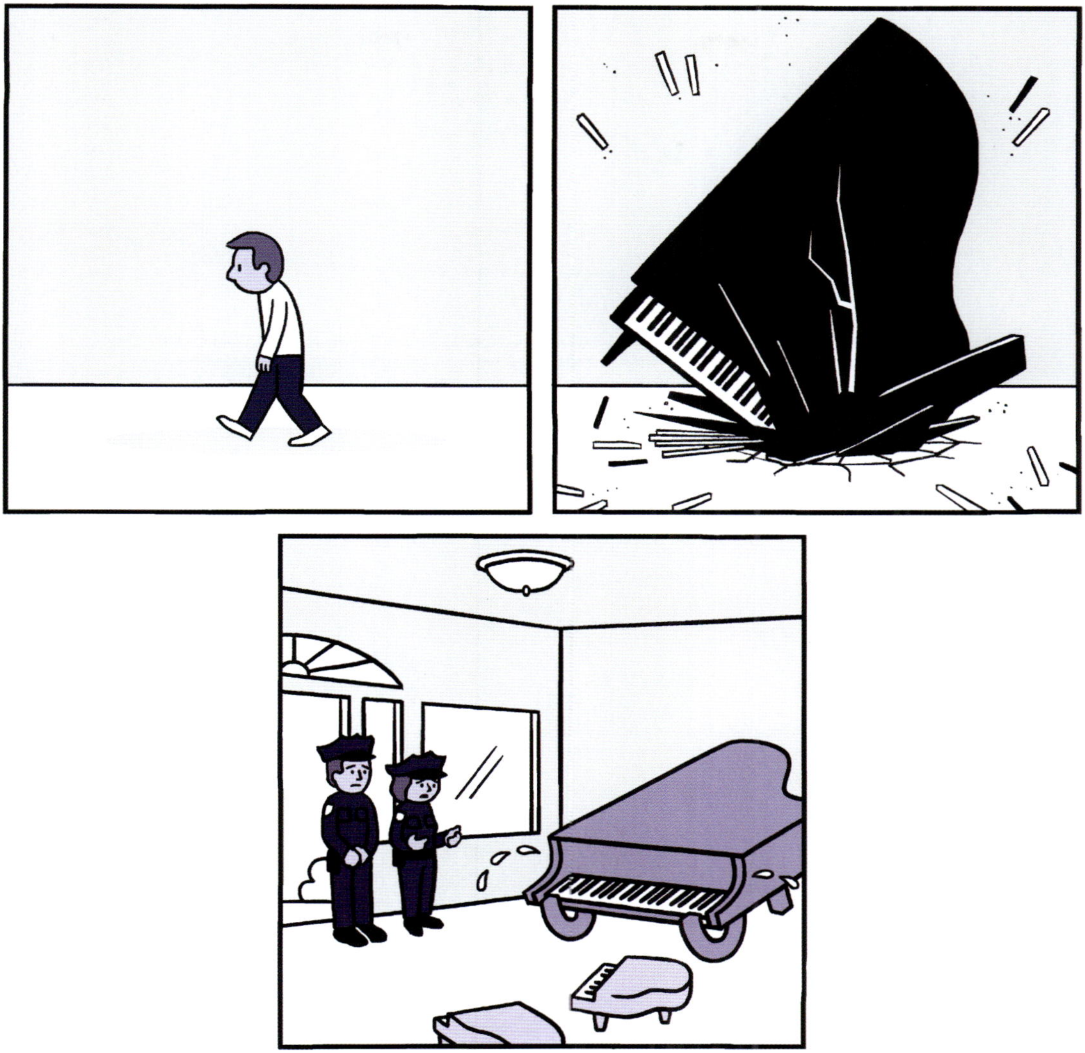

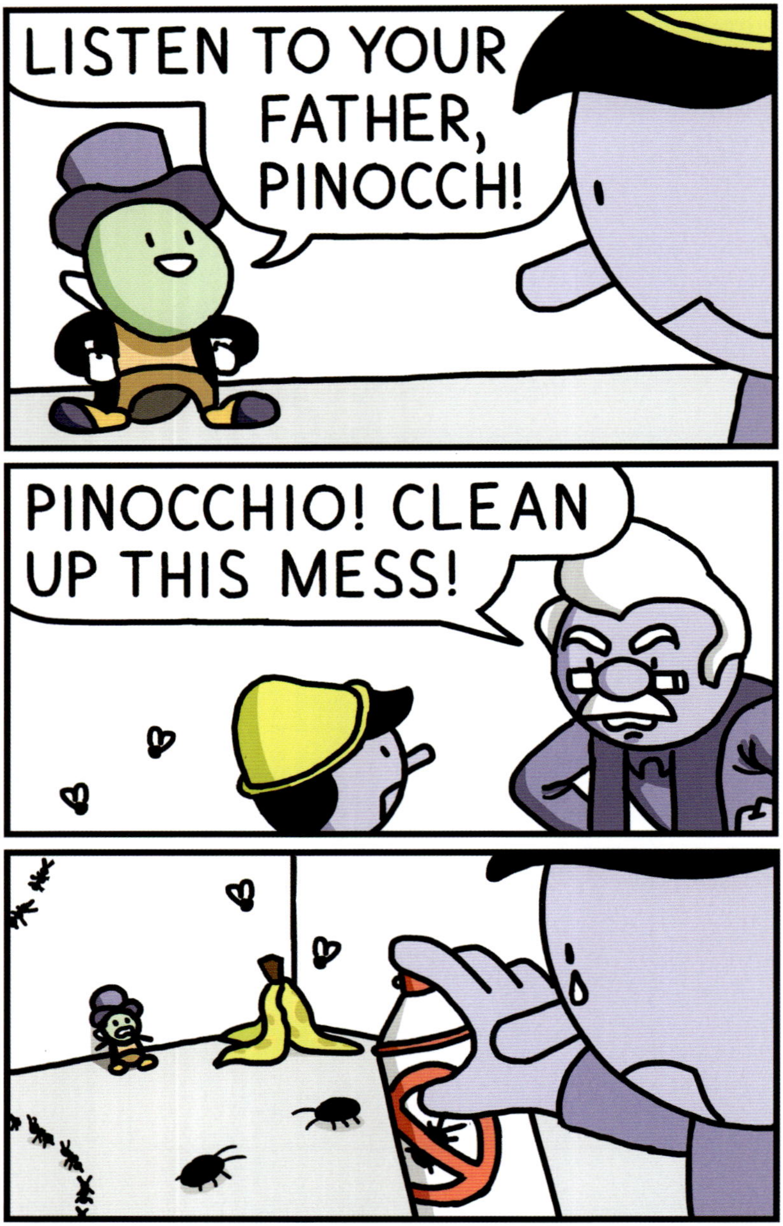
LISTEN TO YOUR FATHER, PINOCCH!
PINOCCHIO! CLEAN UP THIS MESS!

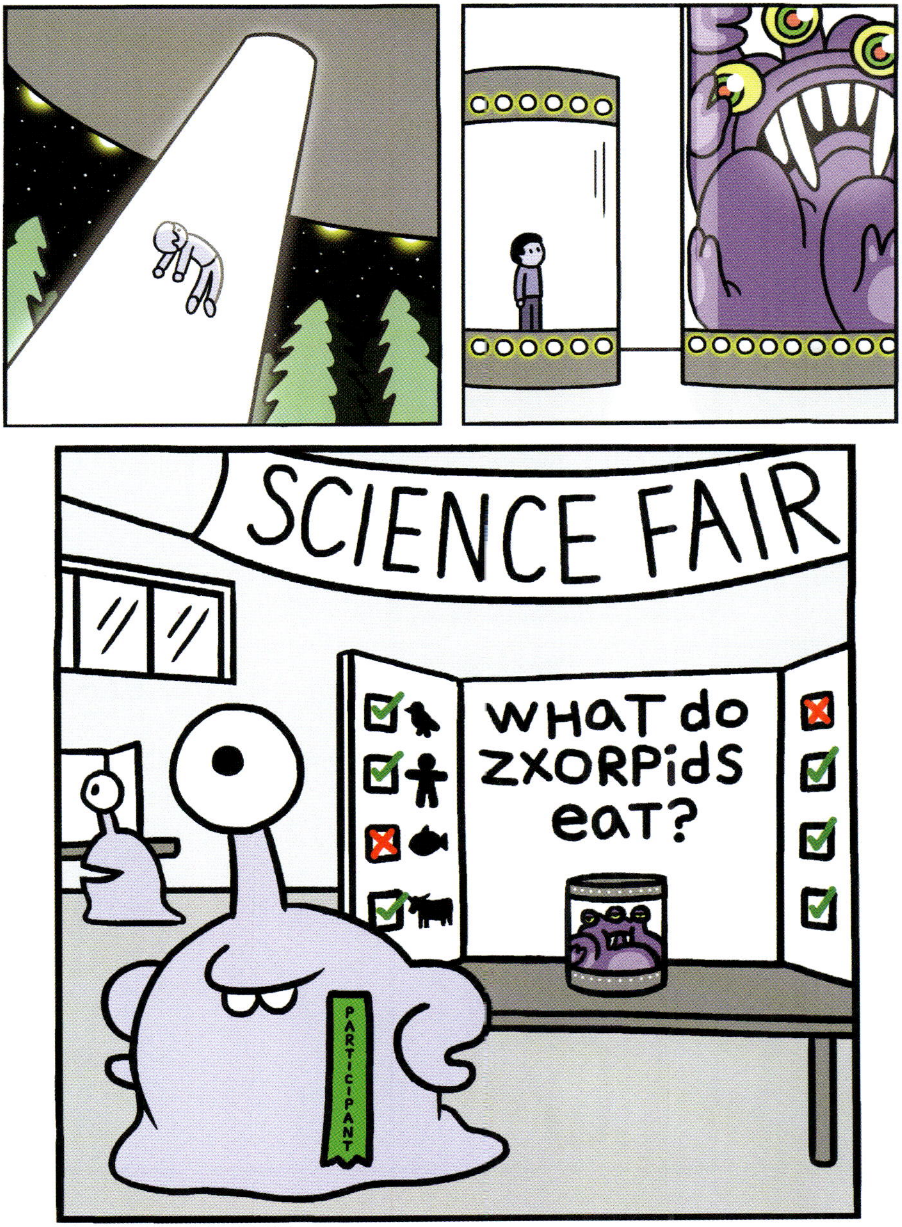
SCIENCE FAIR
WHAT do ZXORPids eaT?
PARTICIPANT

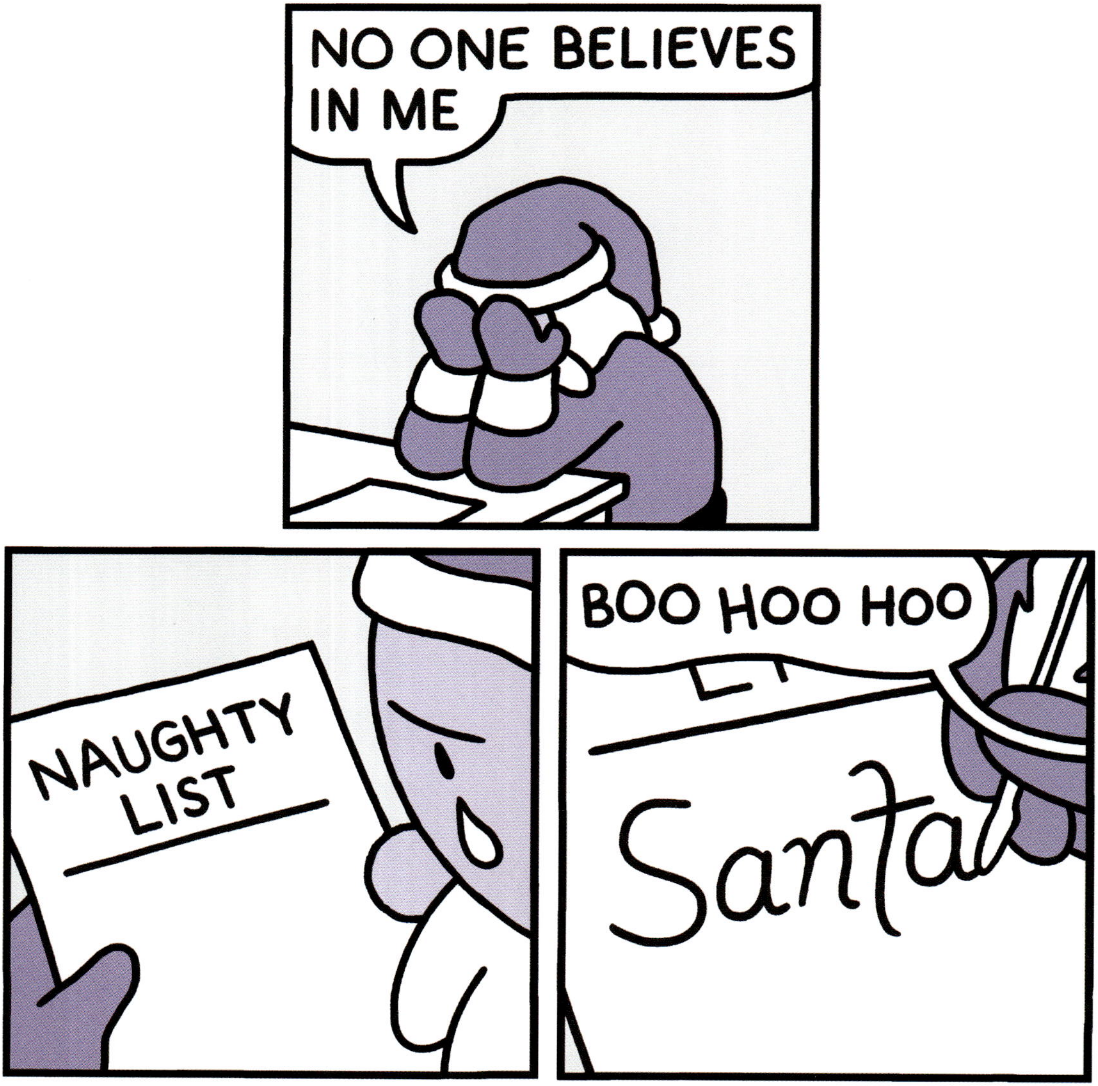
NO ONE BELIEVES IN ME
NAUGHTY LIST
BOO HOO HOO
Santa

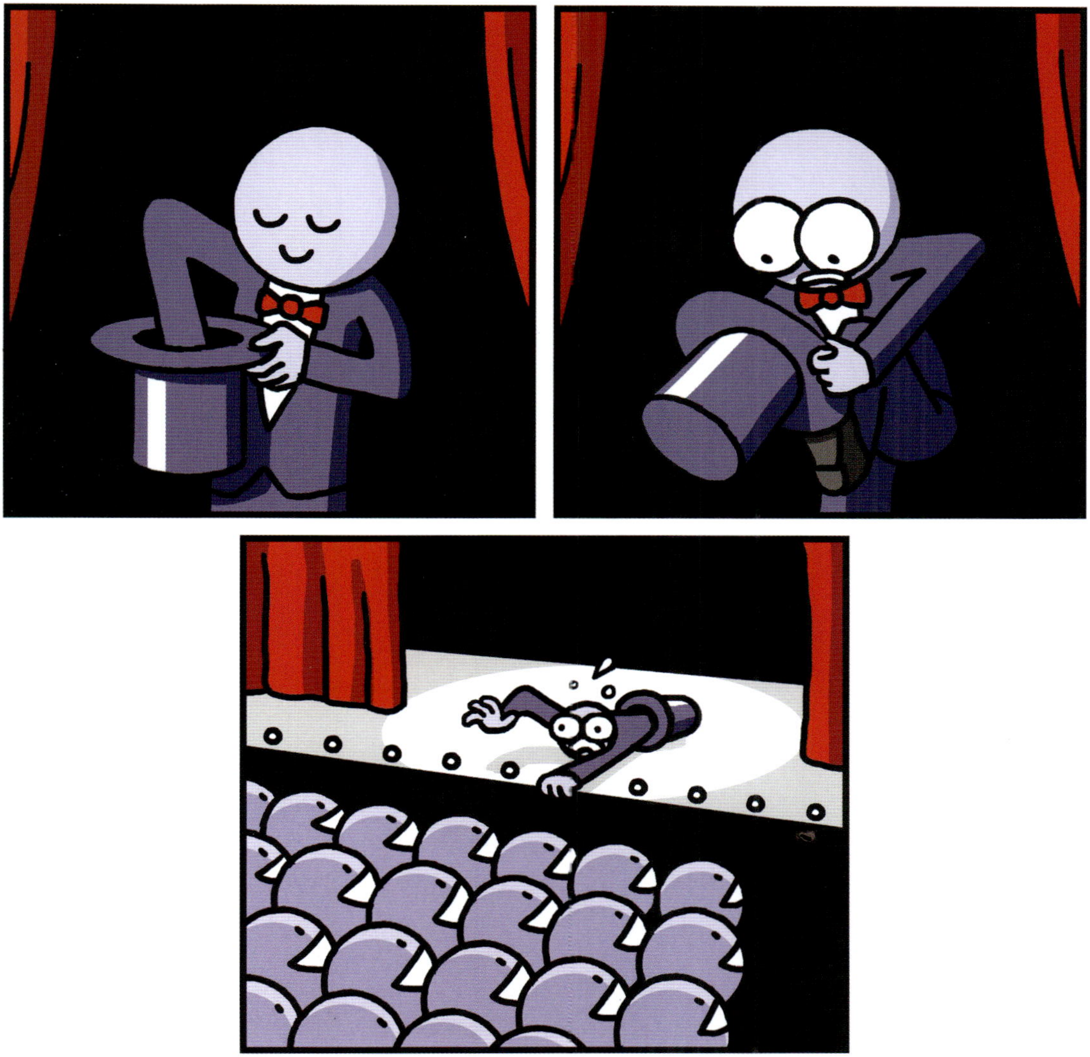

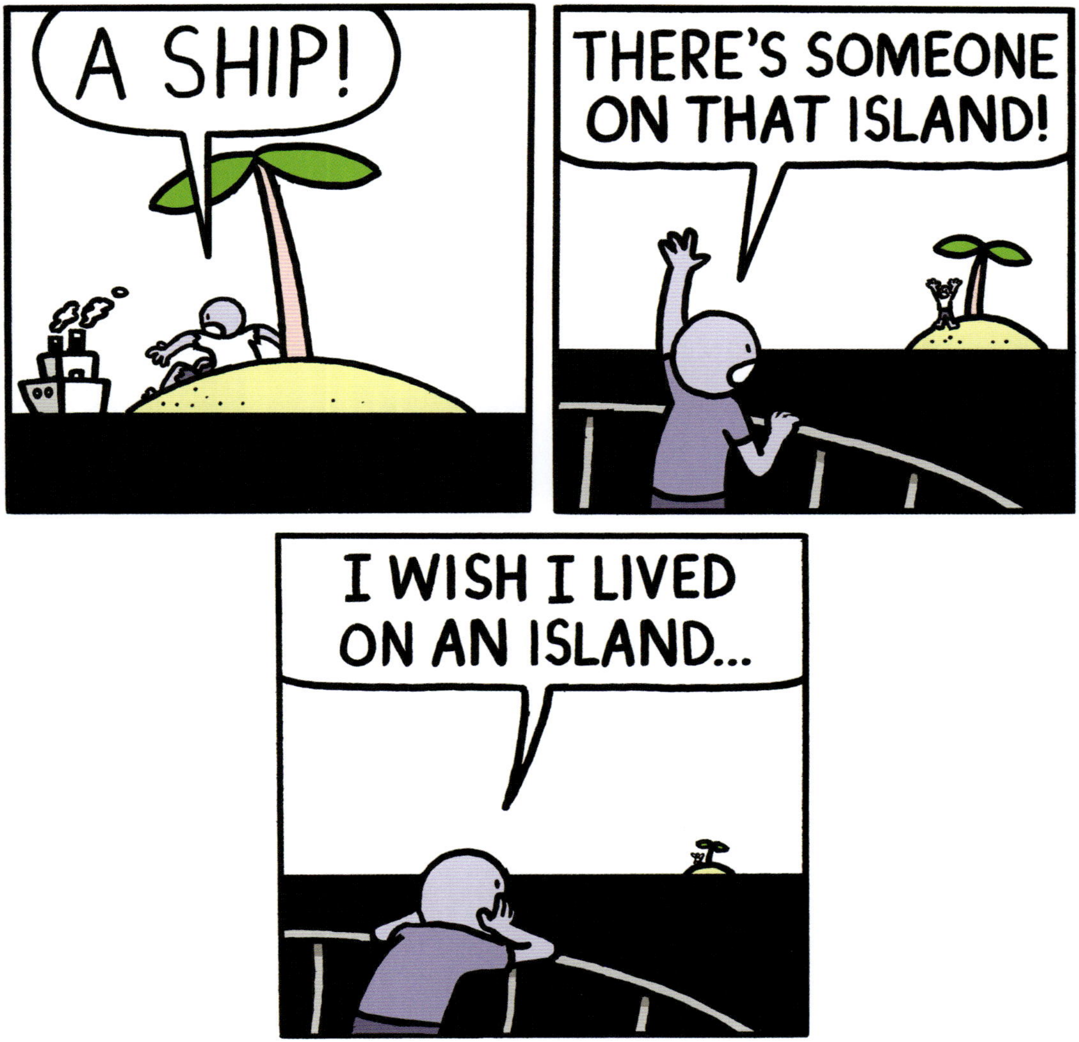
A SHIP!
THERE'S SOMEONE ON THAT ISLAND!
I WISH I LIVED ON AN ISLAND...

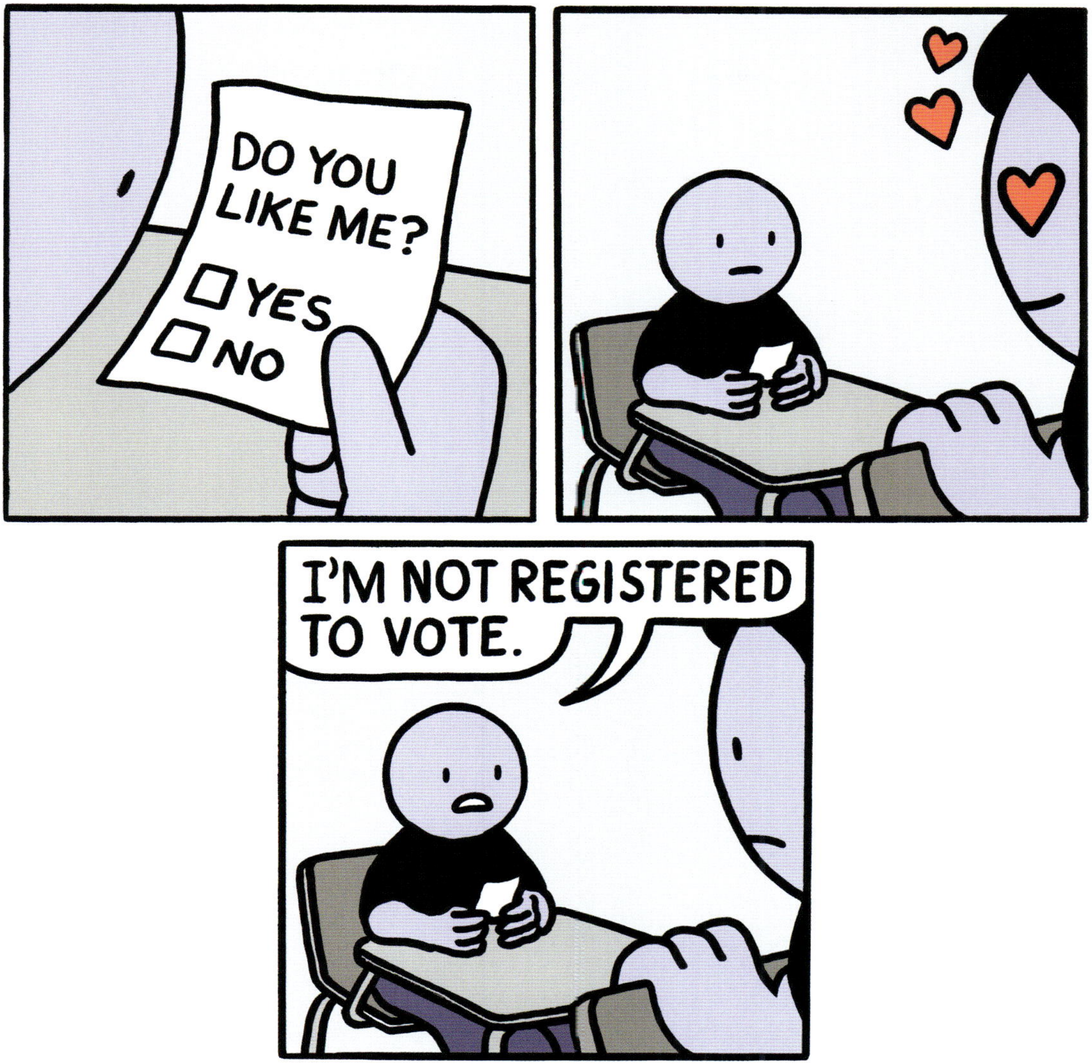
DO YOU LIKE ME?
YES
NO
I'M NOT REGISTERED TO VOTE.

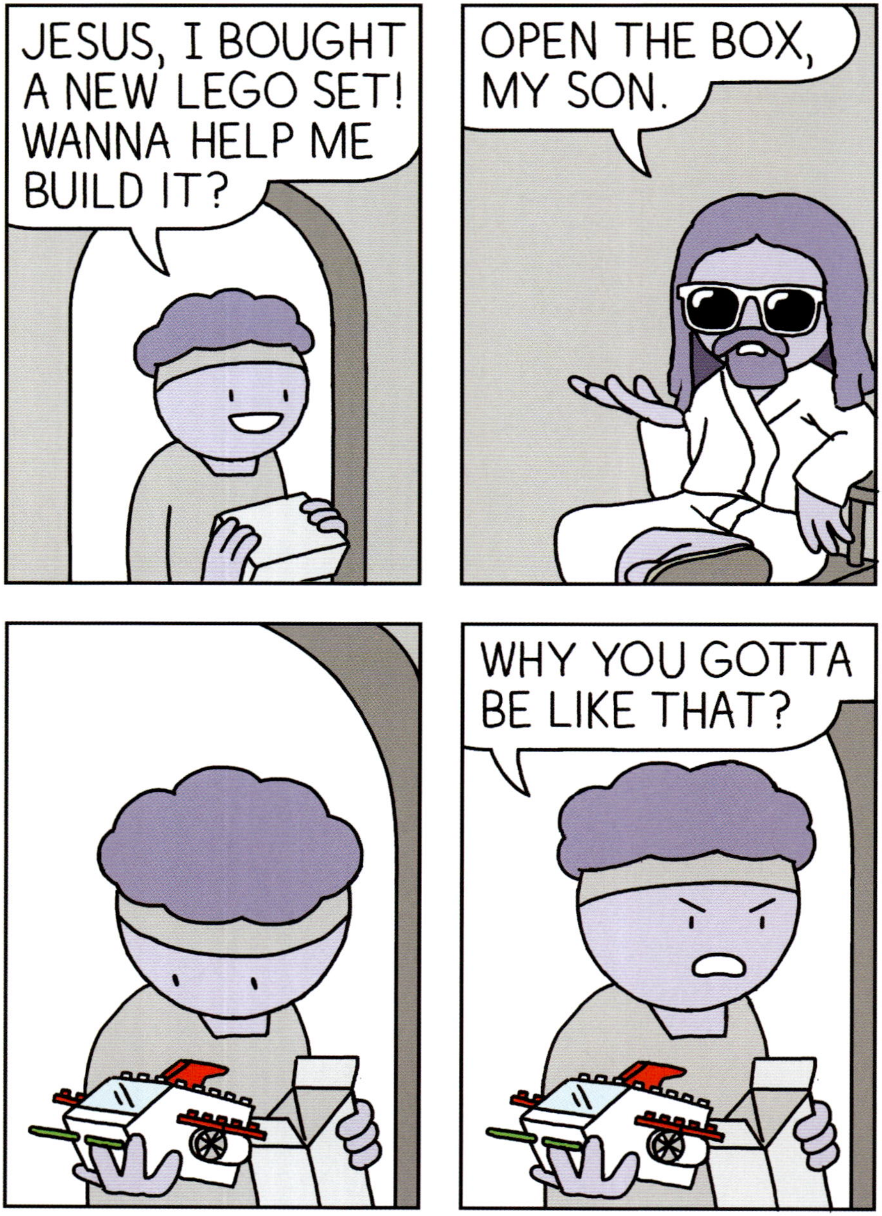
JESUS, I BOUGHT A NEW LEGO SET! WANNA HELP ME BUILD IT?
OPEN THE BOX, MY SON.
WHY YOU GOTTA BE LIKE THAT?

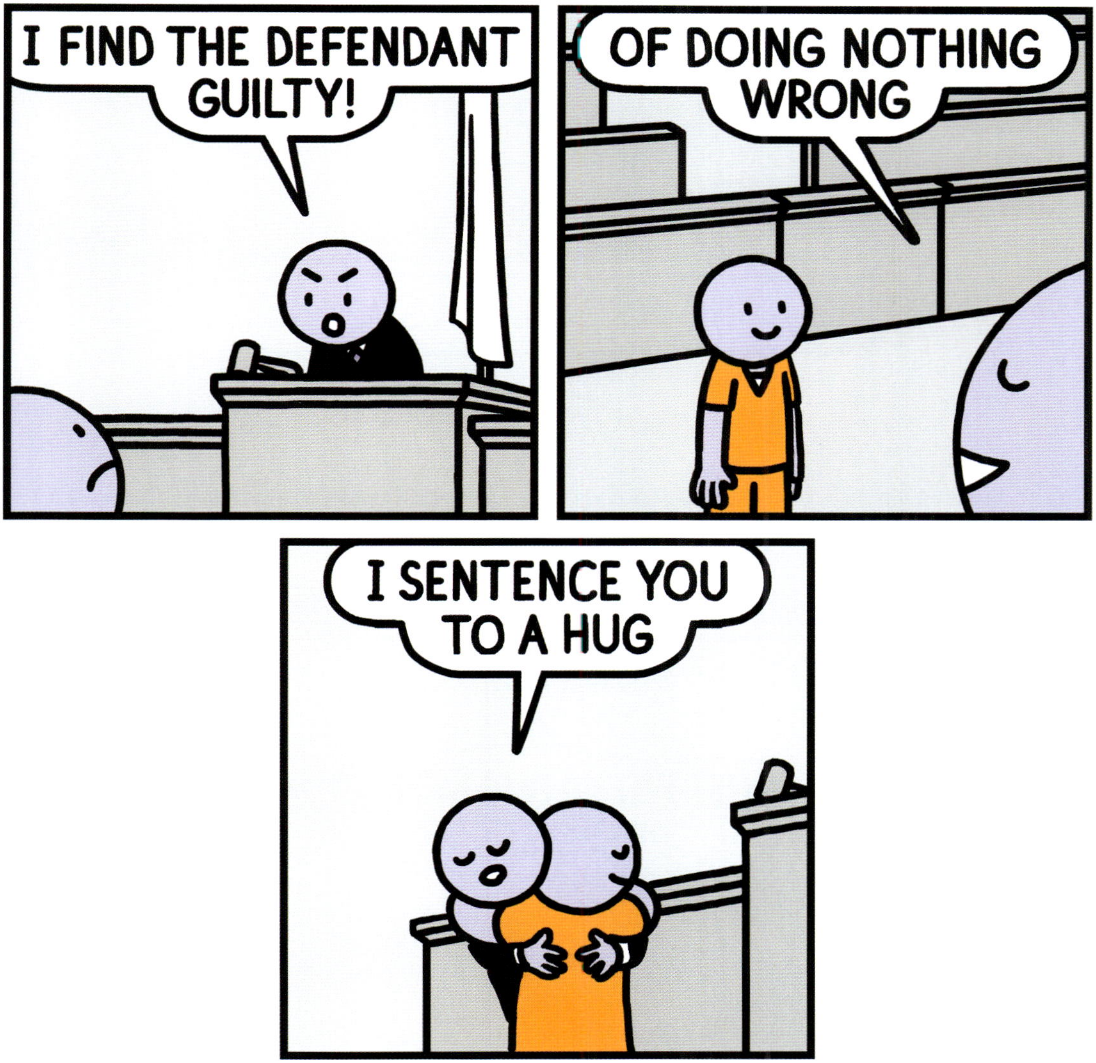
I FIND THE DEFENDANT GUILTY!
OF DOING NOTHING WRONG
I SENTENCE YOU TO A HUG

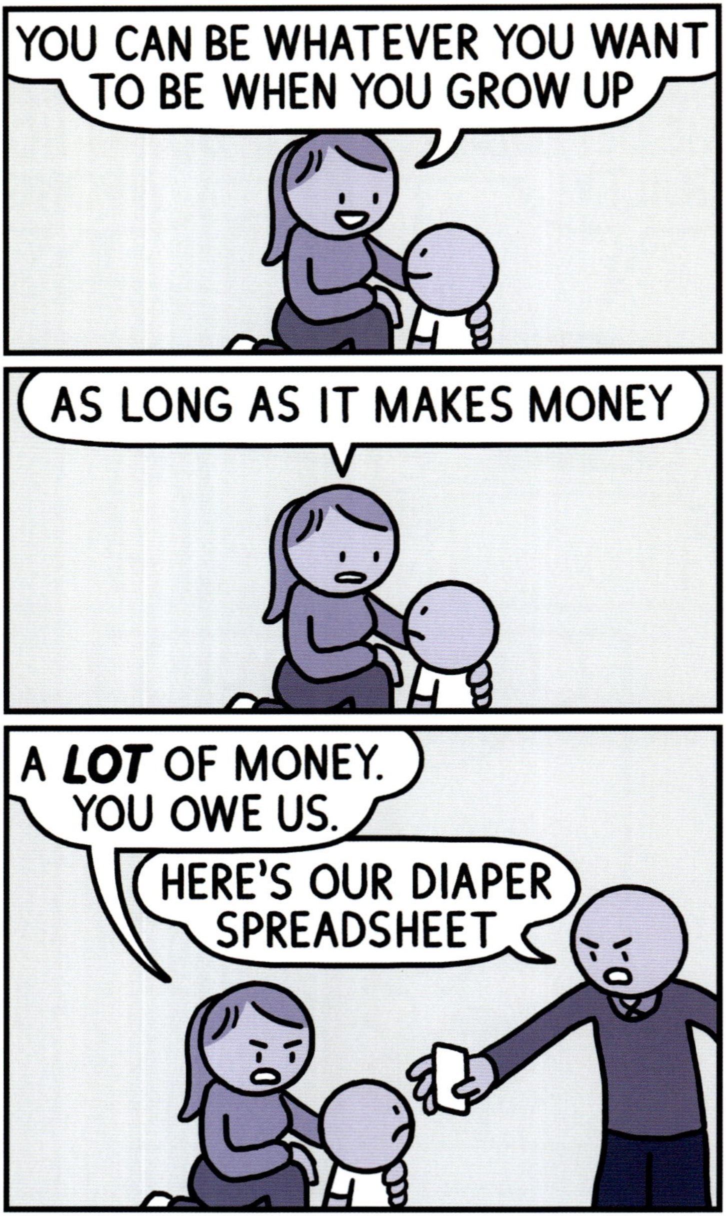
YOU CAN BE WHATEVER YOU WANT TO BE WHEN YOU GROW UP
AS LONG AS IT MAKES MONEY
A *LOT* OF MONEY. YOU OWE US.
HERE'S OUR DIAPER SPREADSHEET

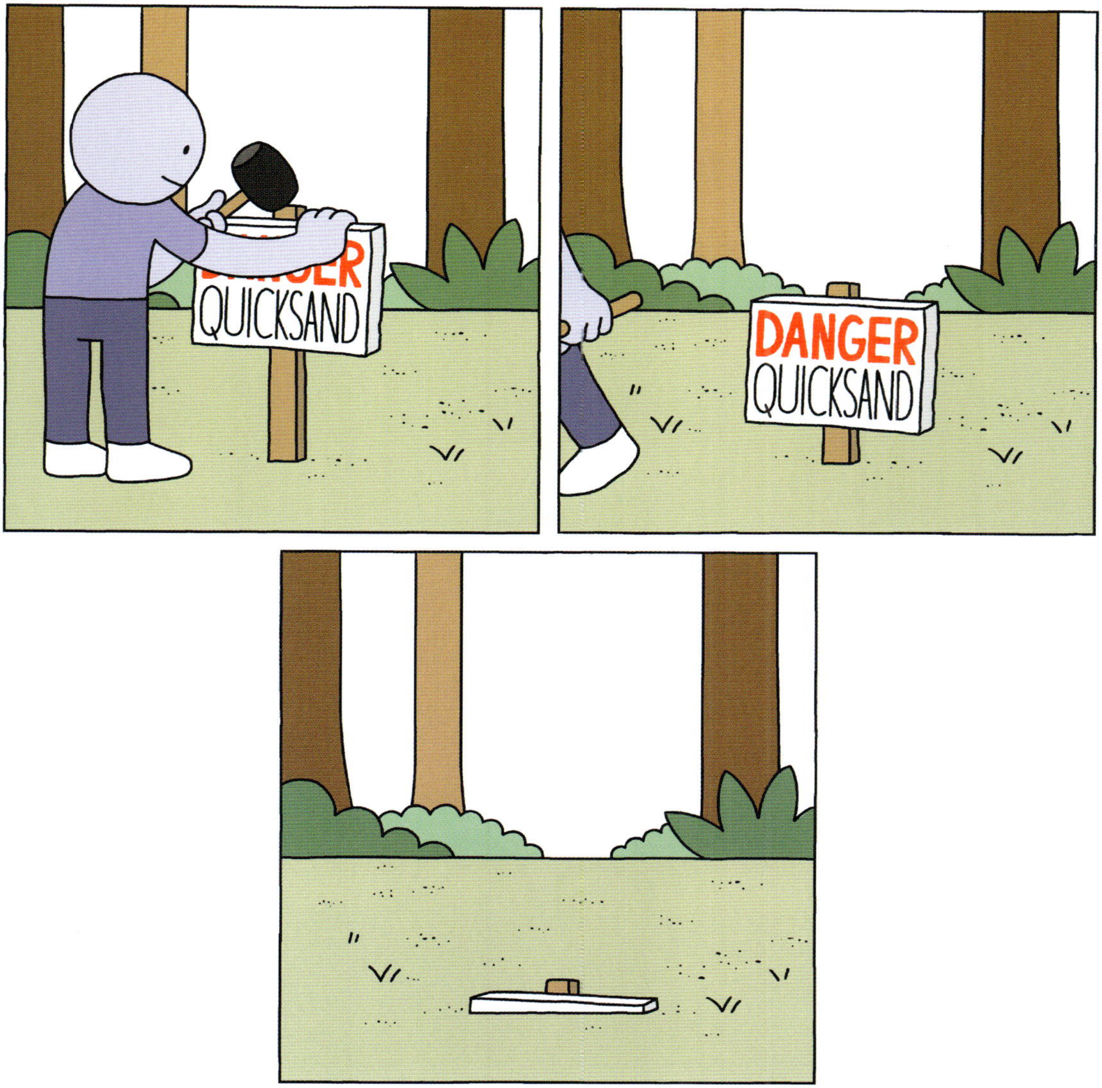
QUICKSAND
DANGER
QUICKSAND

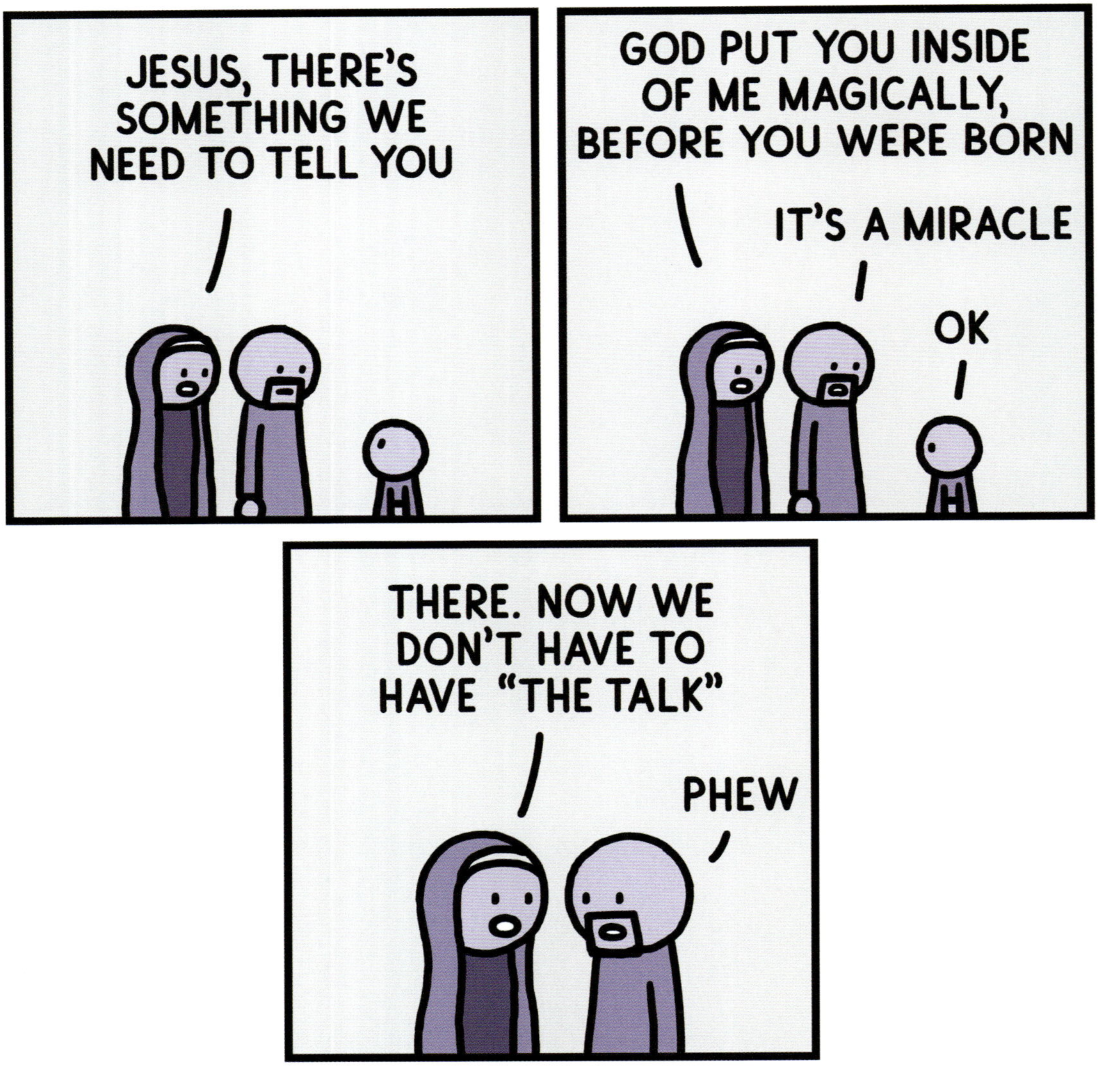
JESUS, THERE'S SOMETHING WE NEED TO TELL YOU
GOD PUT YOU INSIDE OF ME MAGICALLY, BEFORE YOU WERE BORN
IT'S A MIRACLE
OK
THERE. NOW WE DON'T HAVE TO HAVE "THE TALK"
PHEW

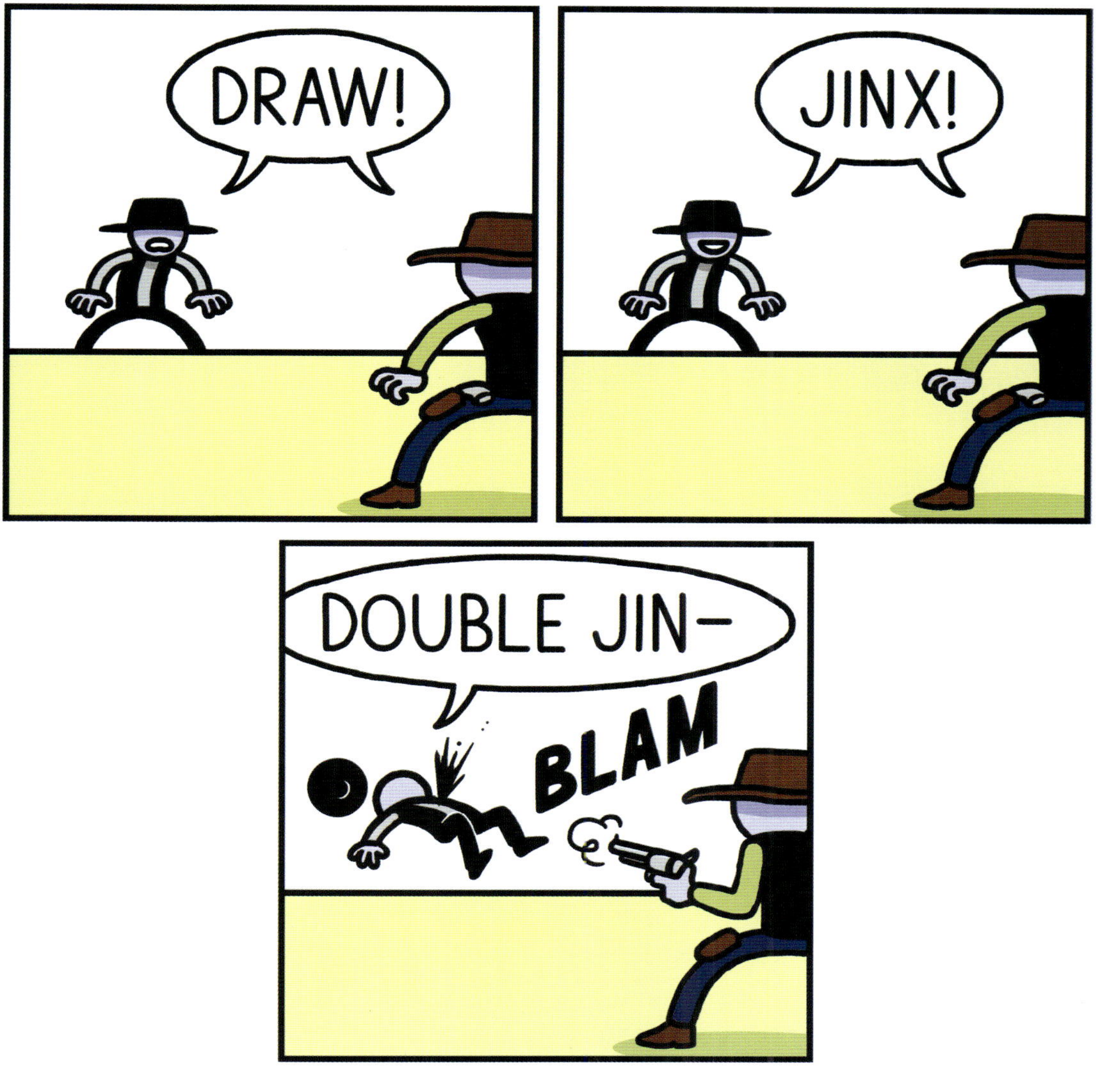
DRAW!
JINX!
DOUBLE JIN–
BLAM

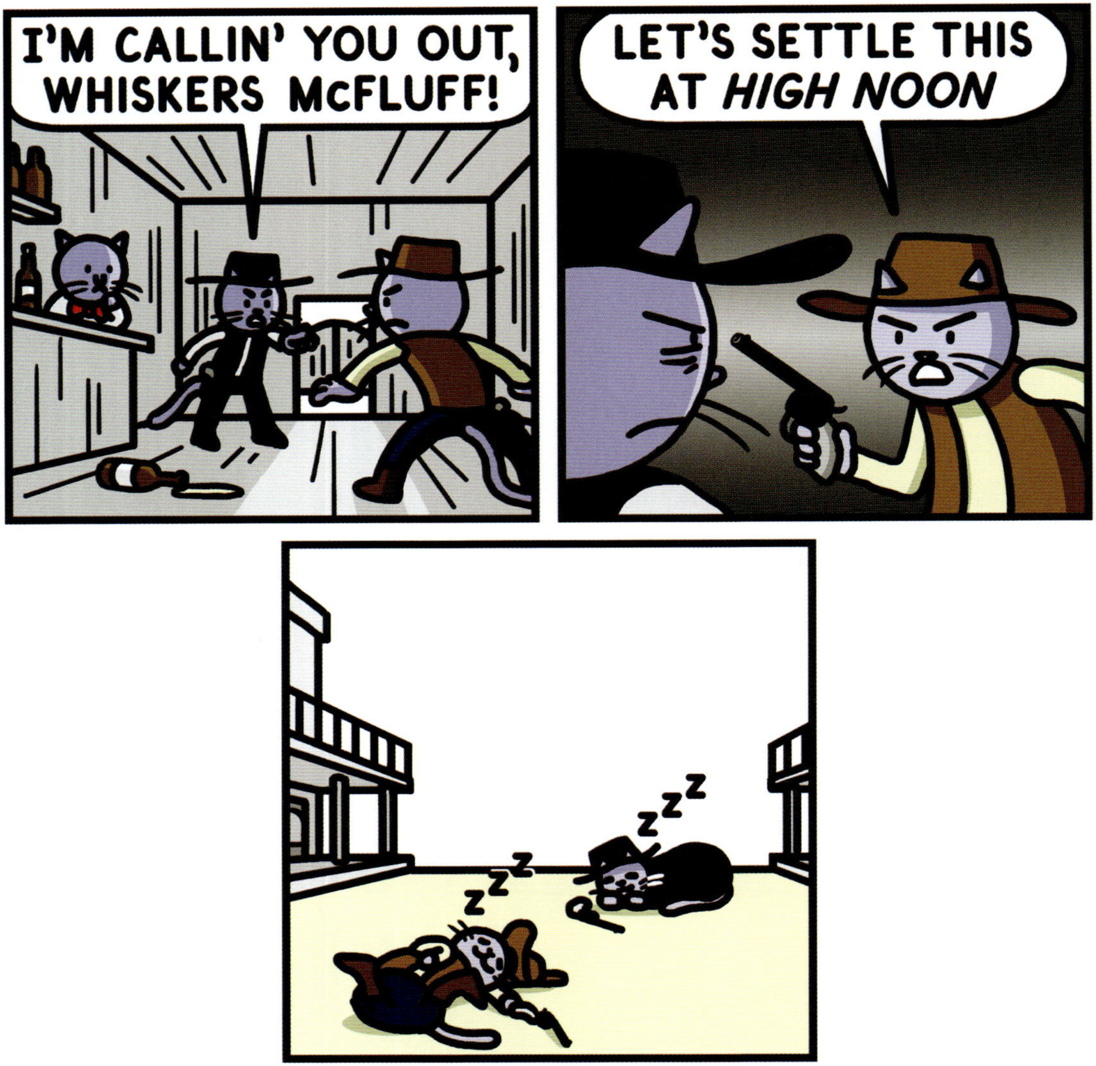
I'M CALLIN' YOU OUT, WHISKERS McFLUFF!
LET'S SETTLE THIS AT *HIGH NOON*
ZZZZ
ZZZ

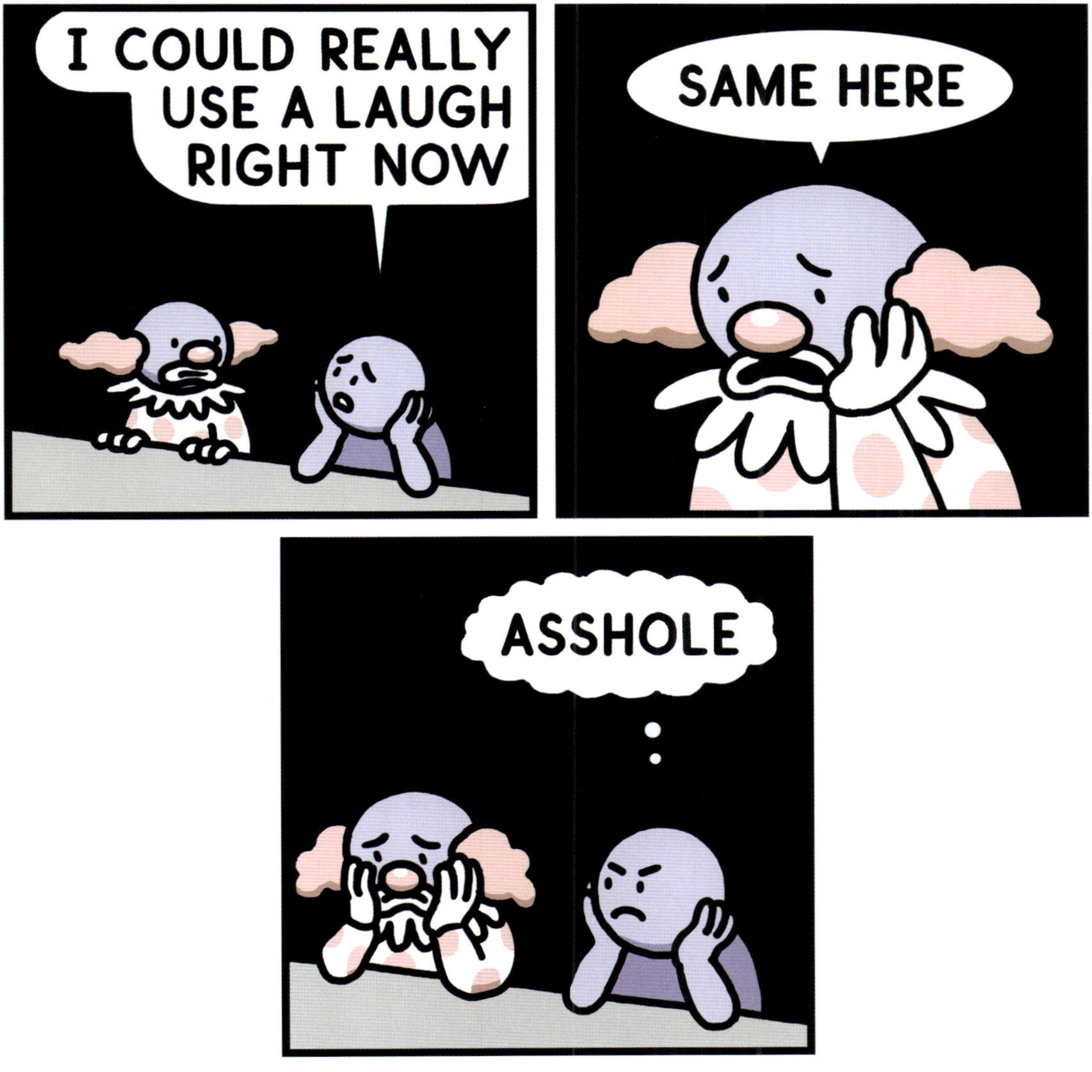
I COULD REALLY USE A LAUGH RIGHT NOW
SAME HERE
ASSHOLE

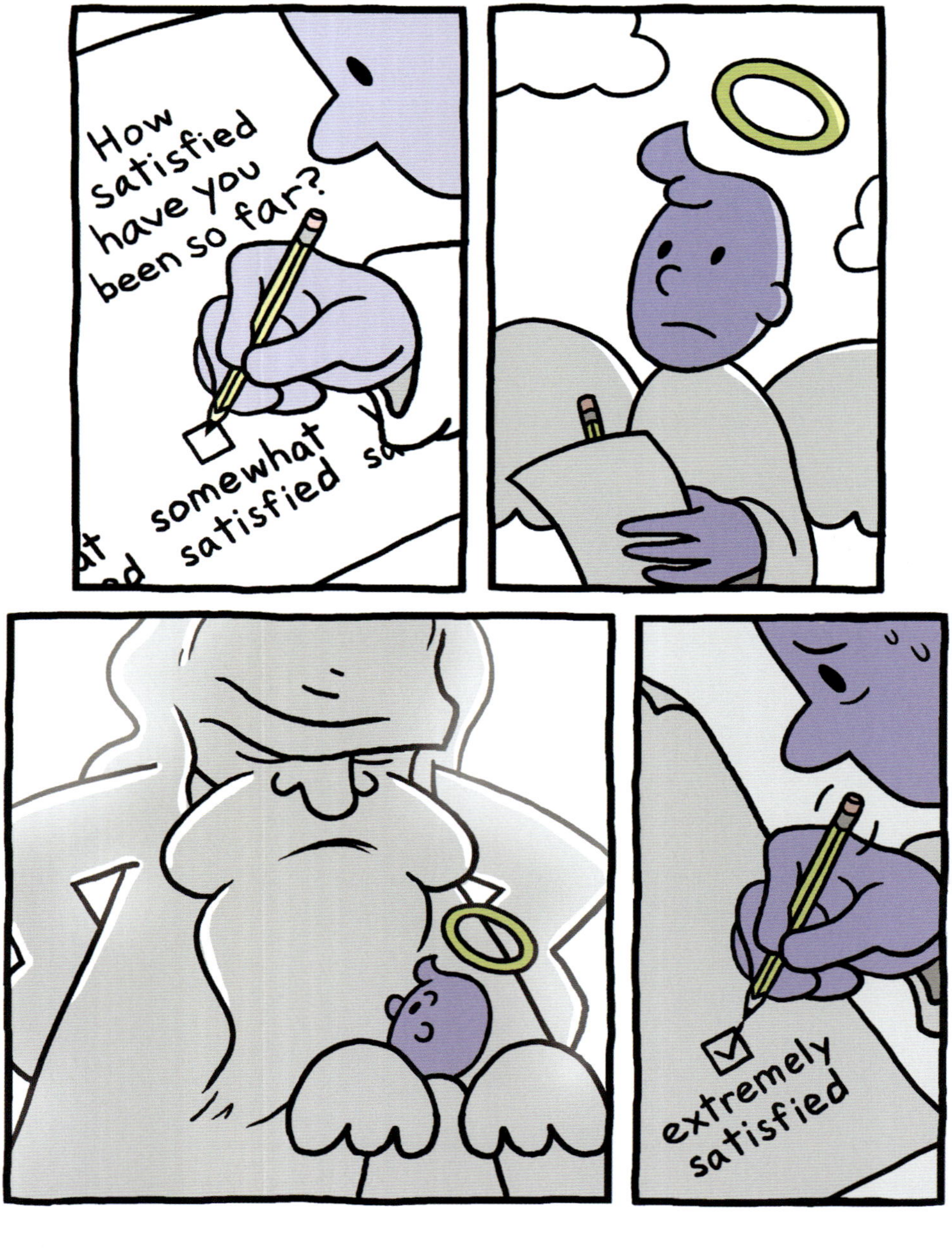
How satisfied have you been so far?
somewhat satisfied
extremely satisfied

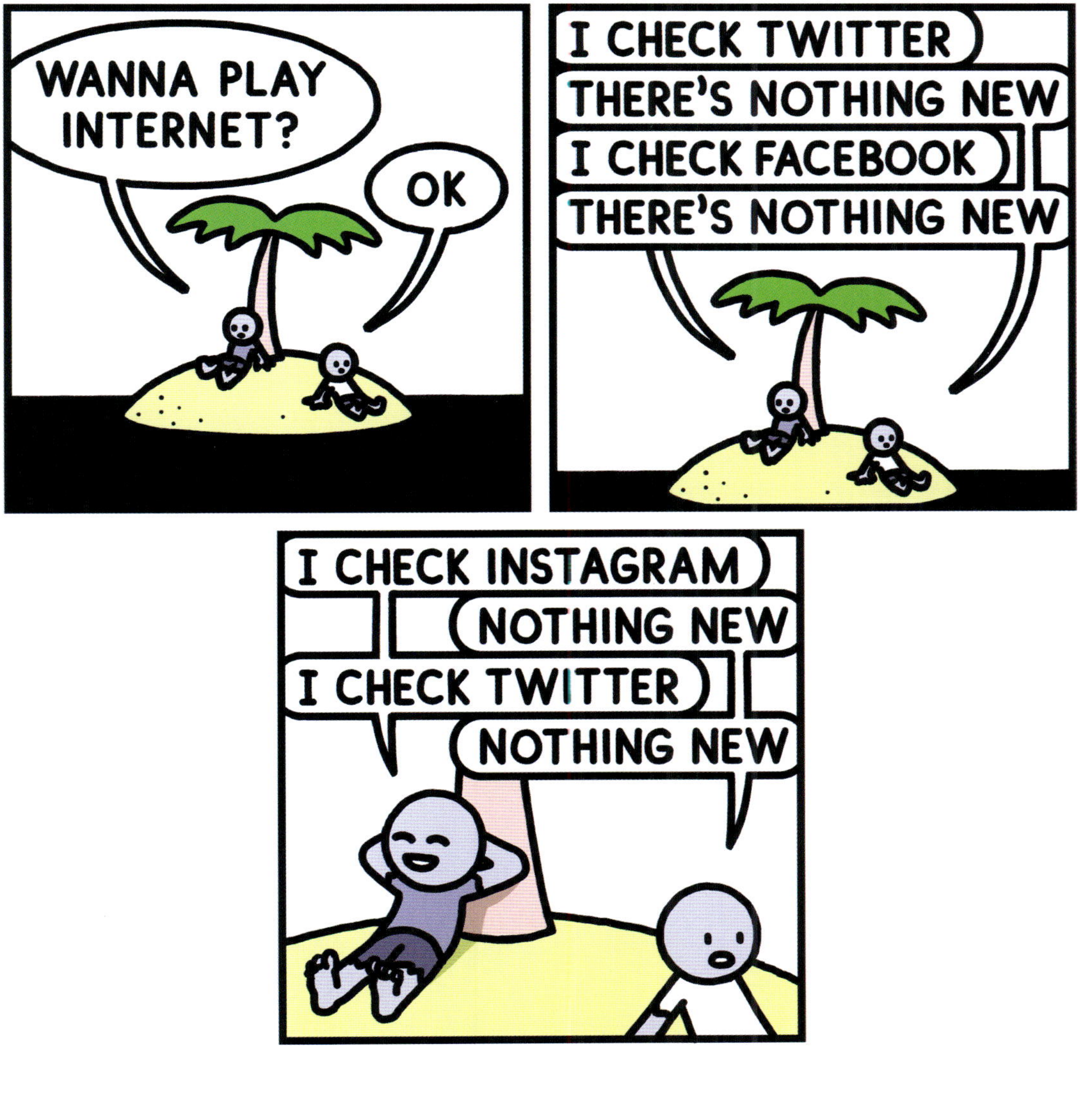
WANNA PLAY INTERNET?
OK
I CHECK TWITTER
THERE'S NOTHING NEW
I CHECK FACEBOOK
THERE'S NOTHING NEW
I CHECK INSTAGRAM
NOTHING NEW
I CHECK TWITTER
NOTHING NEW

I BOUGHT A BLIMP! LET'S GO FOR A RIDE!
PFFFFFFFT

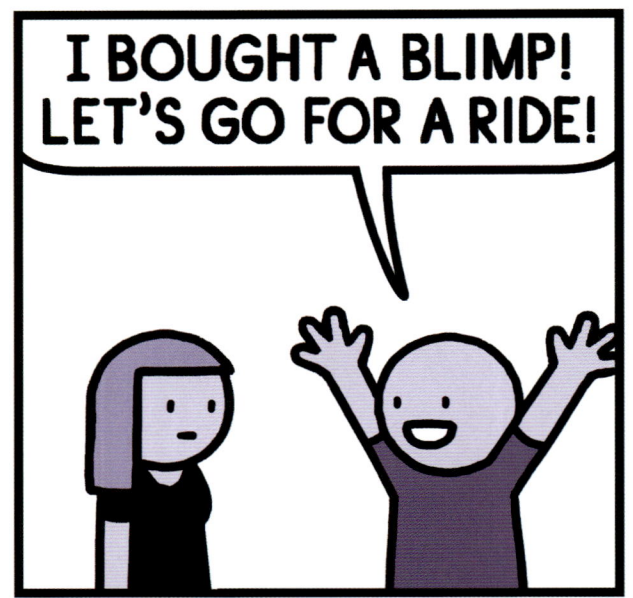

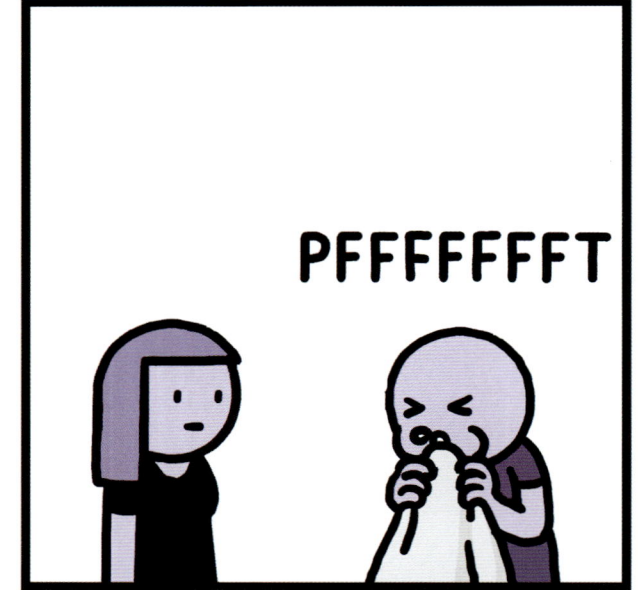

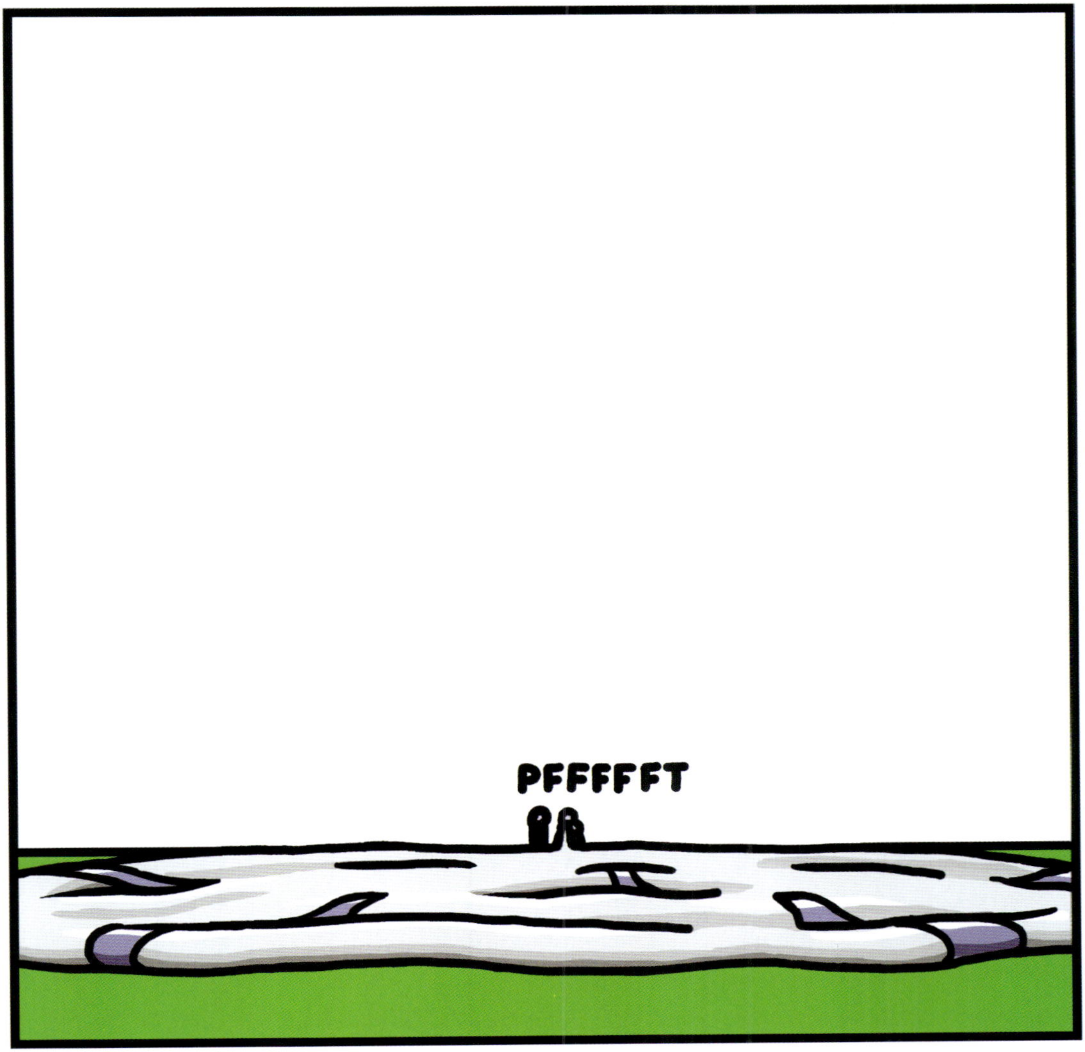
PFFFFFT

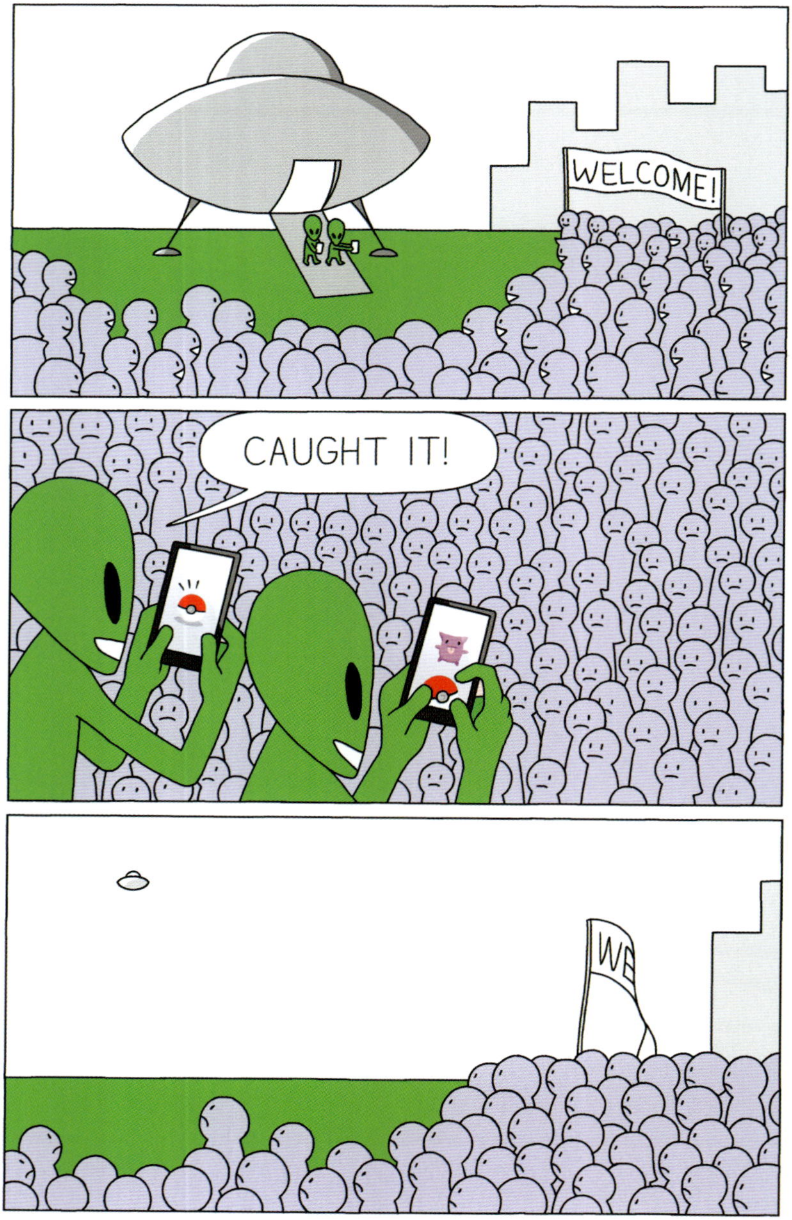
WELCOME!
CAUGHT IT!

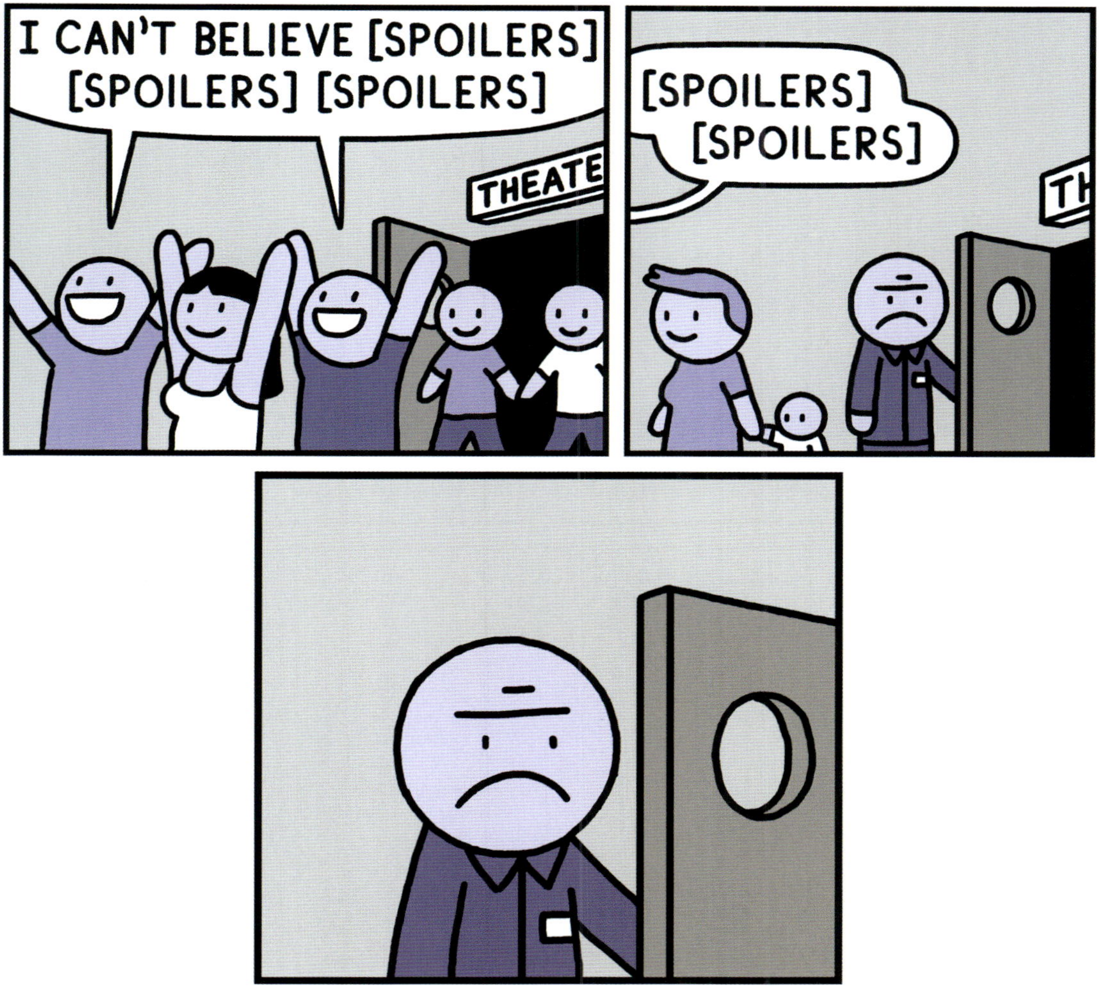
I CAN'T BELIEVE [SPOILERS] [SPOILERS] [SPOILERS]
THEATE
[SPOILERS] [SPOILERS]
TH

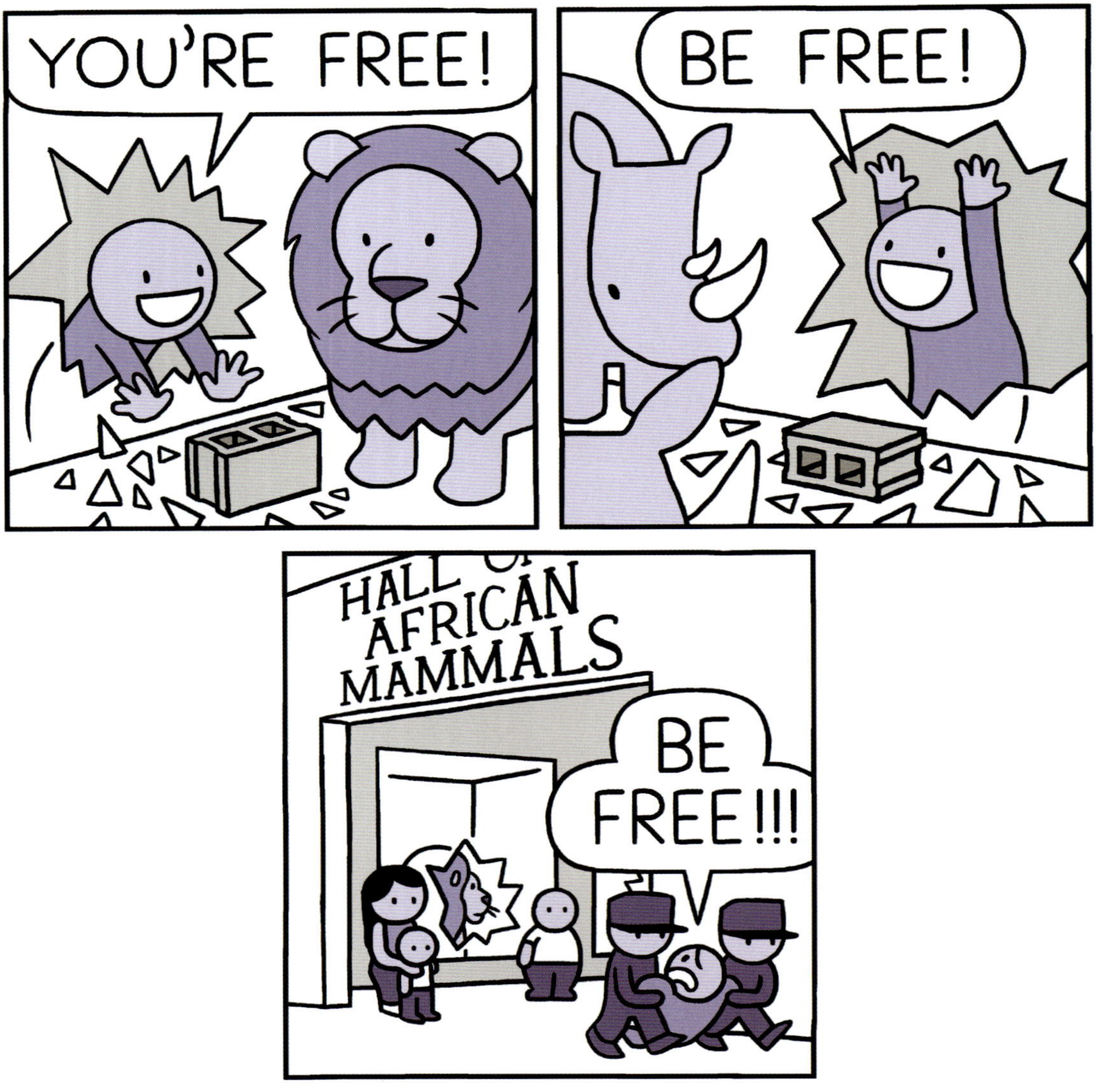
YOU'RE FREE!
BE FREE!
HALL
AFRICAN
MAMMALS
BE FREE!!!

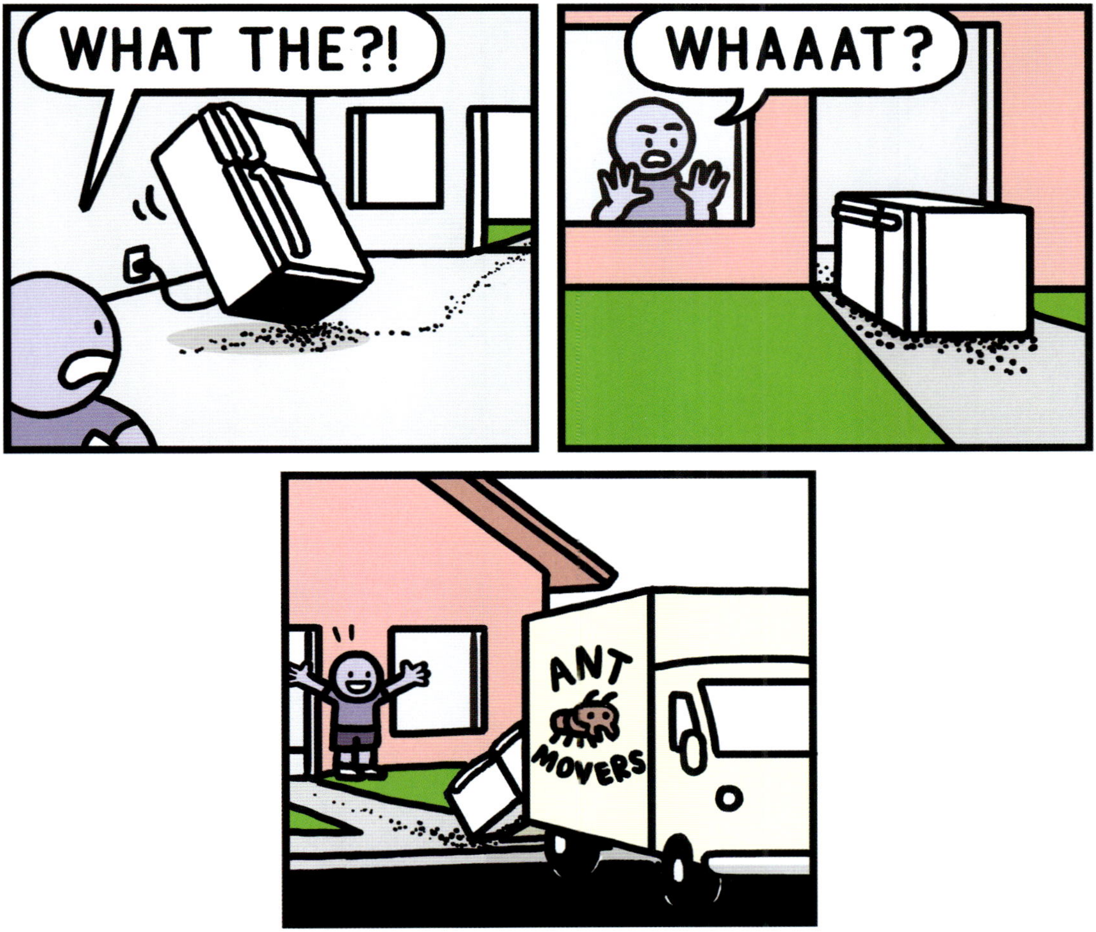
WHAT THE?!
WHAAAT?
ANT
MOVERS

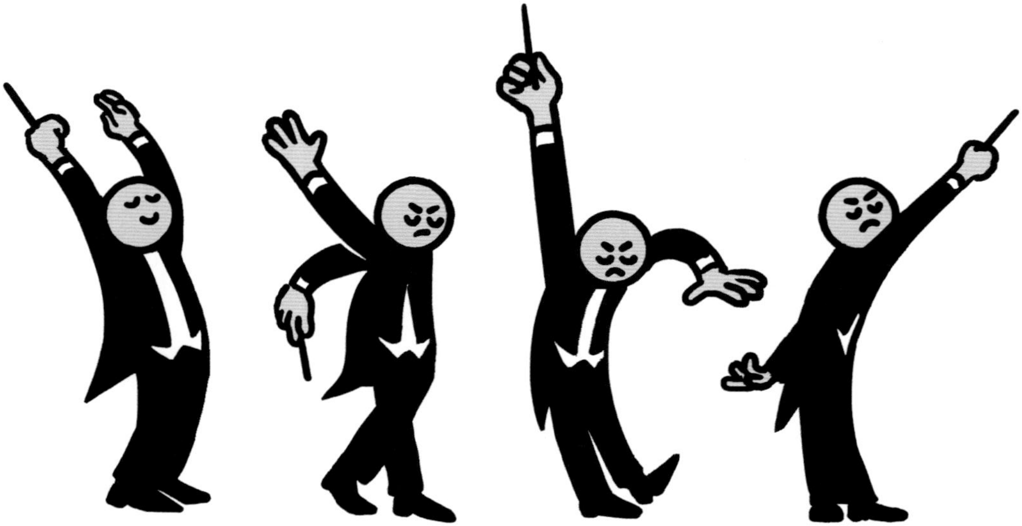

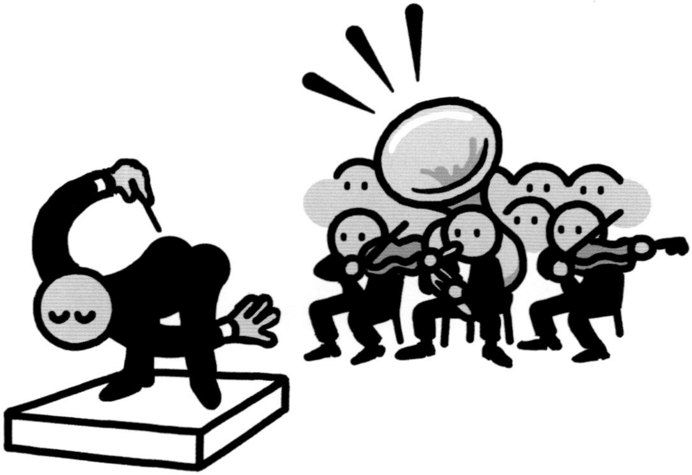

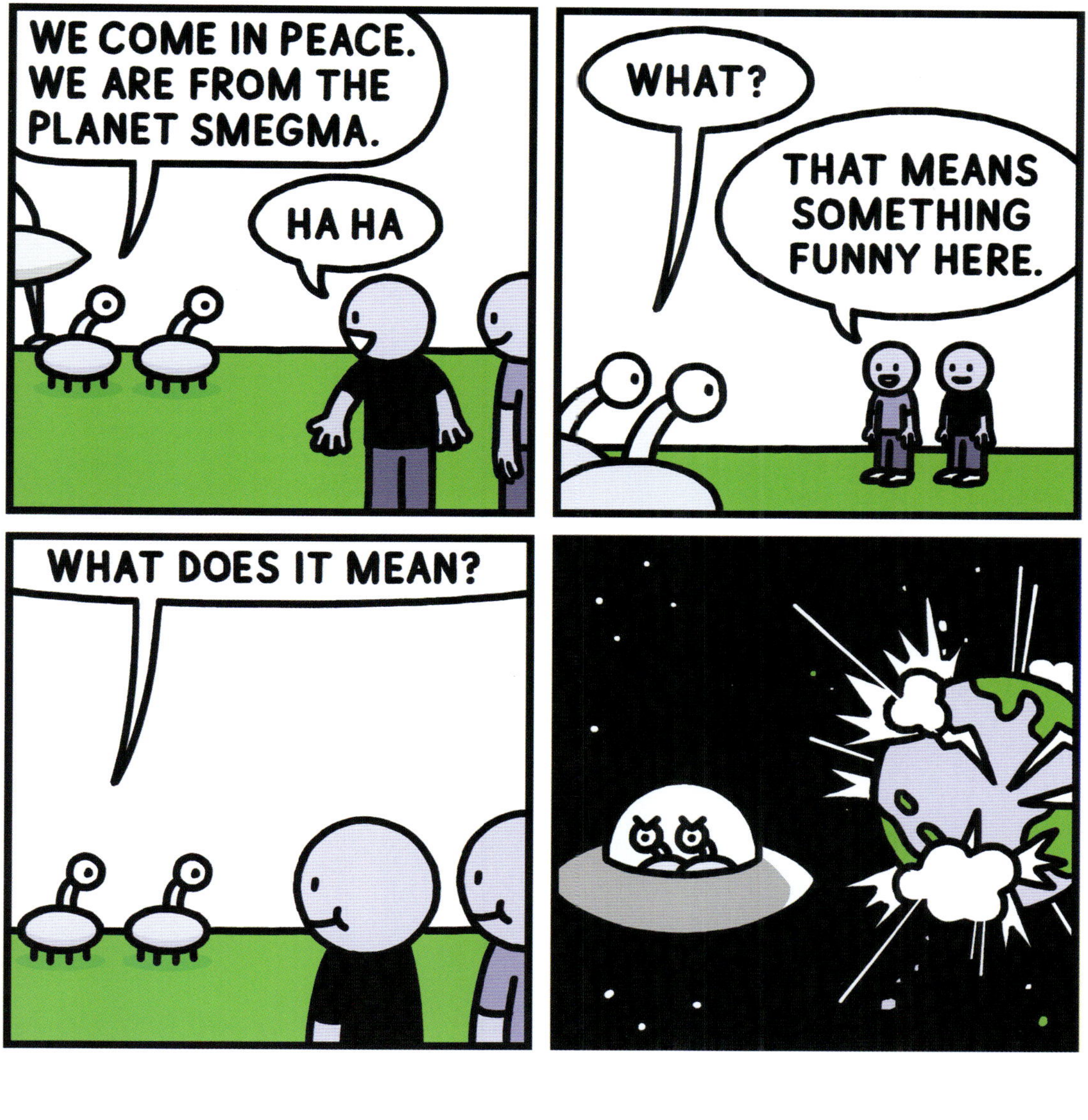
WE COME IN PEACE. WE ARE FROM THE PLANET SMEGMA.
HA HA
WHAT?
THAT MEANS SOMETHING FUNNY HERE.
WHAT DOES IT MEAN?

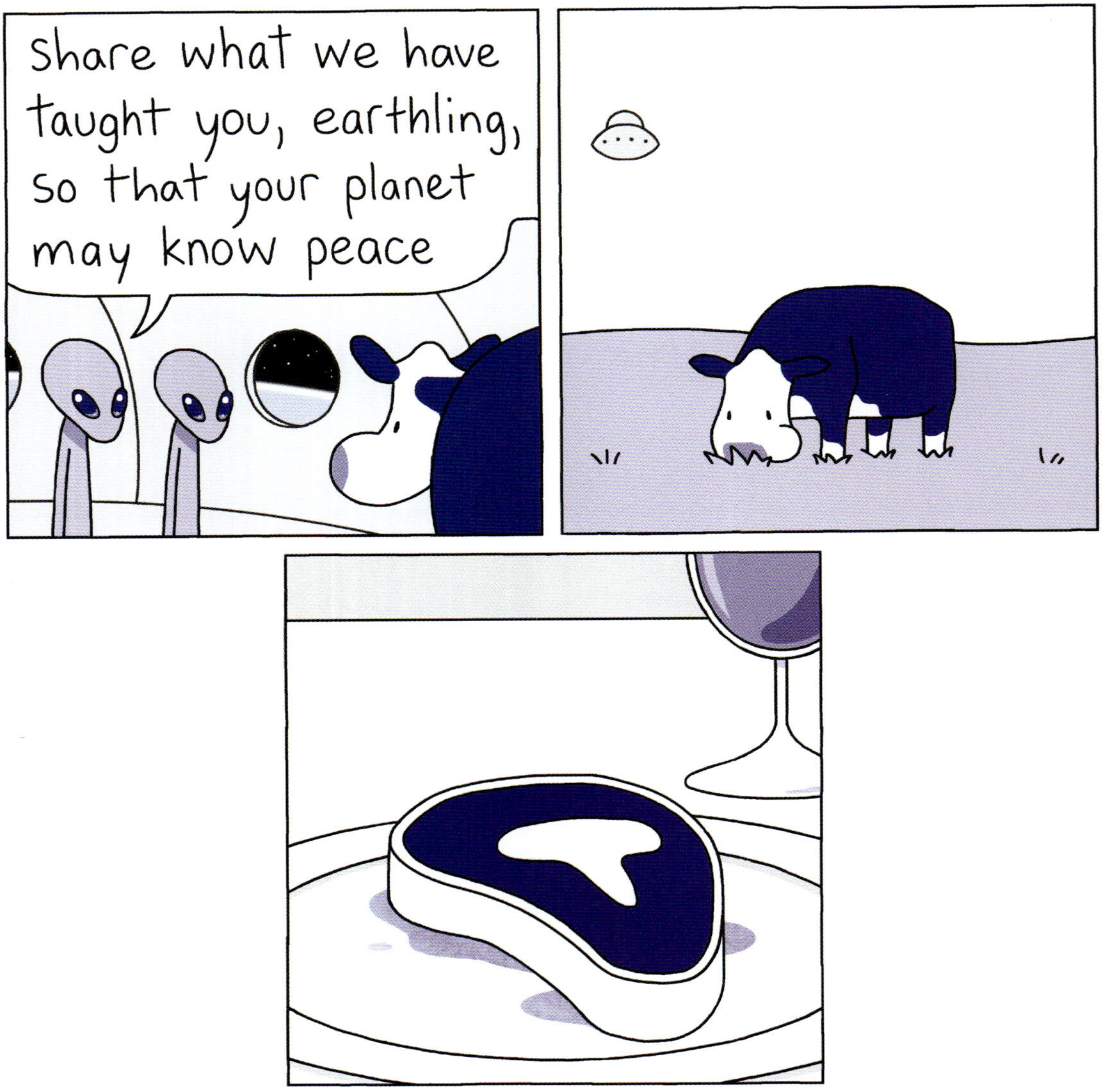
Share what we have taught you, earthling, so that your planet may know peace

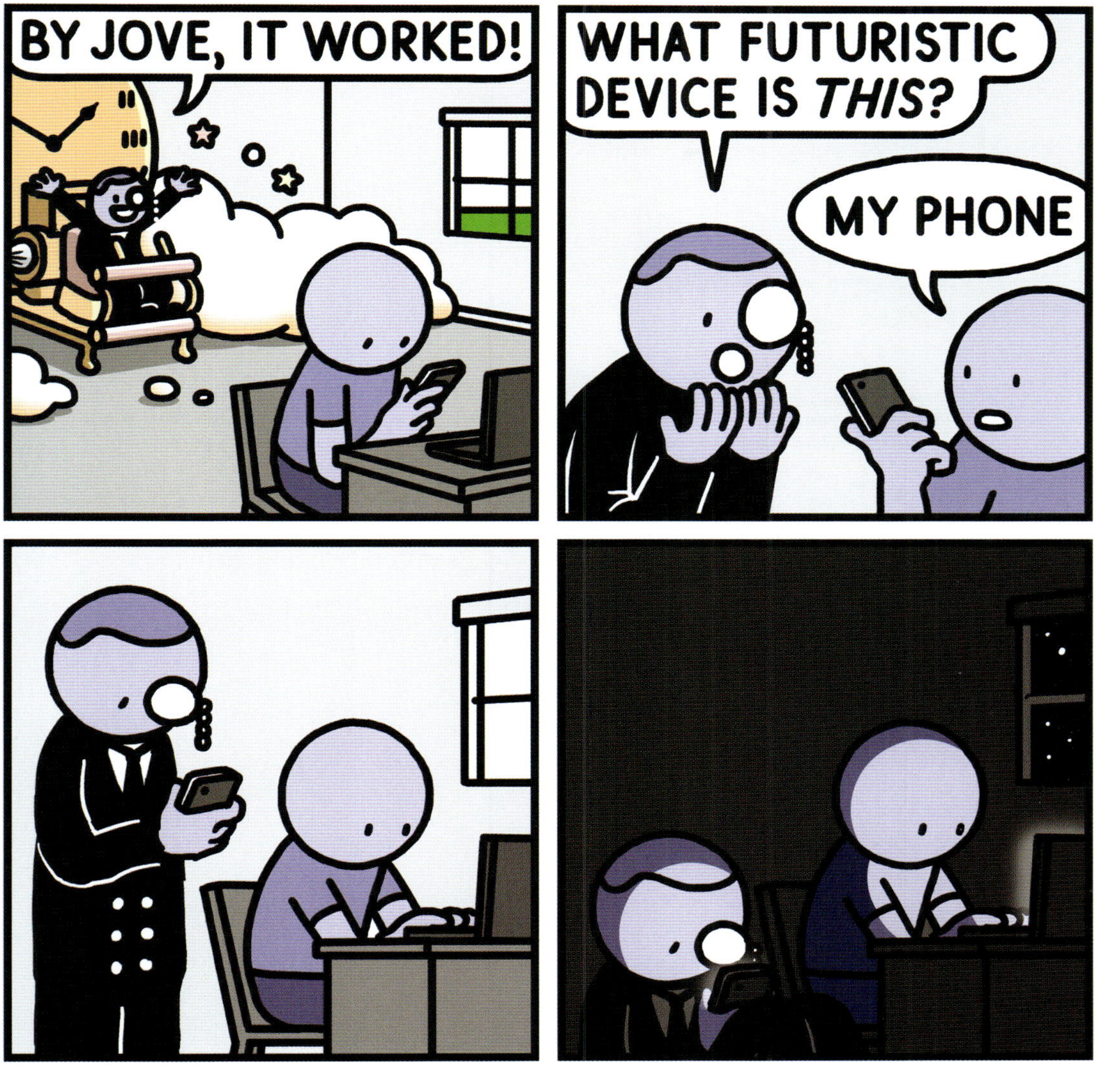
BY JOVE, IT WORKED!
WHAT FUTURISTIC DEVICE IS *THIS*?
MY PHONE

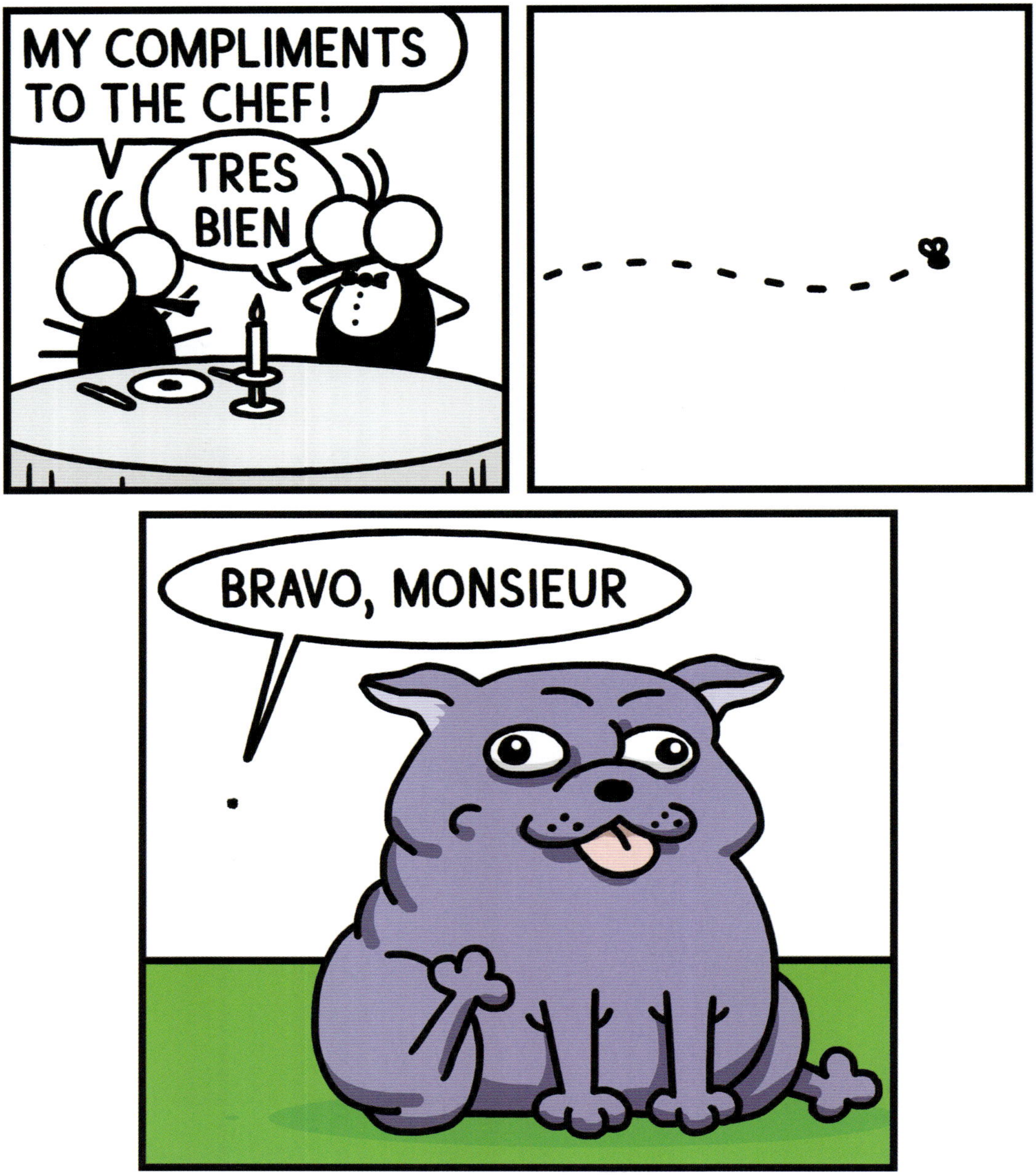
MY COMPLIMENTS TO THE CHEF!
TRES BIEN
BRAVO, MONSIEUR

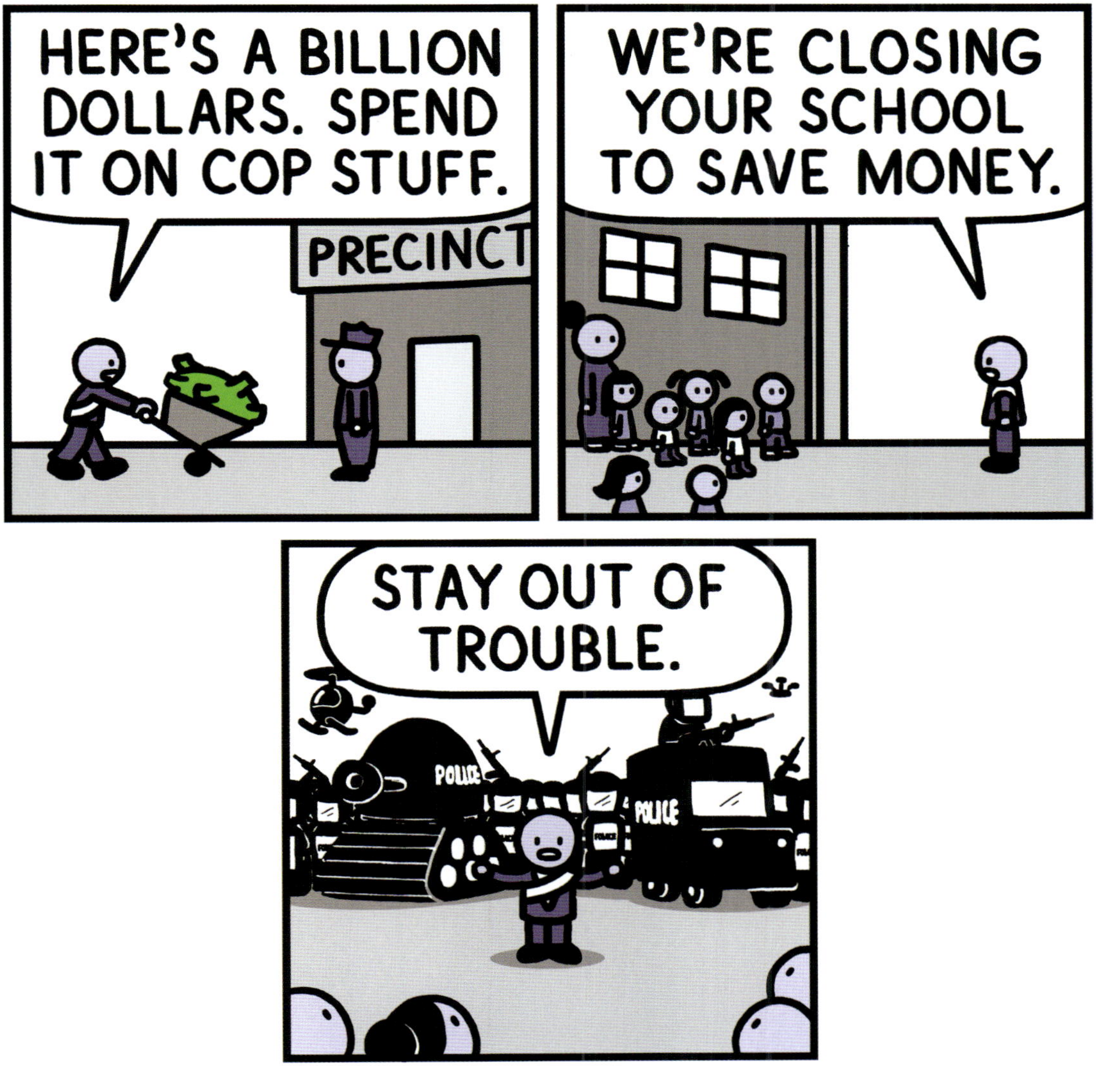
HERE'S A BILLION DOLLARS. SPEND IT ON COP STUFF.
PRECINCT
WE'RE CLOSING YOUR SCHOOL TO SAVE MONEY.
STAY OUT OF TROUBLE.
POLICE
POLICE

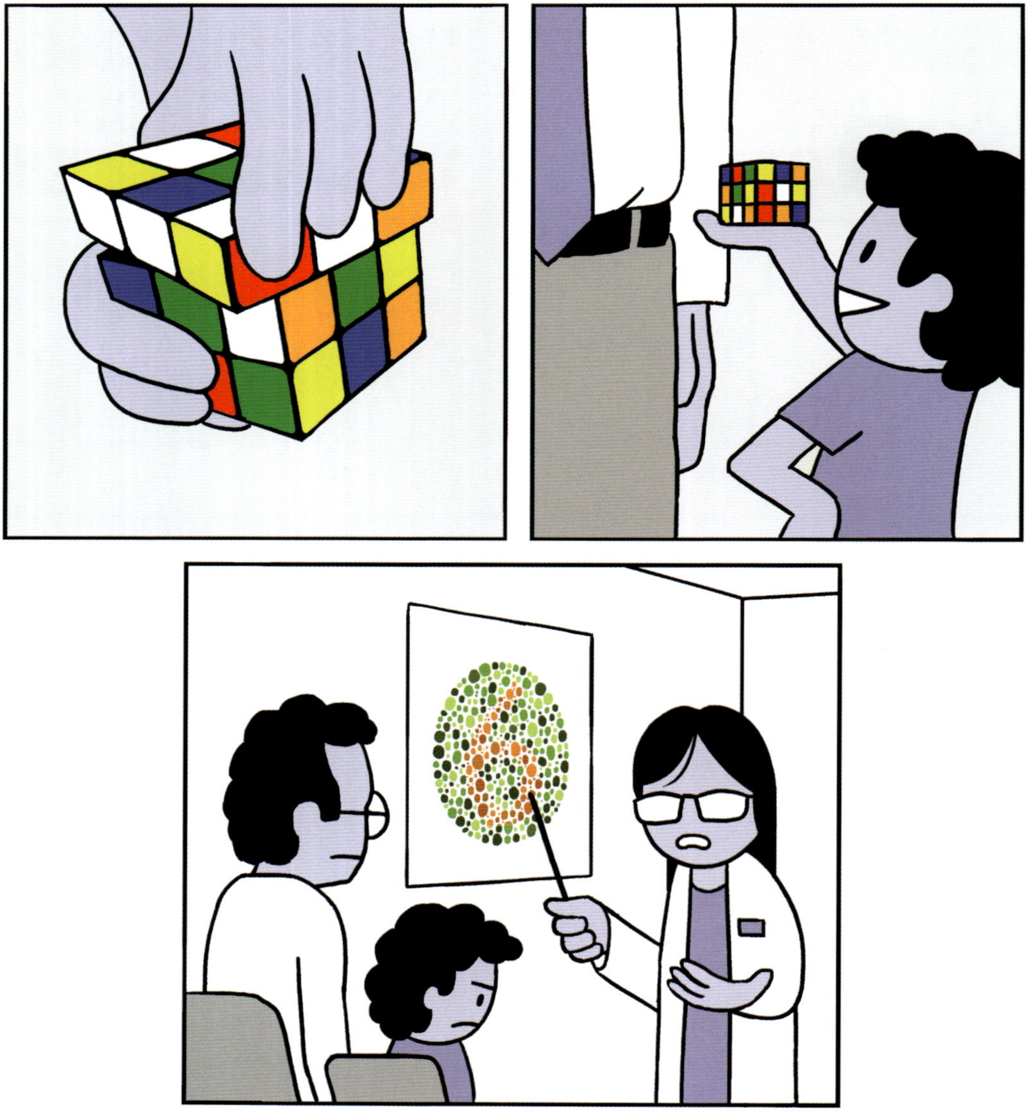

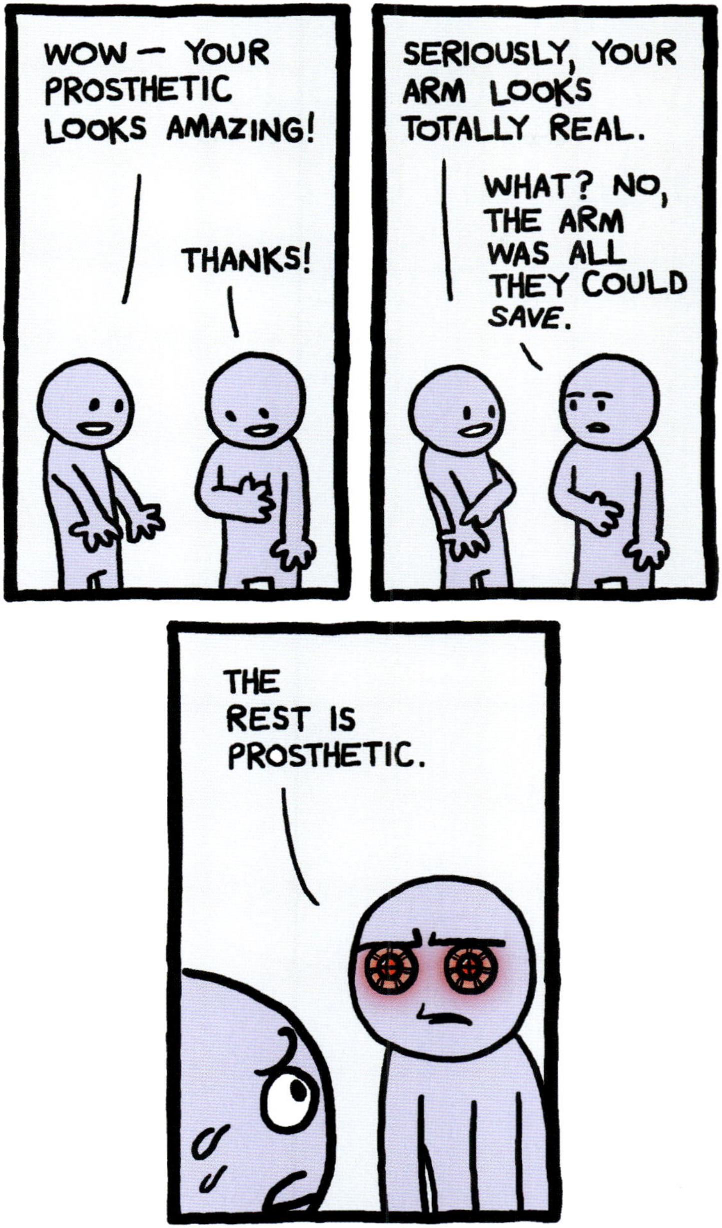
WOW — YOUR PROSTHETIC LOOKS AMAZING!
THANKS!
SERIOUSLY, YOUR ARM LOOKS TOTALLY REAL.
WHAT? NO, THE ARM WAS ALL THEY COULD *SAVE*.
THE REST IS PROSTHETIC.

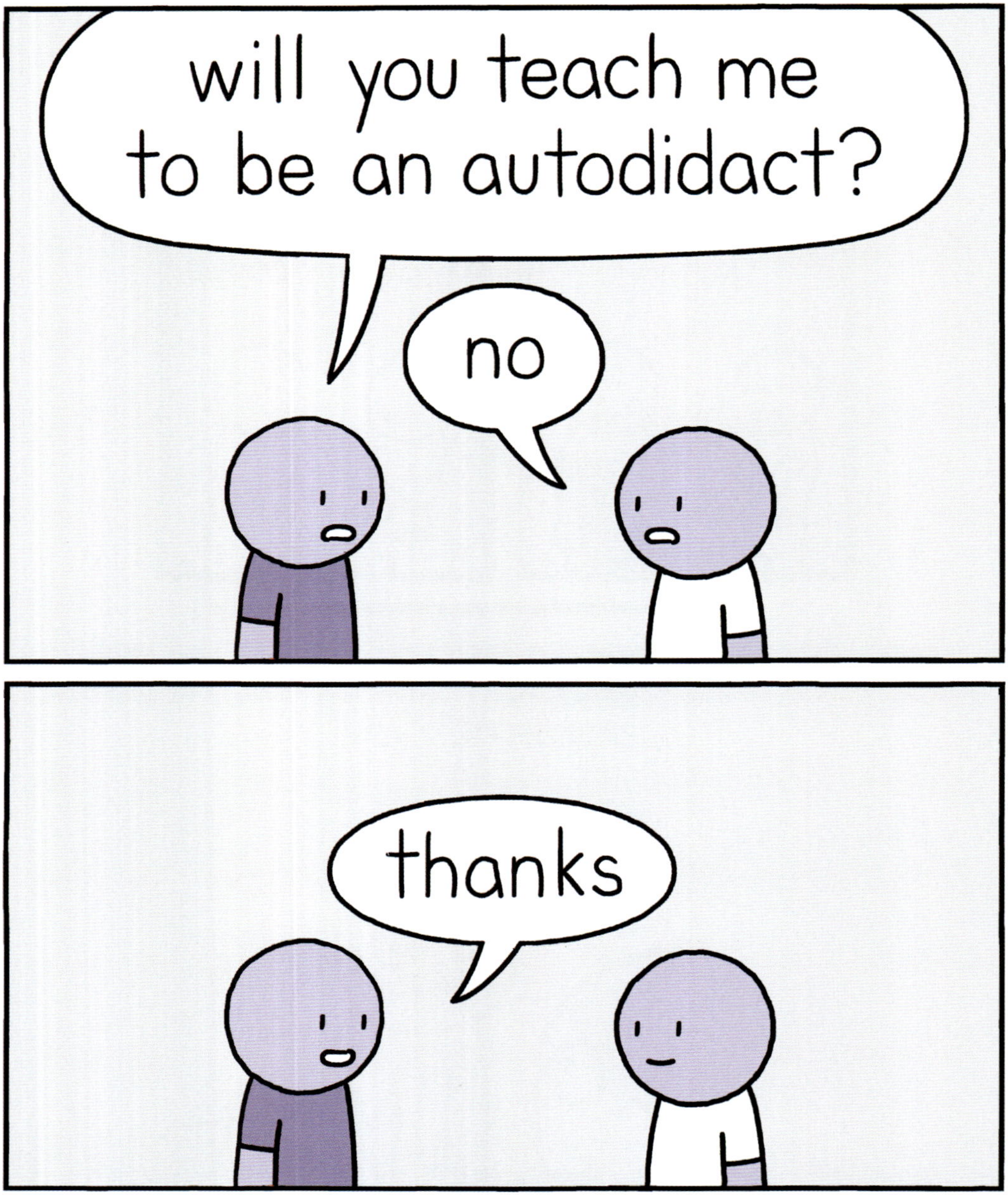
will you teach me to be an autodidact?
no
thanks

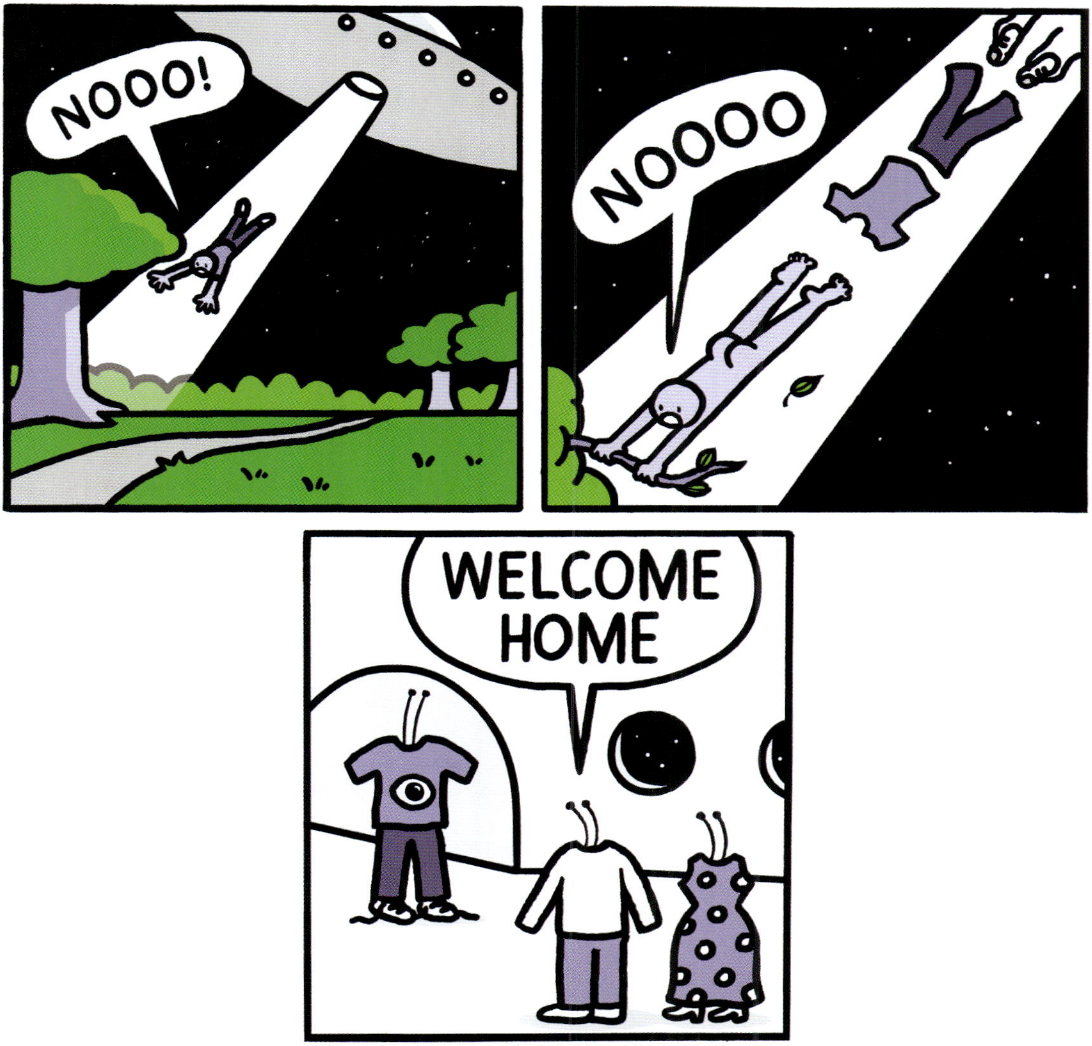
NOOO!
NOOOO
WELCOME HOME

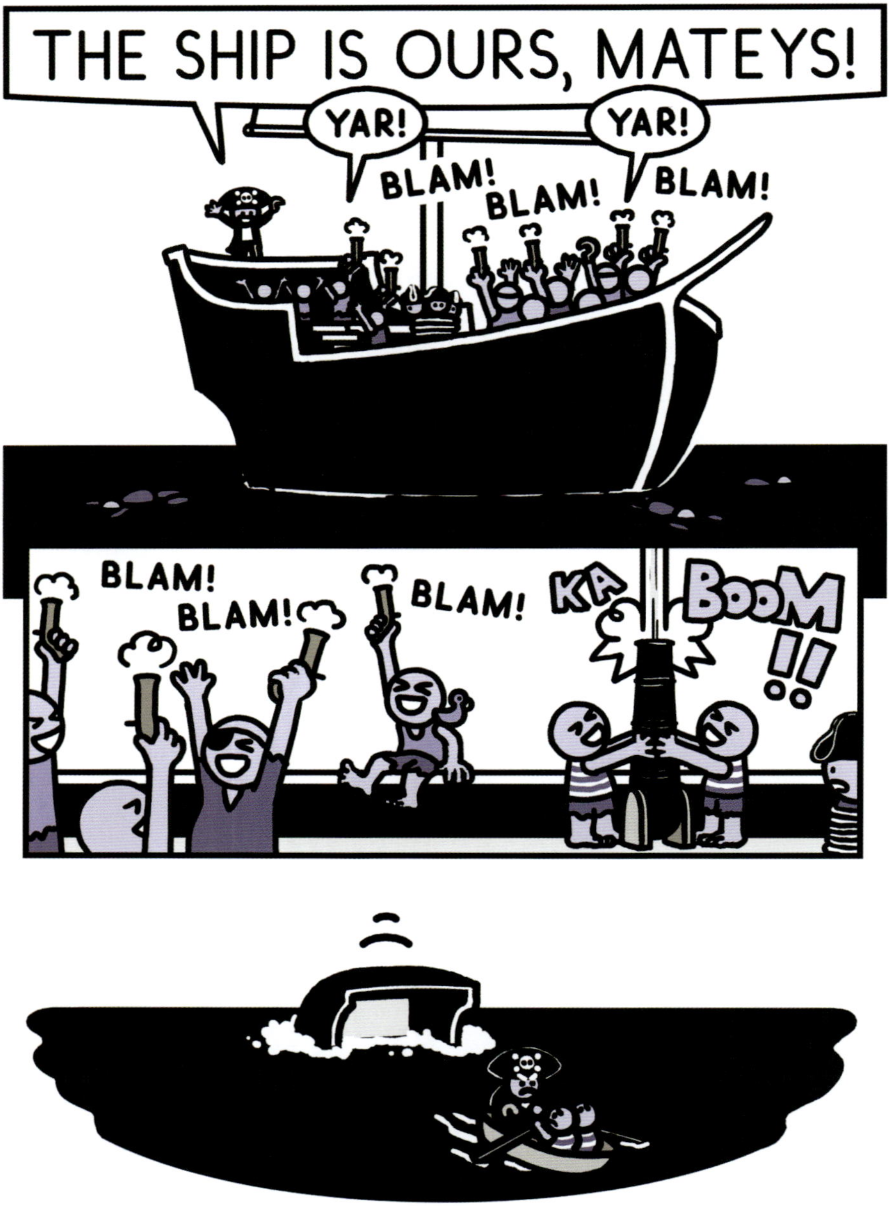
THE SHIP IS OURS, MATEYS!
YAR!
YAR!
BLAM!
BLAM!
BLAM!
BLAM!
BLAM!
BLAM!
KA BOOM!!

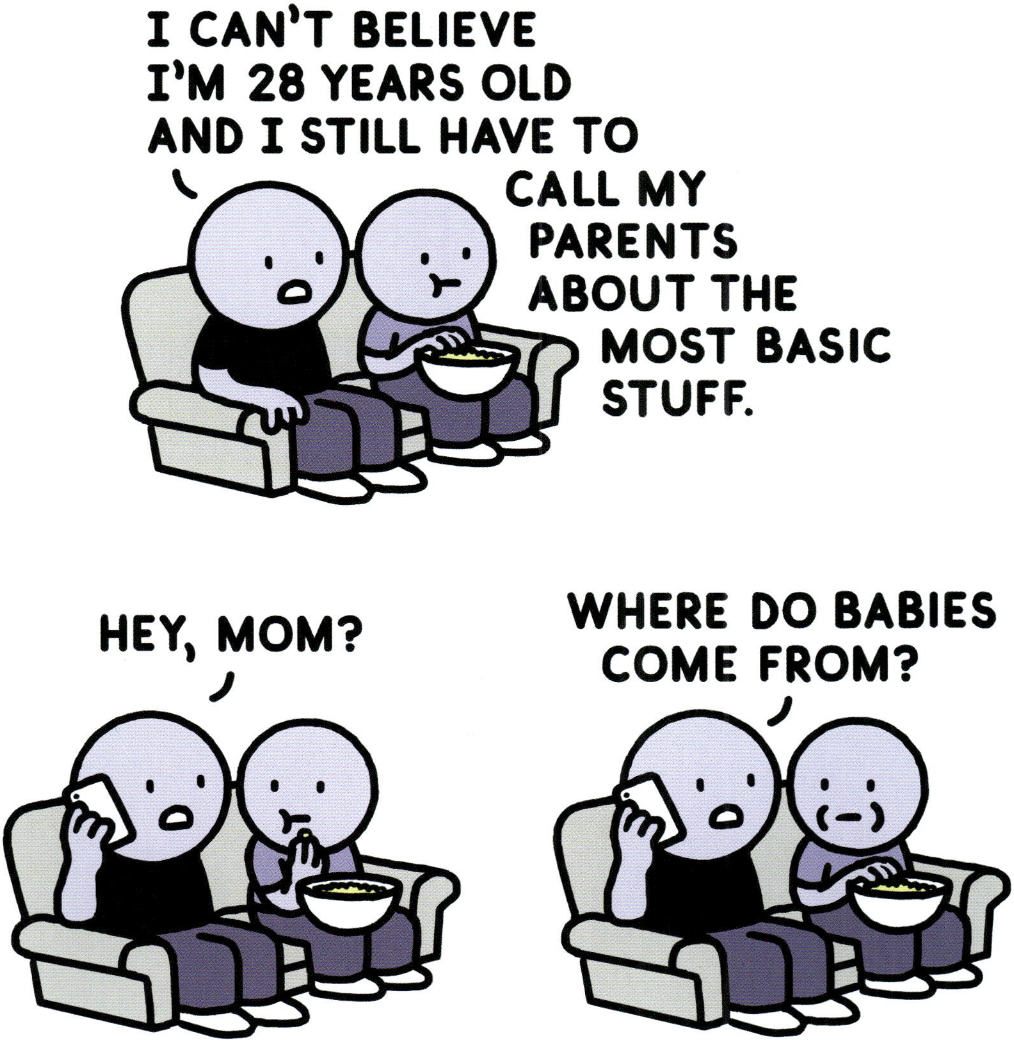
I CAN'T BELIEVE I'M 28 YEARS OLD AND I STILL HAVE TO CALL MY PARENTS ABOUT THE MOST BASIC STUFF.
HEY, MOM?
WHERE DO BABIES COME FROM?

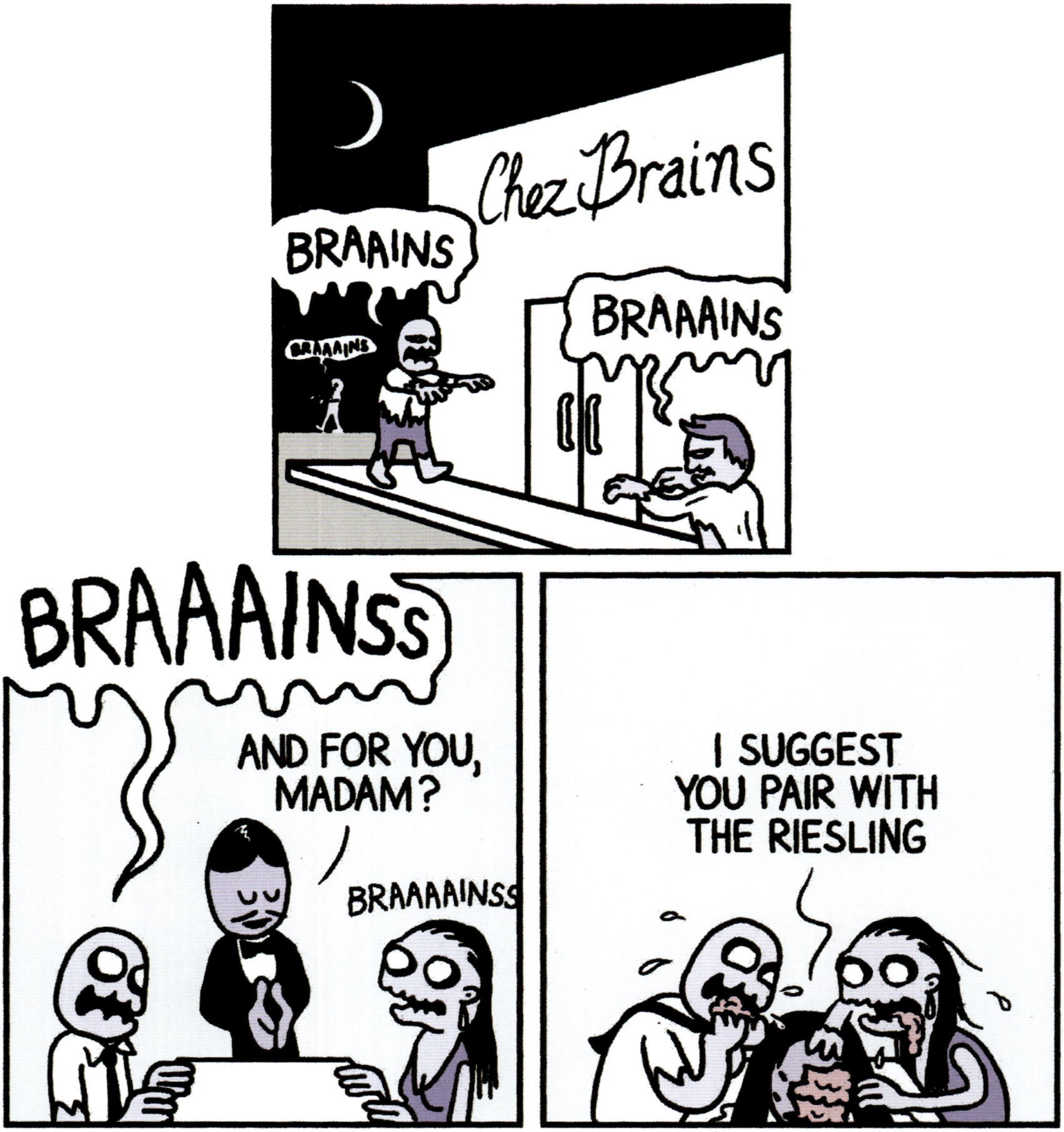
Chez Brains
BRAAINS
BRAAAINS
BRAAAINS
BRAAAINSS
AND FOR YOU, MADAM?
BRAAAAINSS
I SUGGEST YOU PAIR WITH THE RIESLING

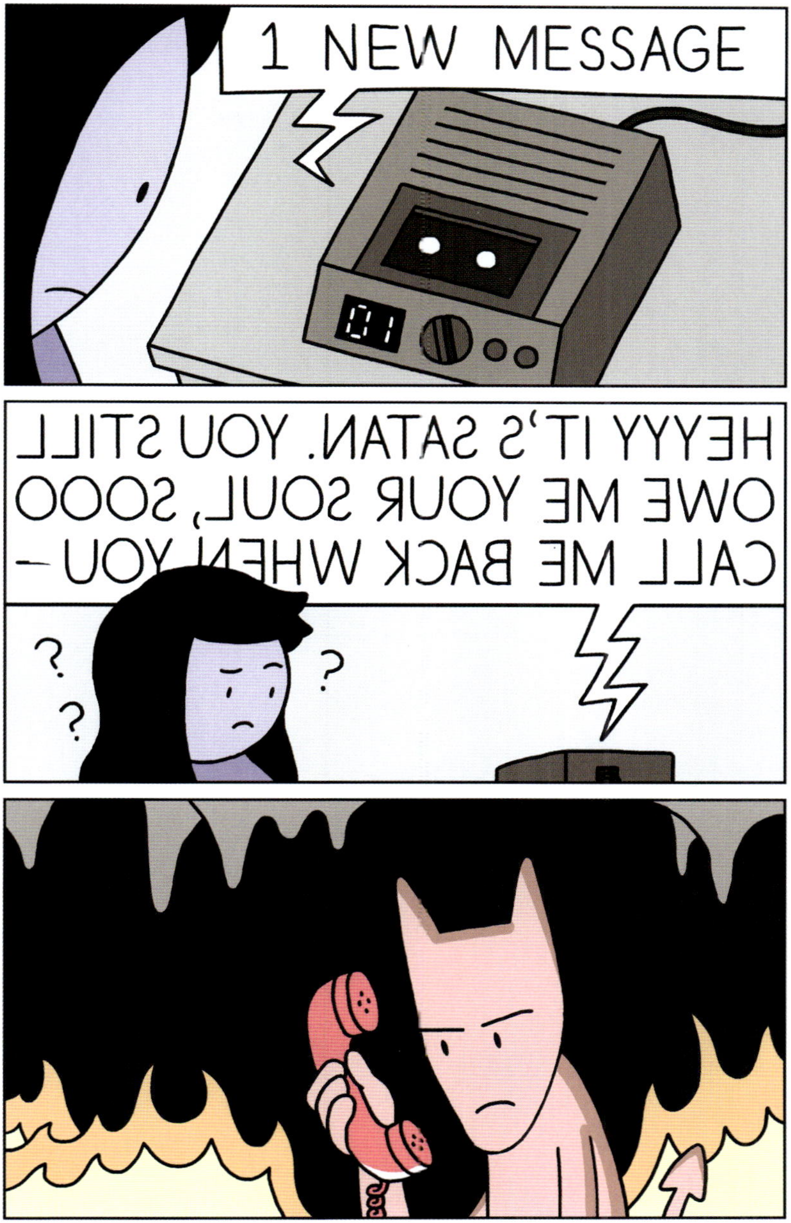
1 NEW MESSAGE
01
HEYYY IT'S SATAN. YOU STILL OWE ME YOUR SOUL, SOOO CALL ME BACK WHEN YOU –
? ? ?

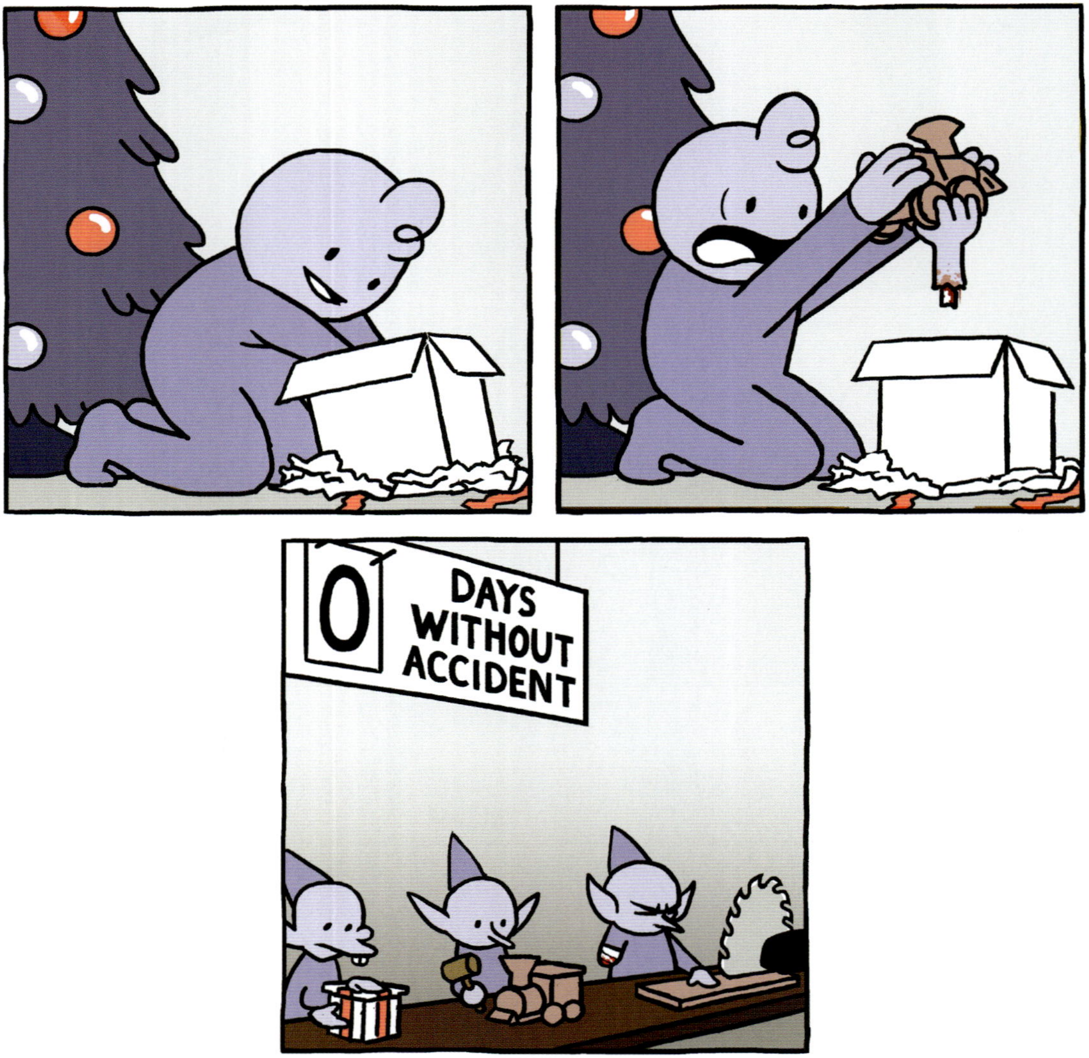
0
DAYS WITHOUT ACCIDENT

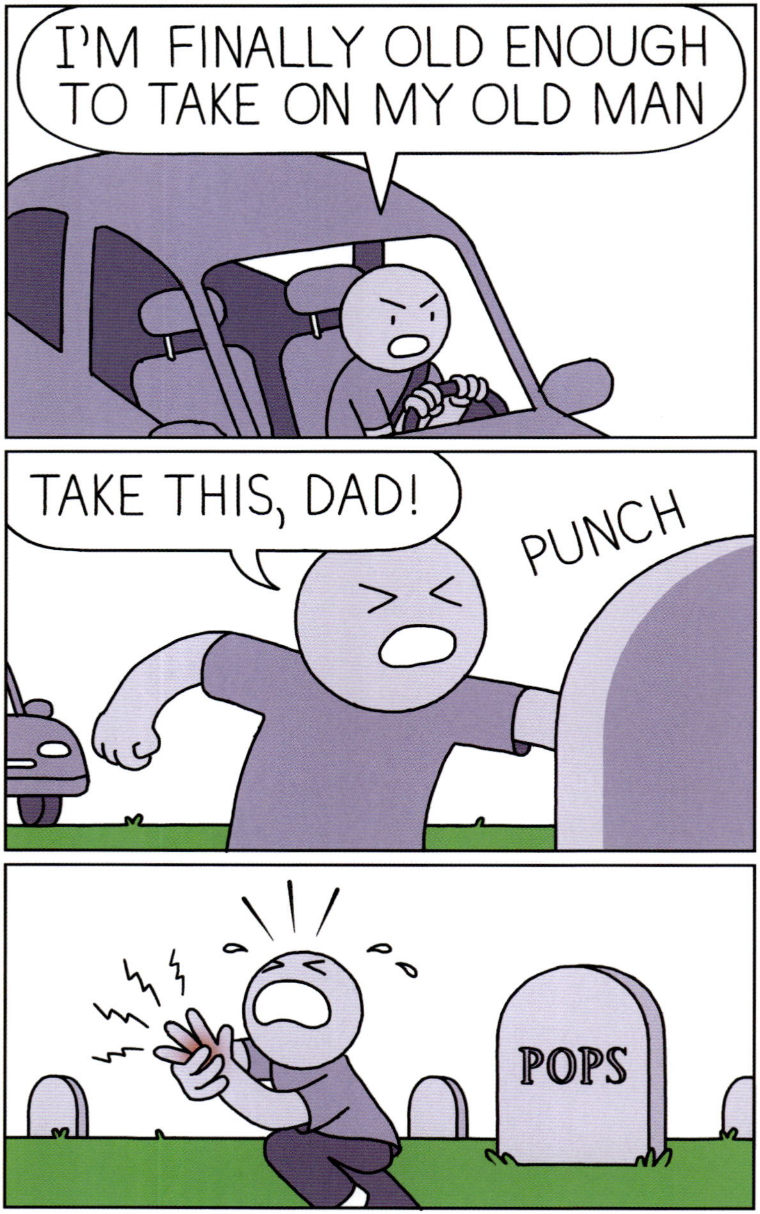
I'M FINALLY OLD ENOUGH TO TAKE ON MY OLD MAN
TAKE THIS, DAD!
PUNCH
POPS

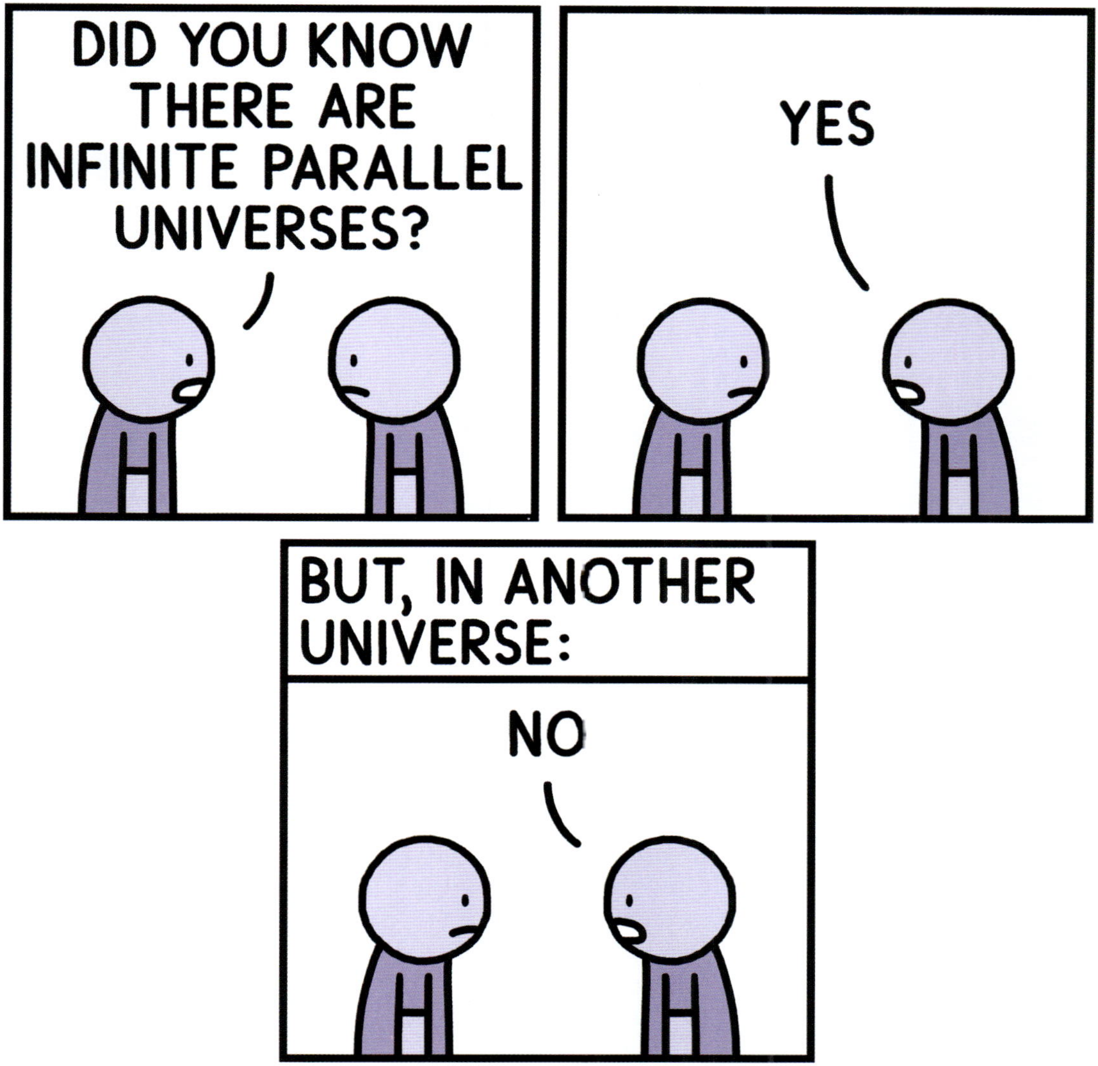
DID YOU KNOW THERE ARE INFINITE PARALLEL UNIVERSES?
YES
BUT, IN ANOTHER UNIVERSE:
NO

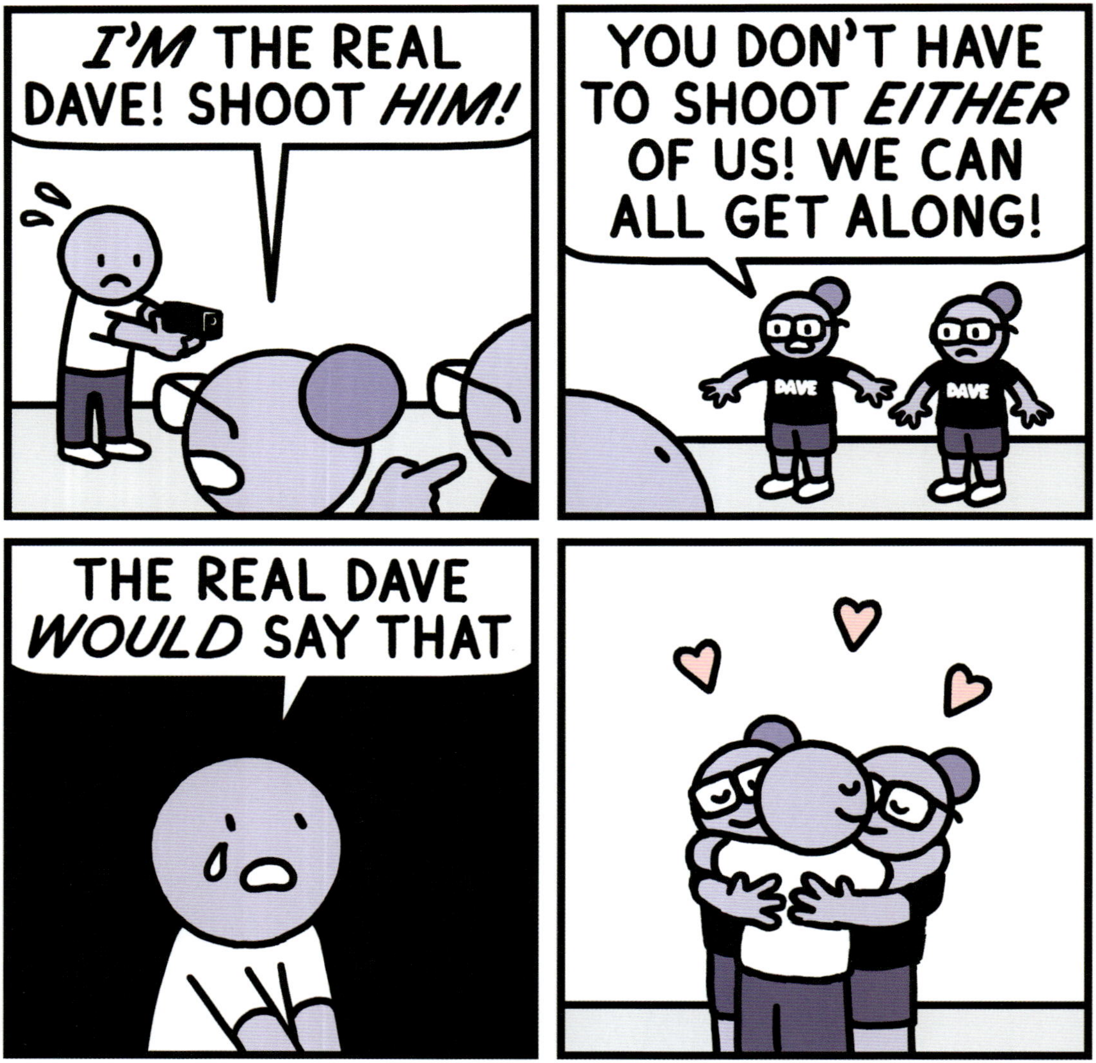
I'M THE REAL DAVE! SHOOT *HIM!*
YOU DON'T HAVE TO SHOOT *EITHER* OF US! WE CAN ALL GET ALONG!
DAVE
DAVE
THE REAL DAVE *WOULD* SAY THAT

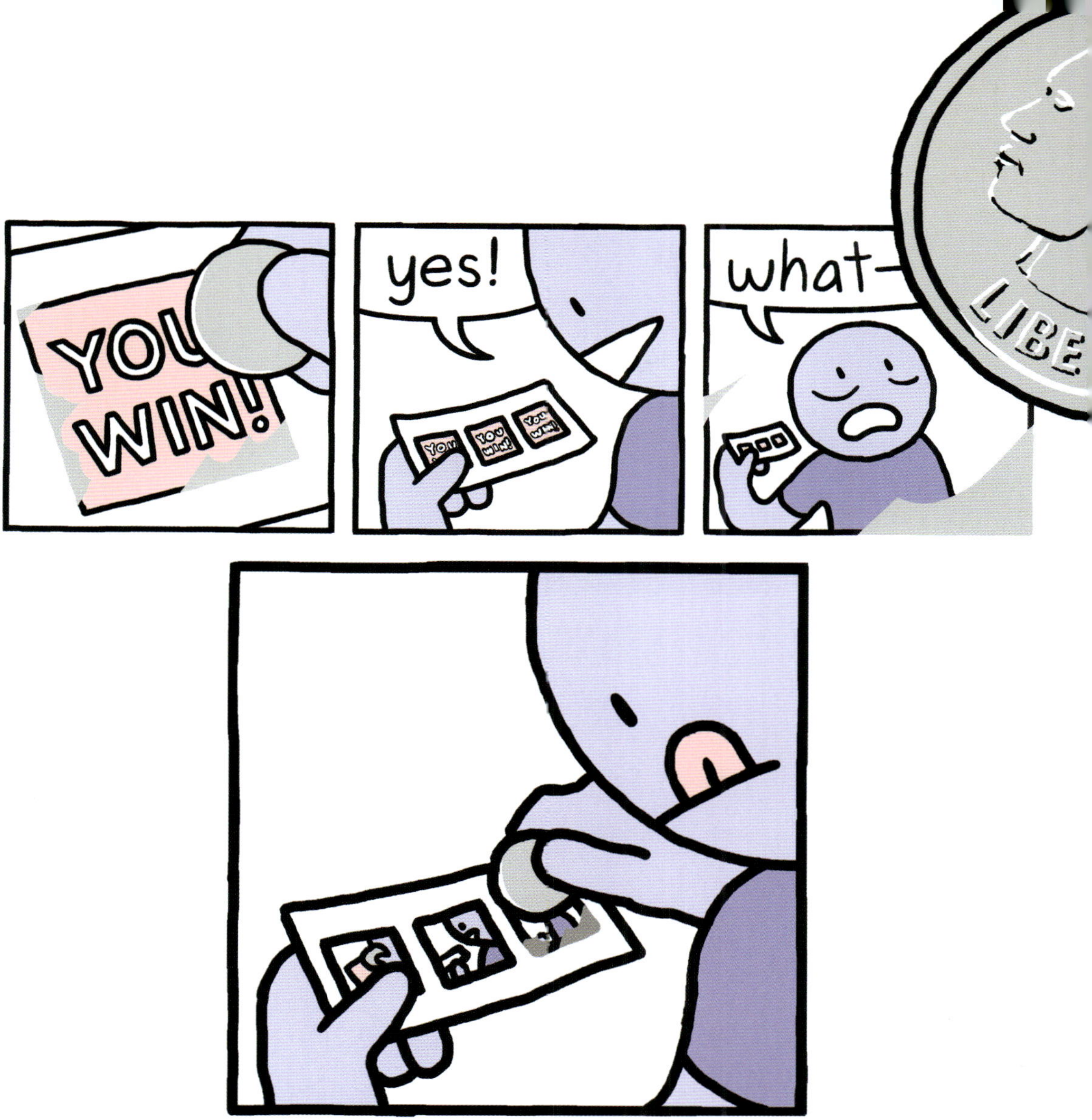
YOU WIN!
yes!
YOU WIN!
YOU WIN!
what-
LIBE

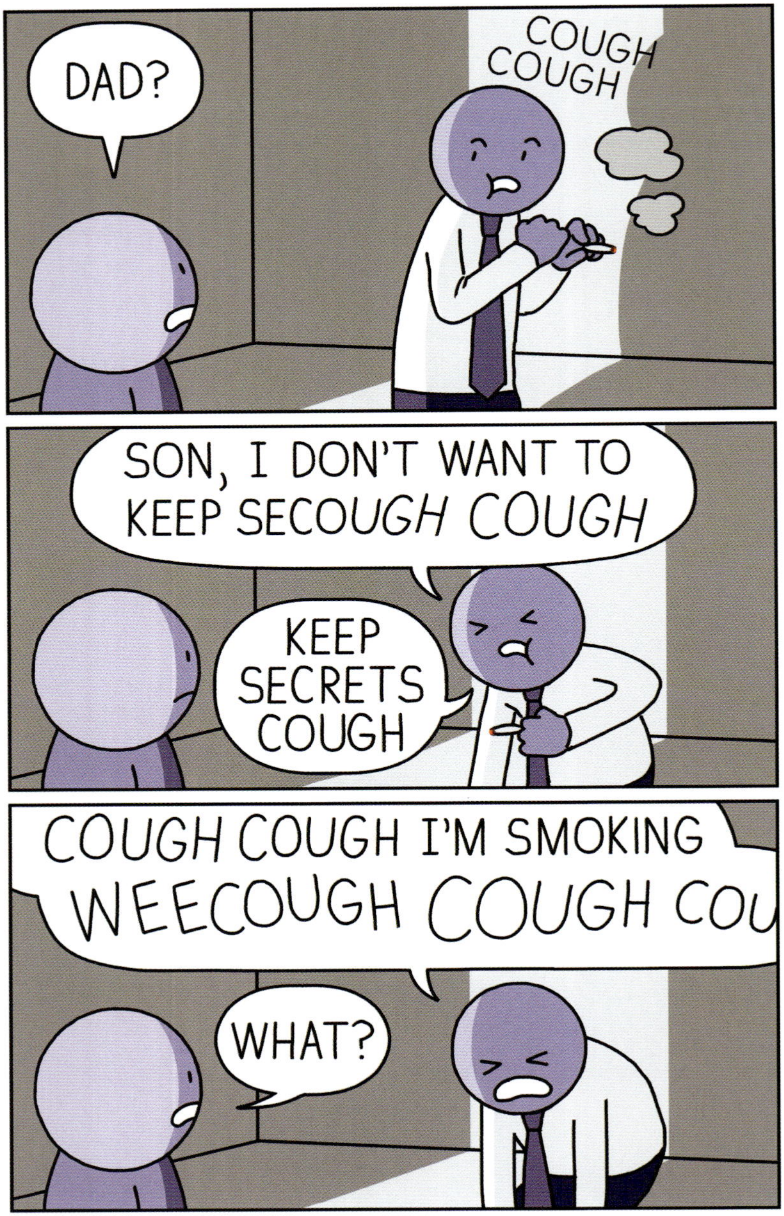
DAD?
COUGH
COUGH
SON, I DON'T WANT TO KEEP SECOUGH COUGH
KEEP SECRETS COUGH
COUGH COUGH I'M SMOKING WEECOUGH COUGH COU
WHAT?

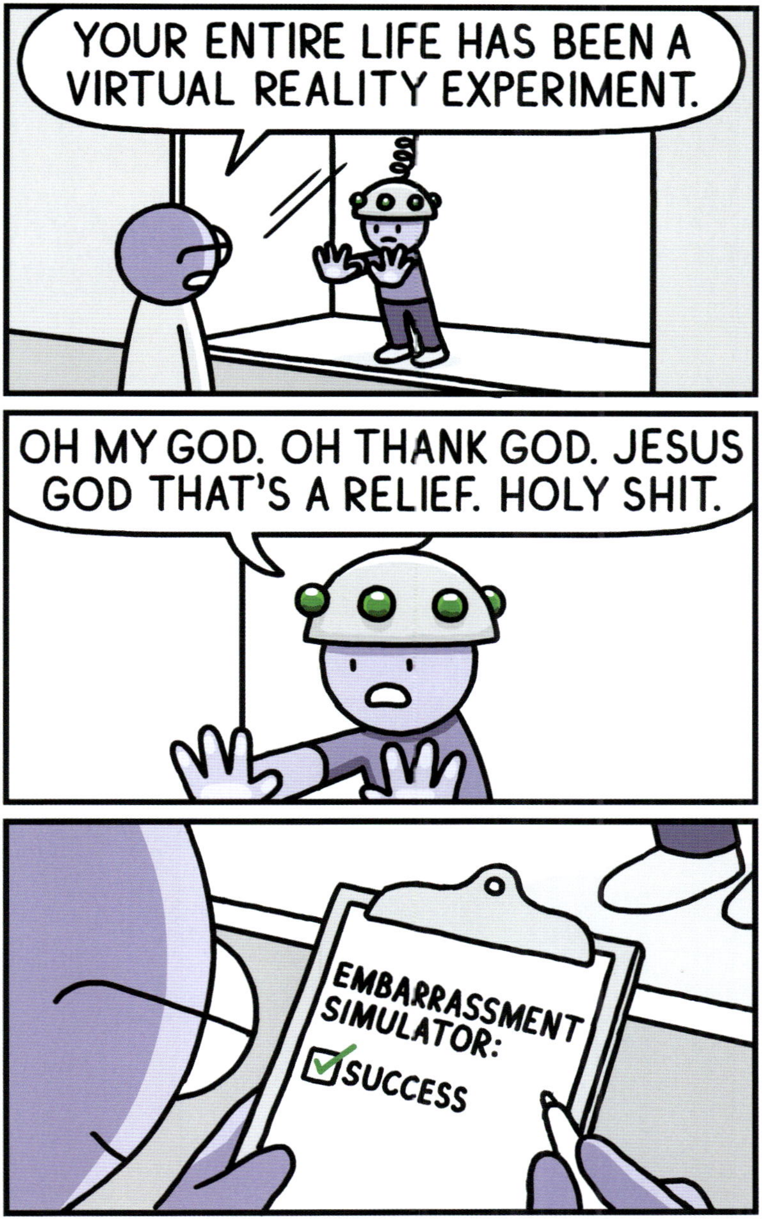
YOUR ENTIRE LIFE HAS BEEN A VIRTUAL REALITY EXPERIMENT.
OH MY GOD. OH THANK GOD. JESUS GOD THAT'S A RELIEF. HOLY SHIT.
EMBARRASSMENT SIMULATOR:
SUCCESS

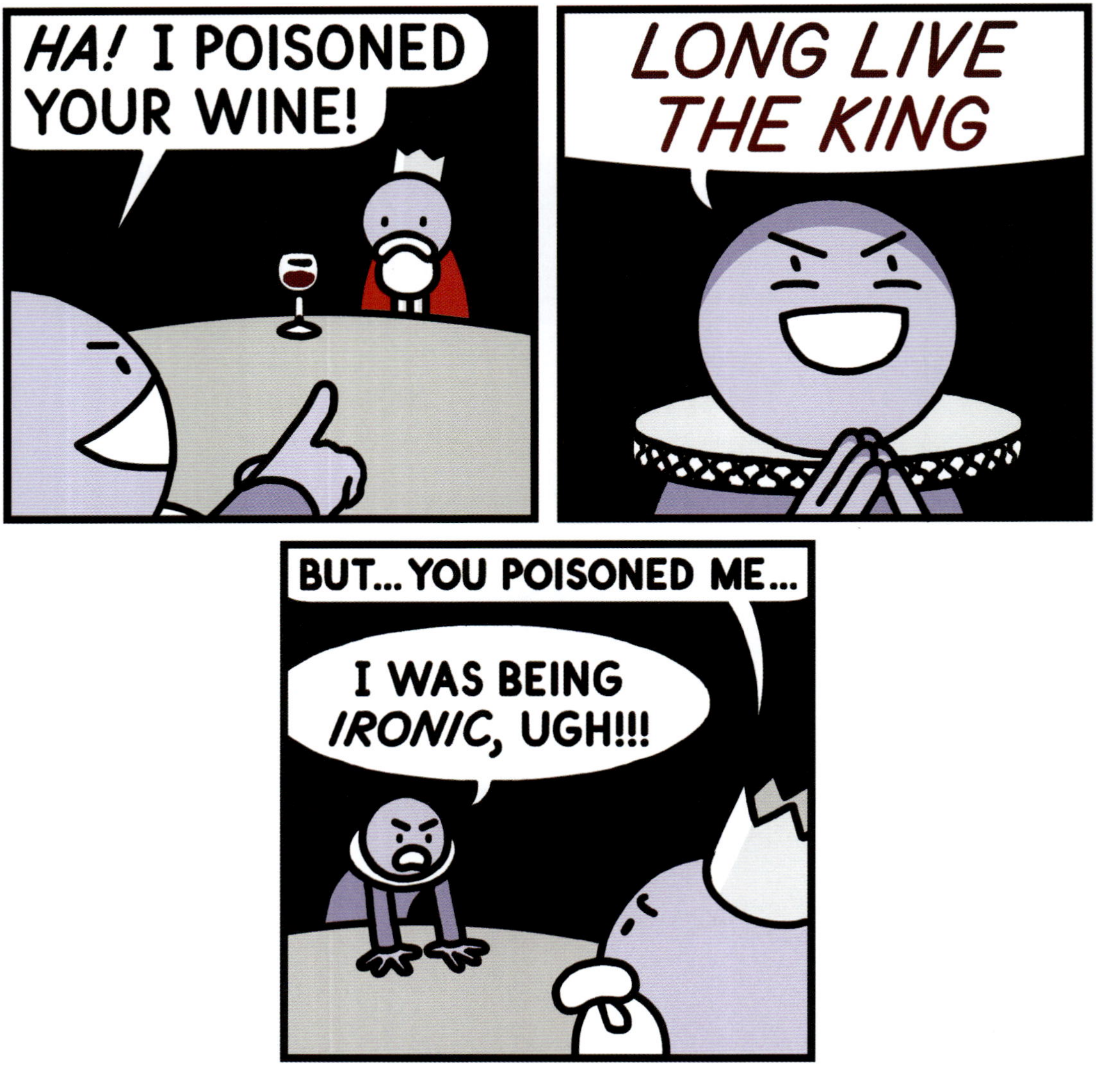
HA! I POISONED YOUR WINE!
LONG LIVE THE KING
BUT... YOU POISONED ME...
I WAS BEING IRONIC, UGH!!!

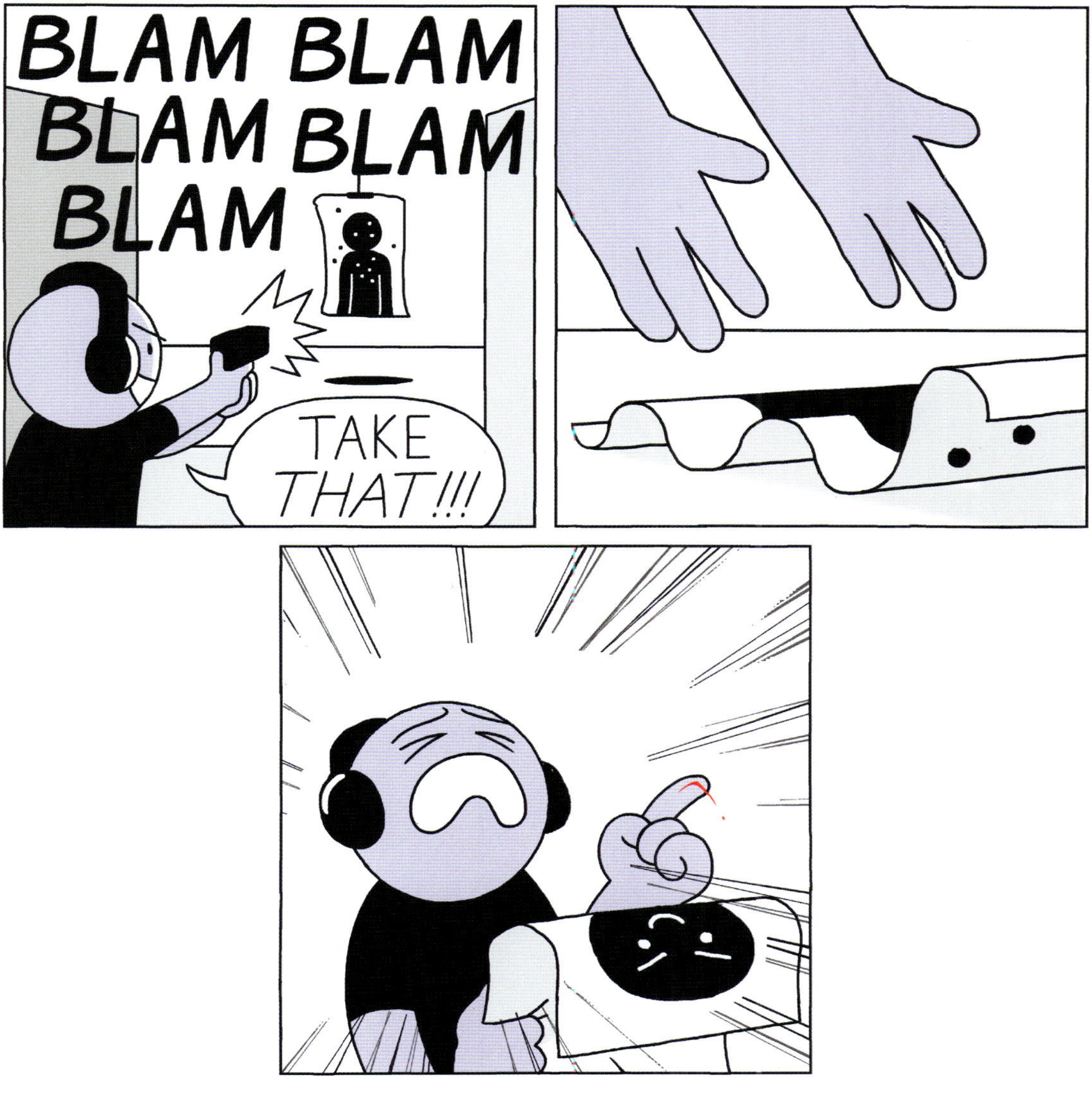
BLAM BLAM
BLAM BLAM
BLAM
TAKE THAT!!!

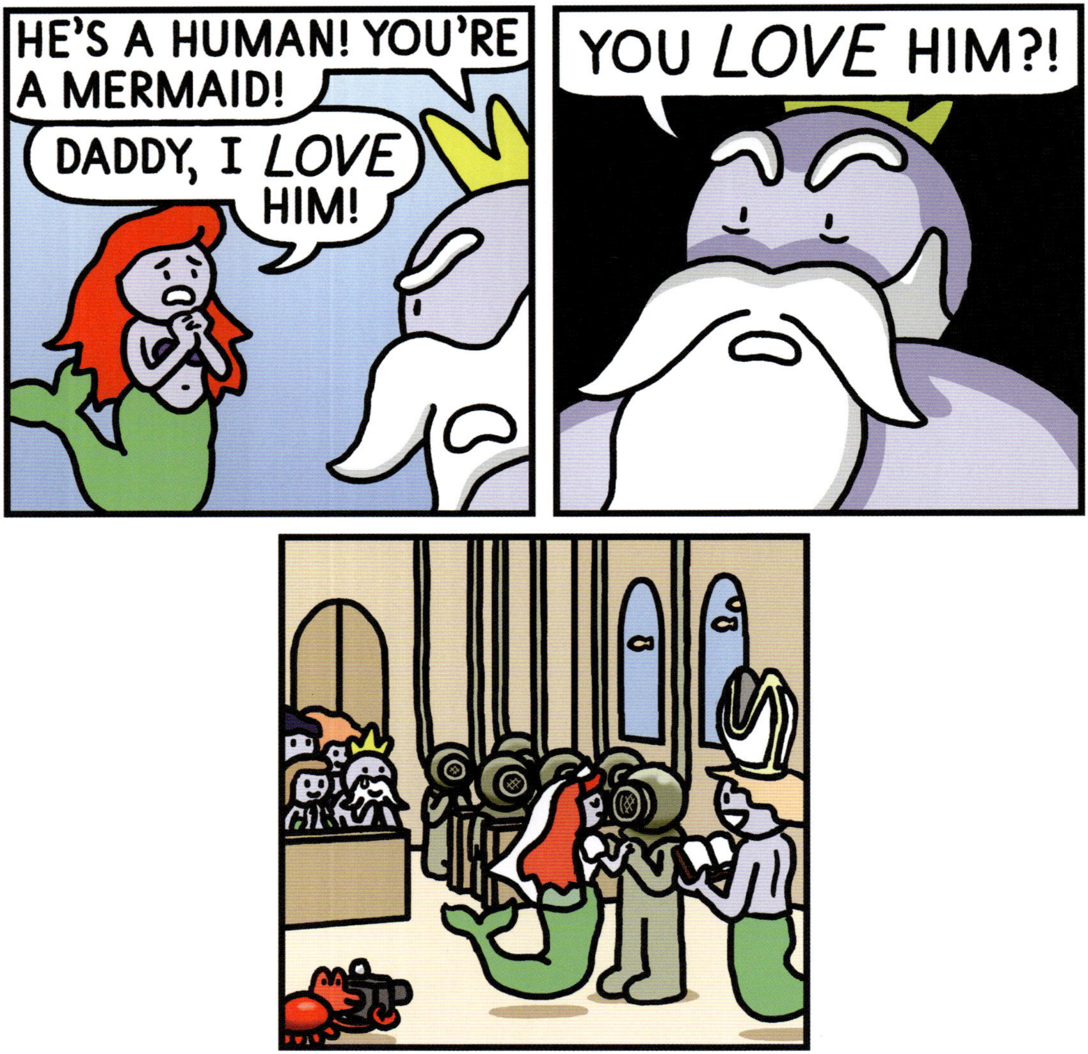
HE'S A HUMAN! YOU'RE A MERMAID!
DADDY, I *LOVE* HIM!
YOU *LOVE* HIM?!

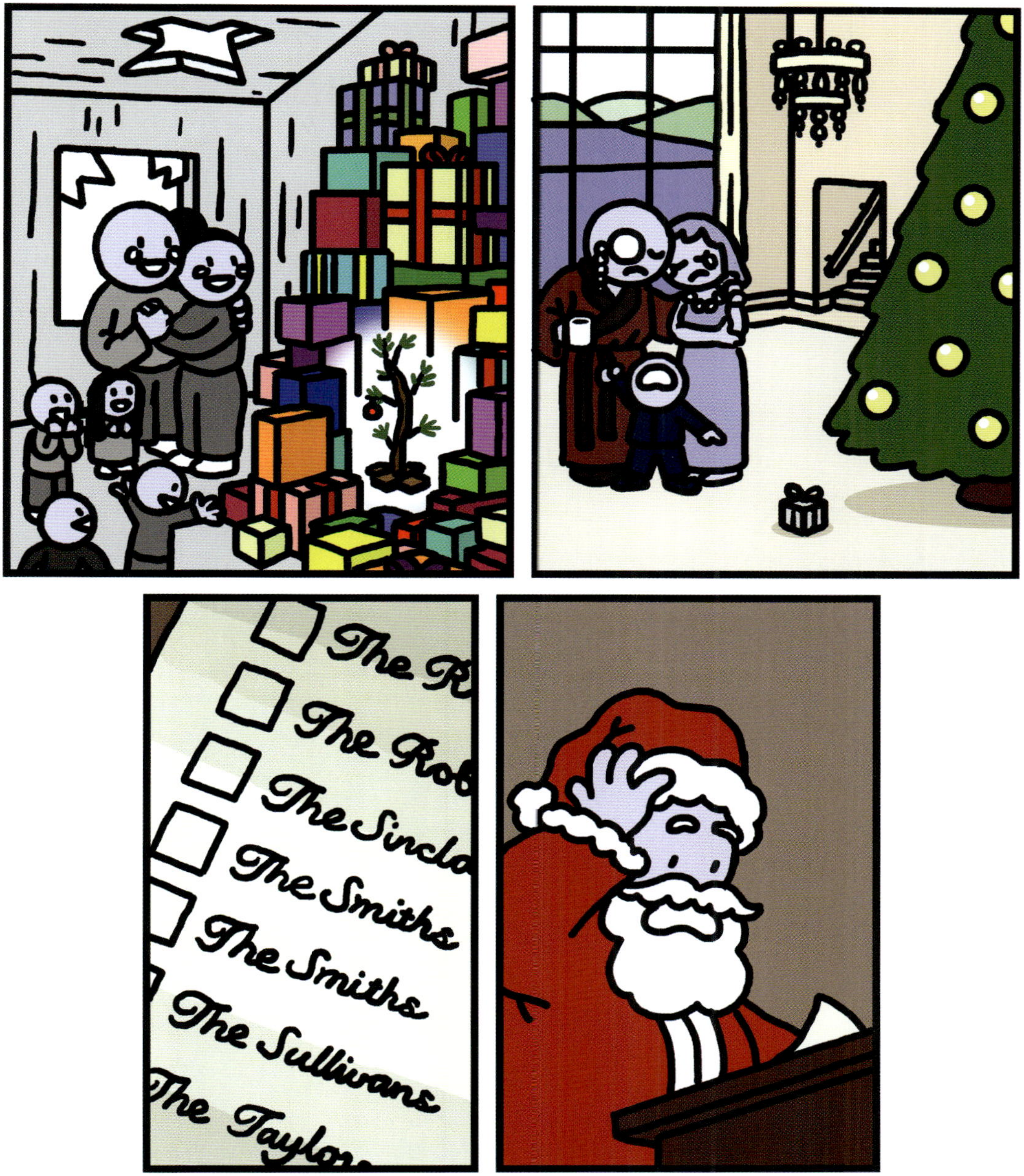
The R
The Rob
The Sincla
The Smiths
The Smiths
The Sullivans
The Taylo

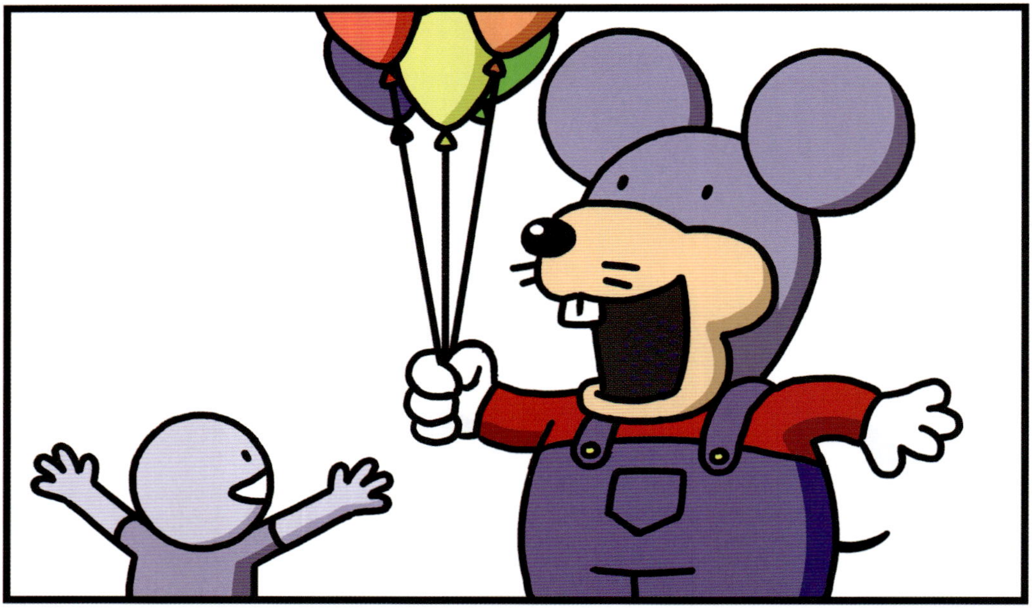

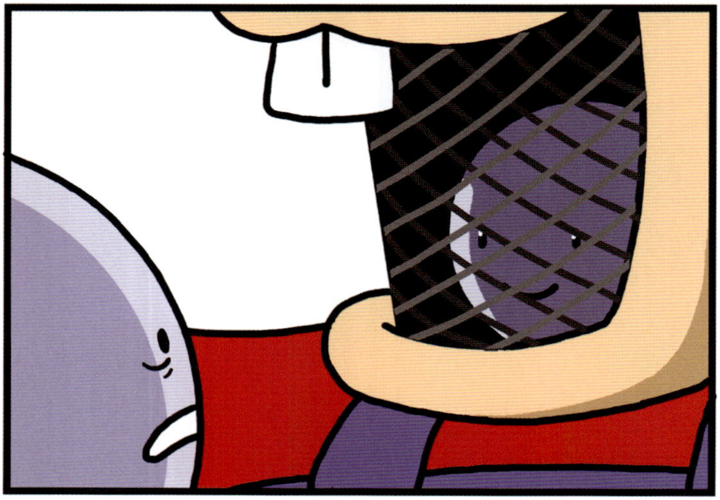

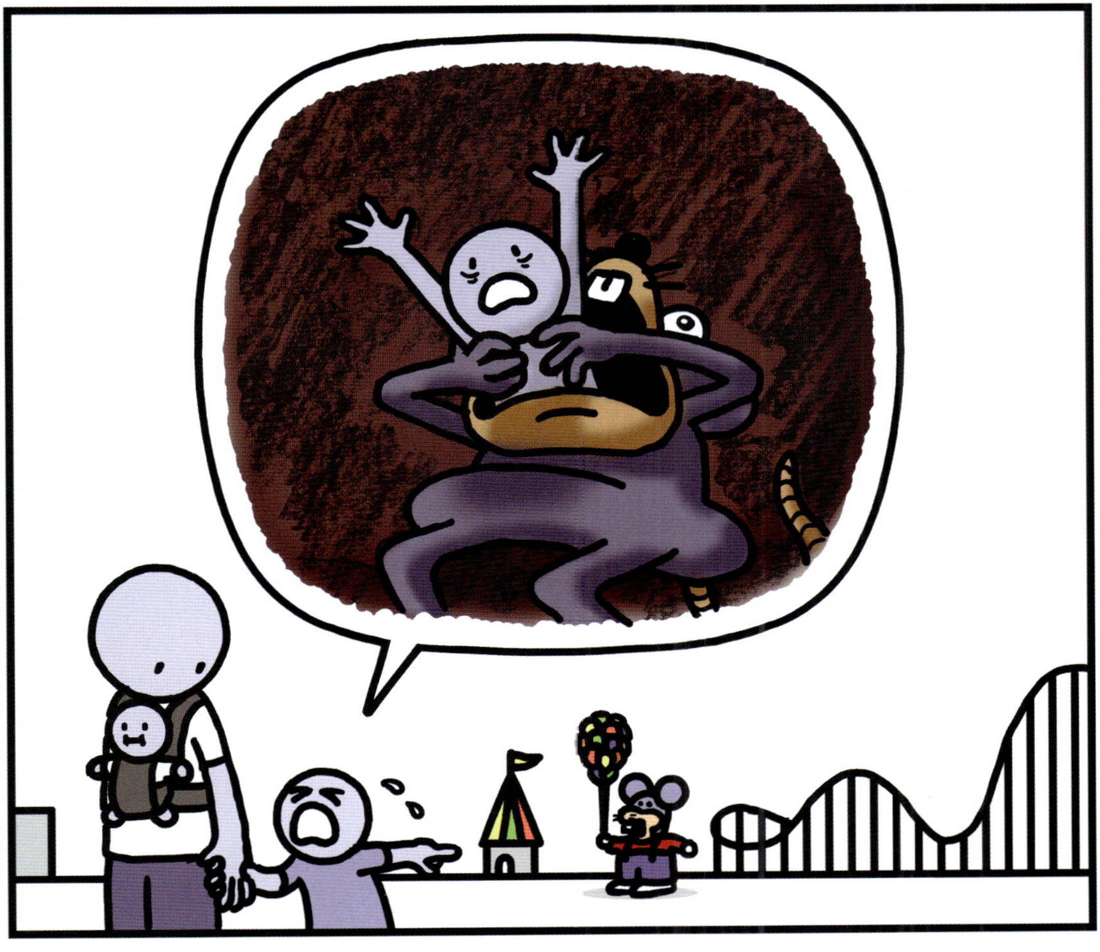

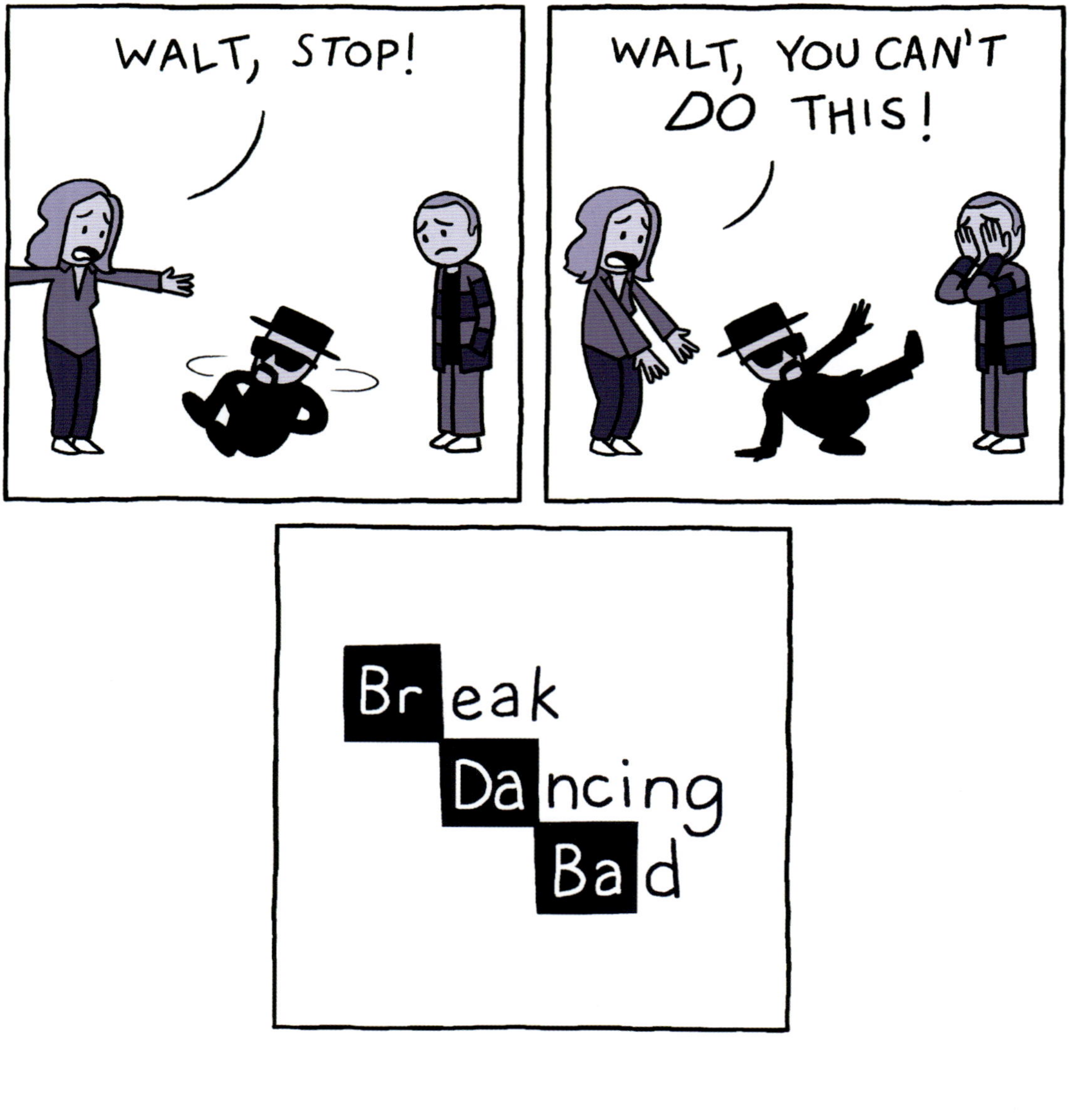
WALT, STOP!
WALT, YOU CAN'T DO THIS!
Break Dancing Bad

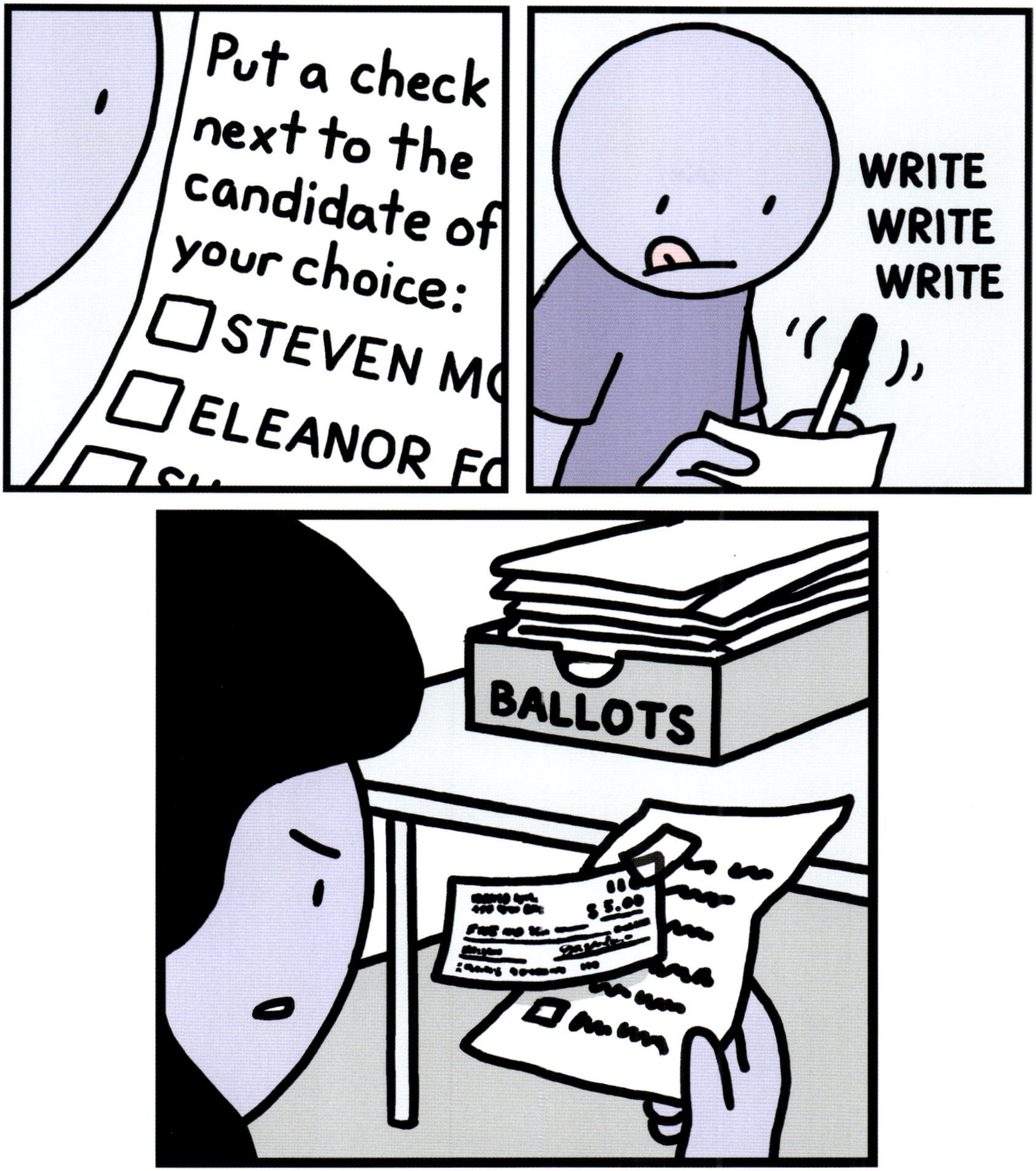
Put a check next to the candidate of your choice:
STEVEN MC
ELEANOR FO
WRITE WRITE WRITE
BALLOTS
$ 5.00

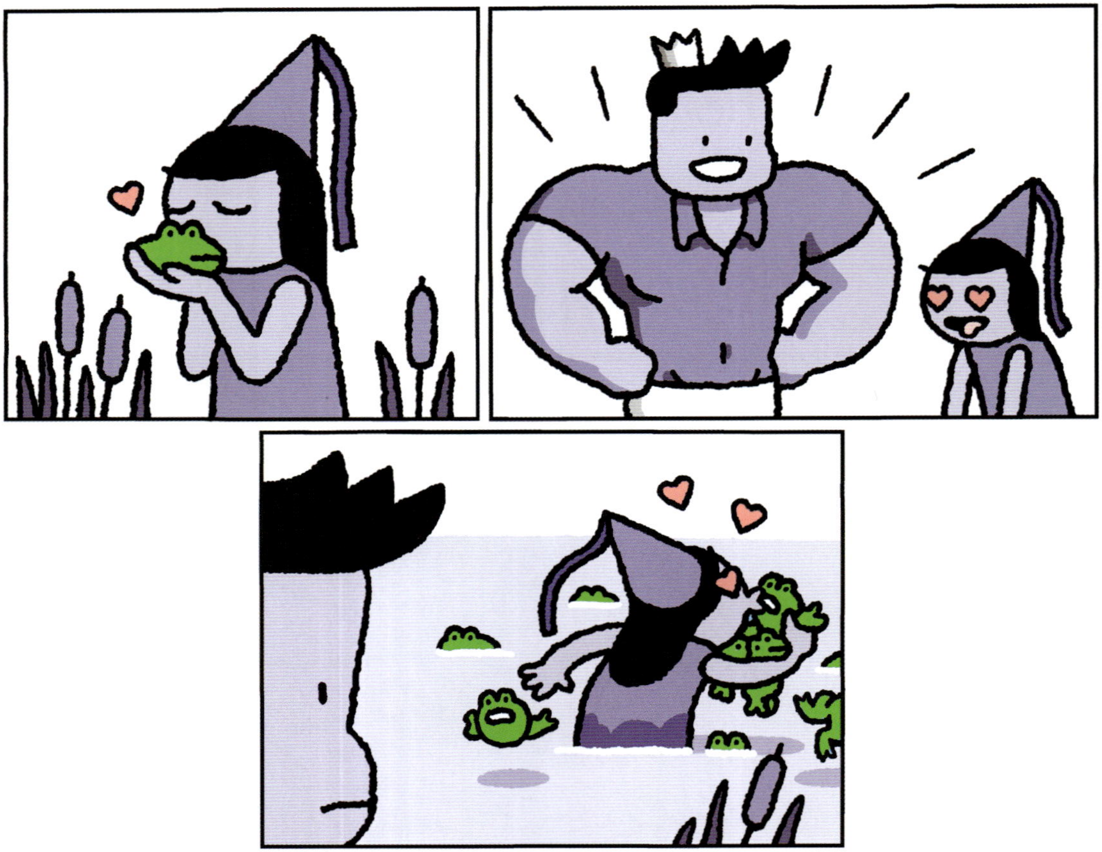

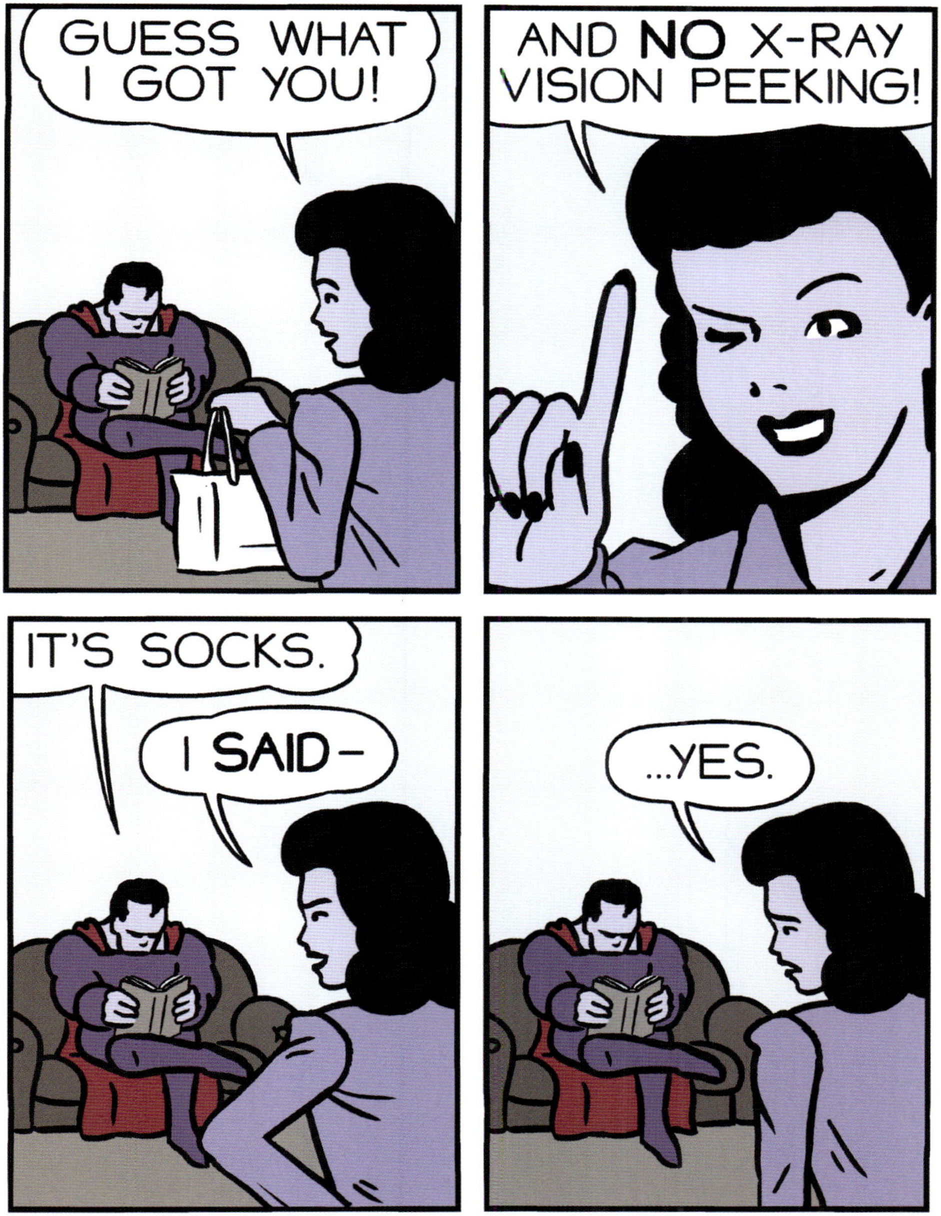
GUESS WHAT I GOT YOU!
AND **NO** X-RAY VISION PEEKING!
IT'S SOCKS.
I **SAID**-
...YES.

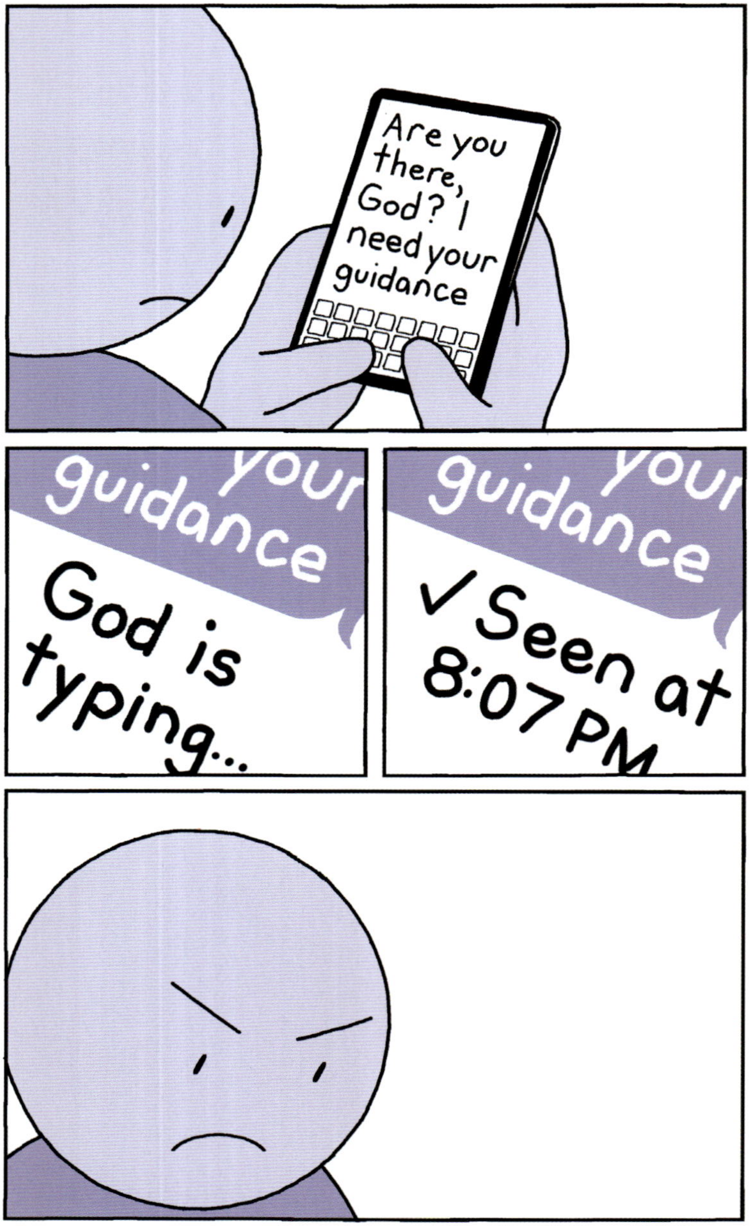
Are you there, God? I need your guidance
your guidance
God is typing...
your guidance
✓Seen at 8:07 PM

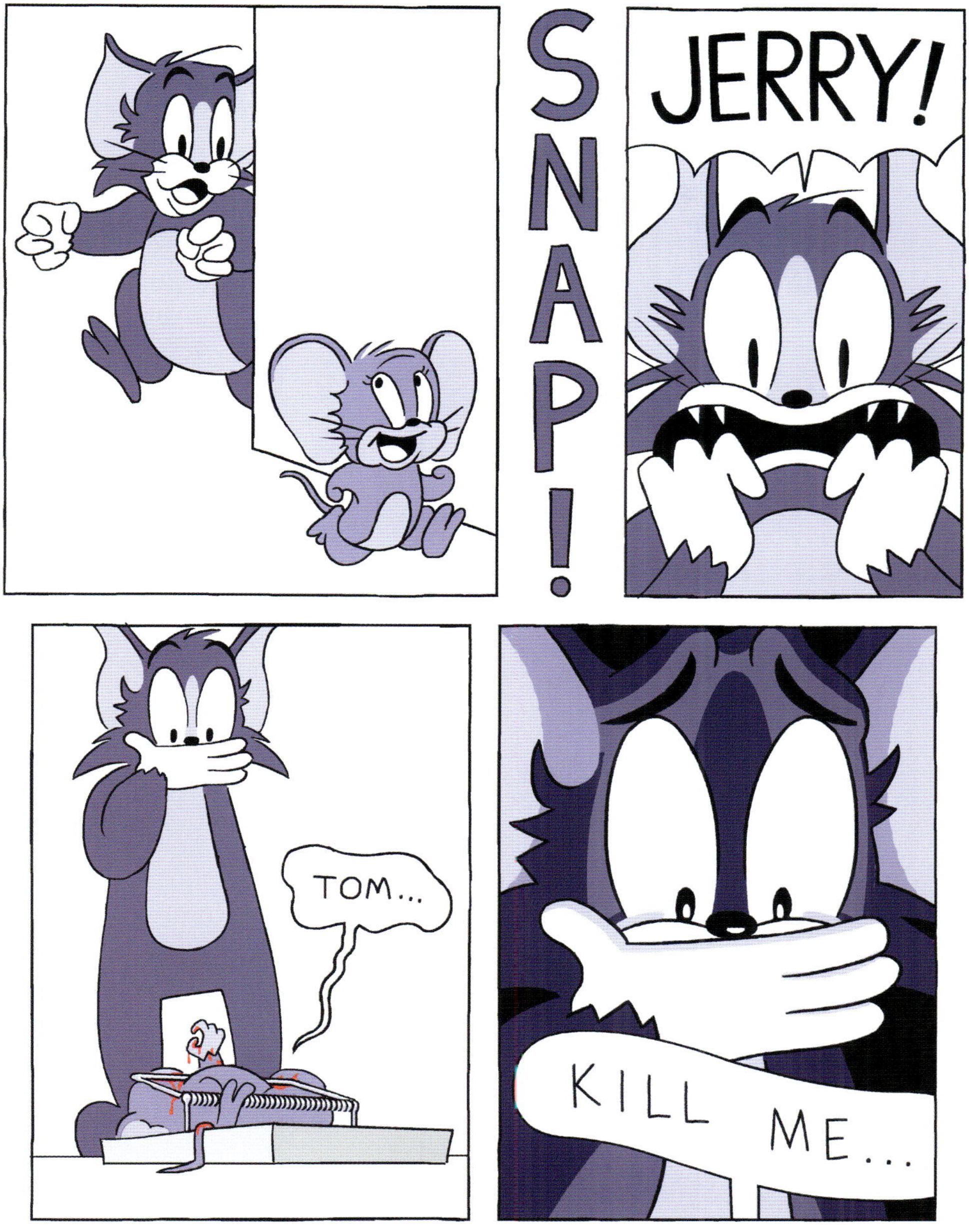
SNAP!
JERRY!
TOM...
KILL ME...

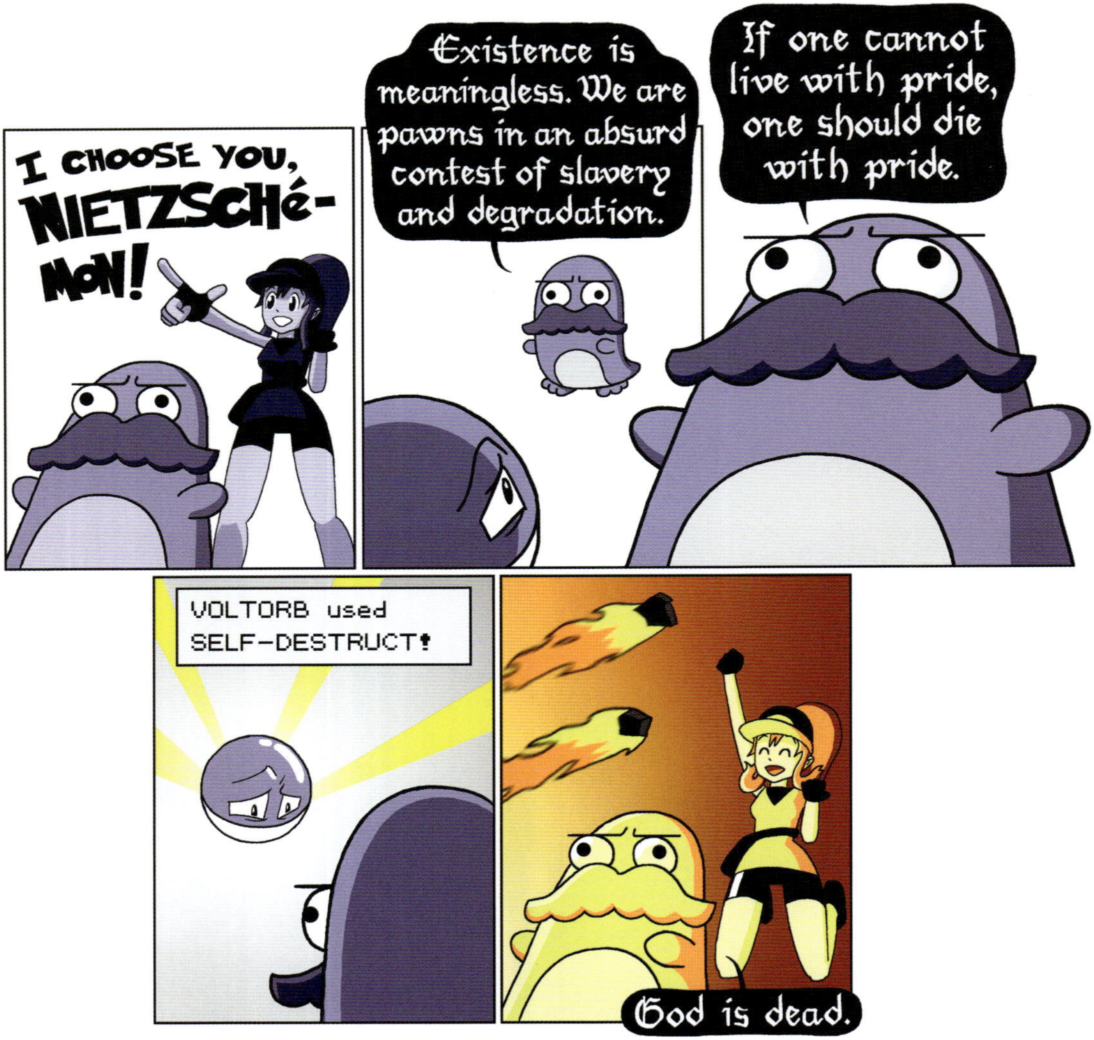
I CHOOSE YOU, NIETZSCHÉ-MON!
Existence is meaningless. We are pawns in an absurd contest of slavery and degradation.
If one cannot live with pride, one should die with pride.
VOLTORB used SELF-DESTRUCT!
God is dead.

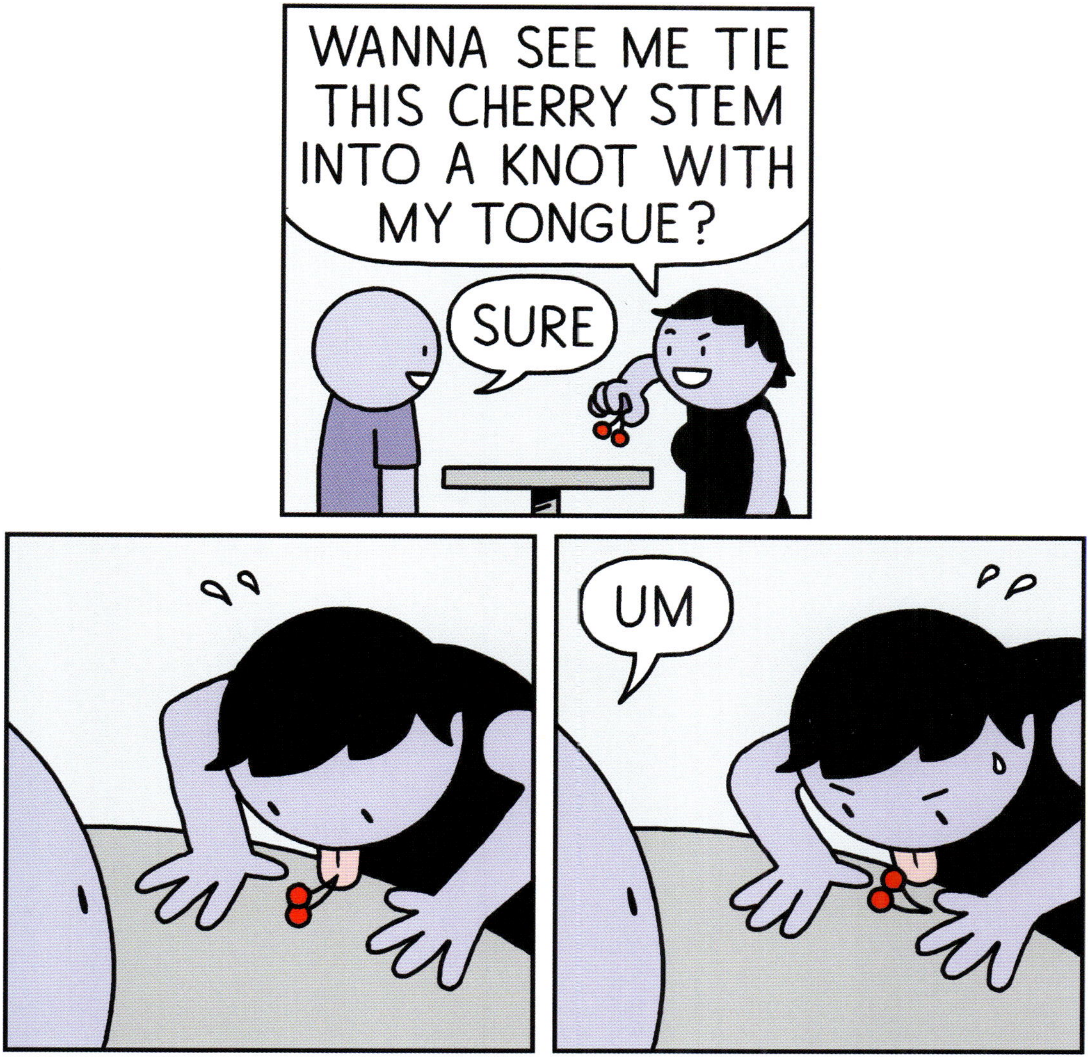
WANNA SEE ME TIE THIS CHERRY STEM INTO A KNOT WITH MY TONGUE?
SURE
UM

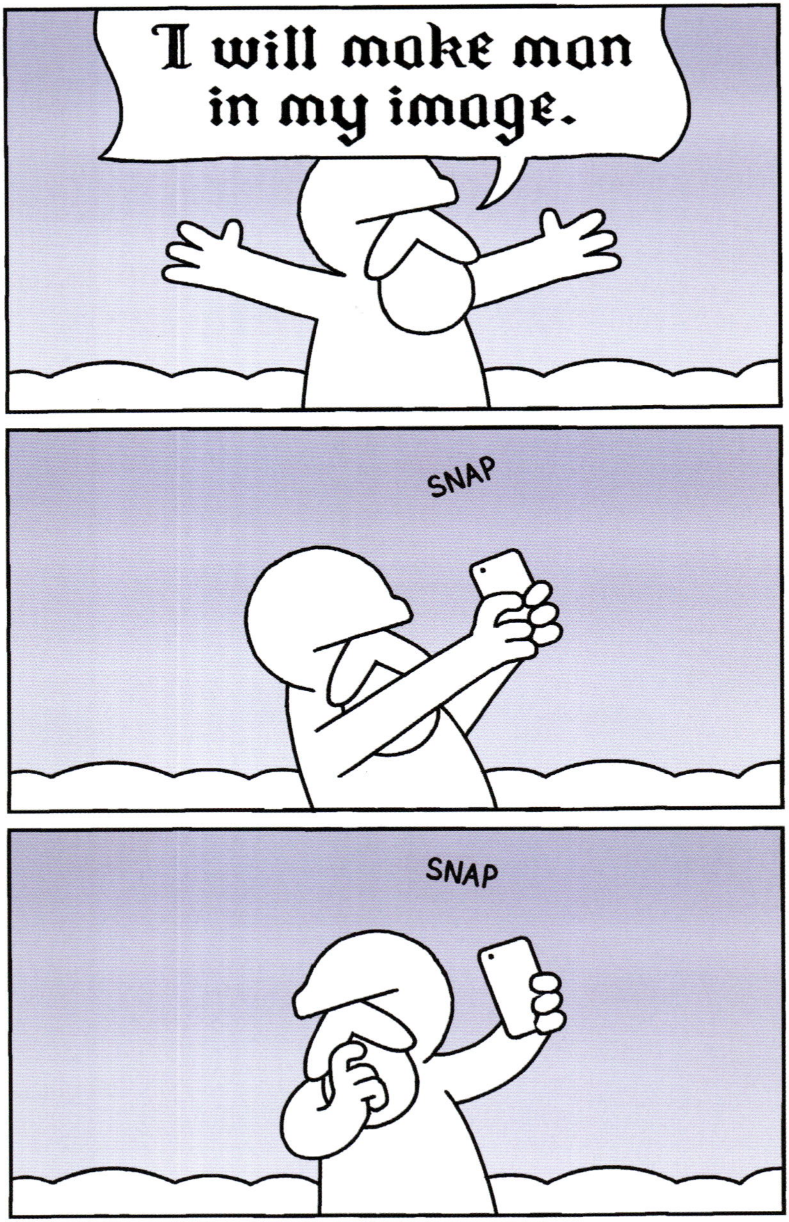
I will make man in my image.
SNAP
SNAP

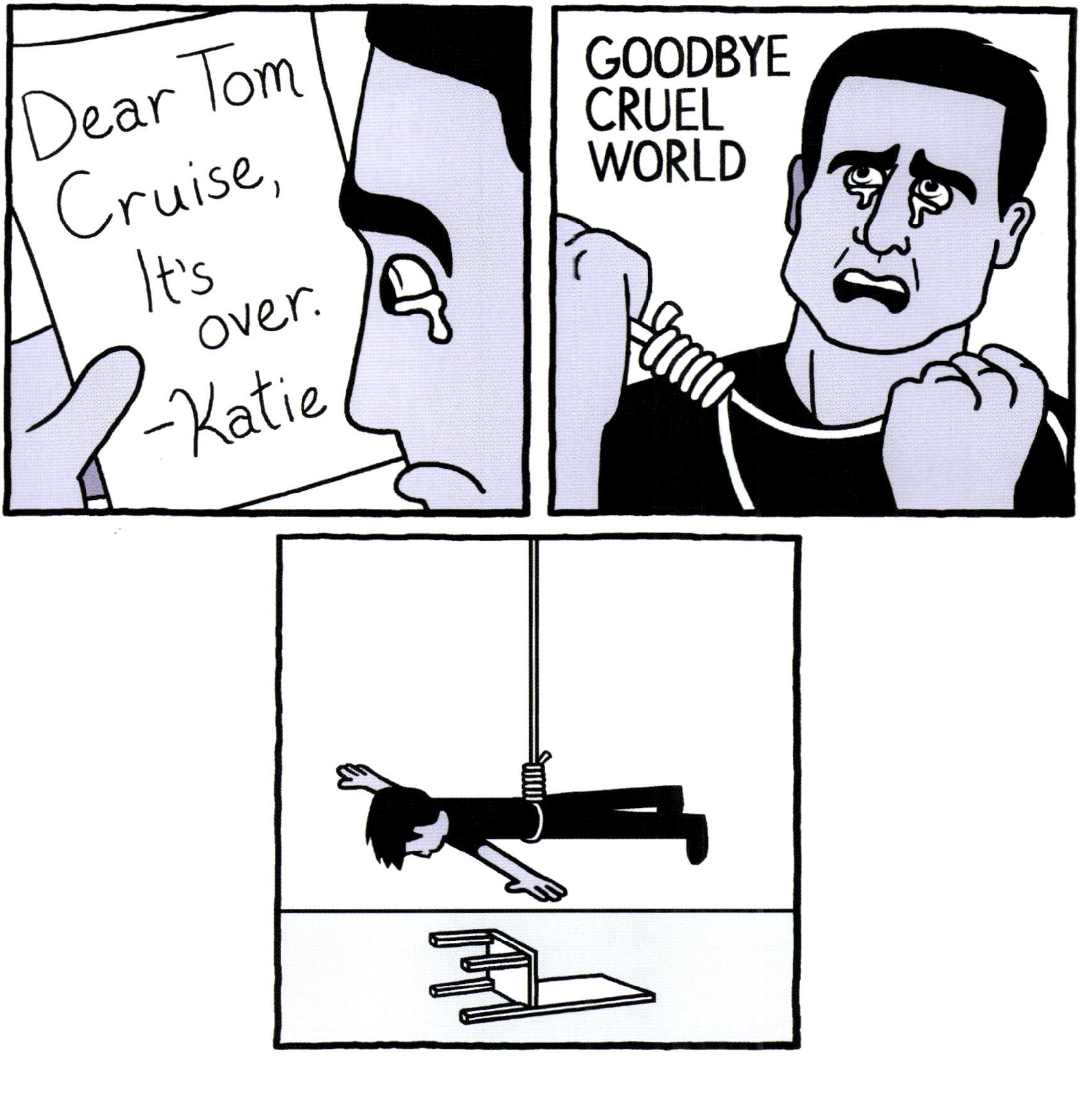
Dear Tom Cruise, It's over. -Katie
GOODBYE CRUEL WORLD

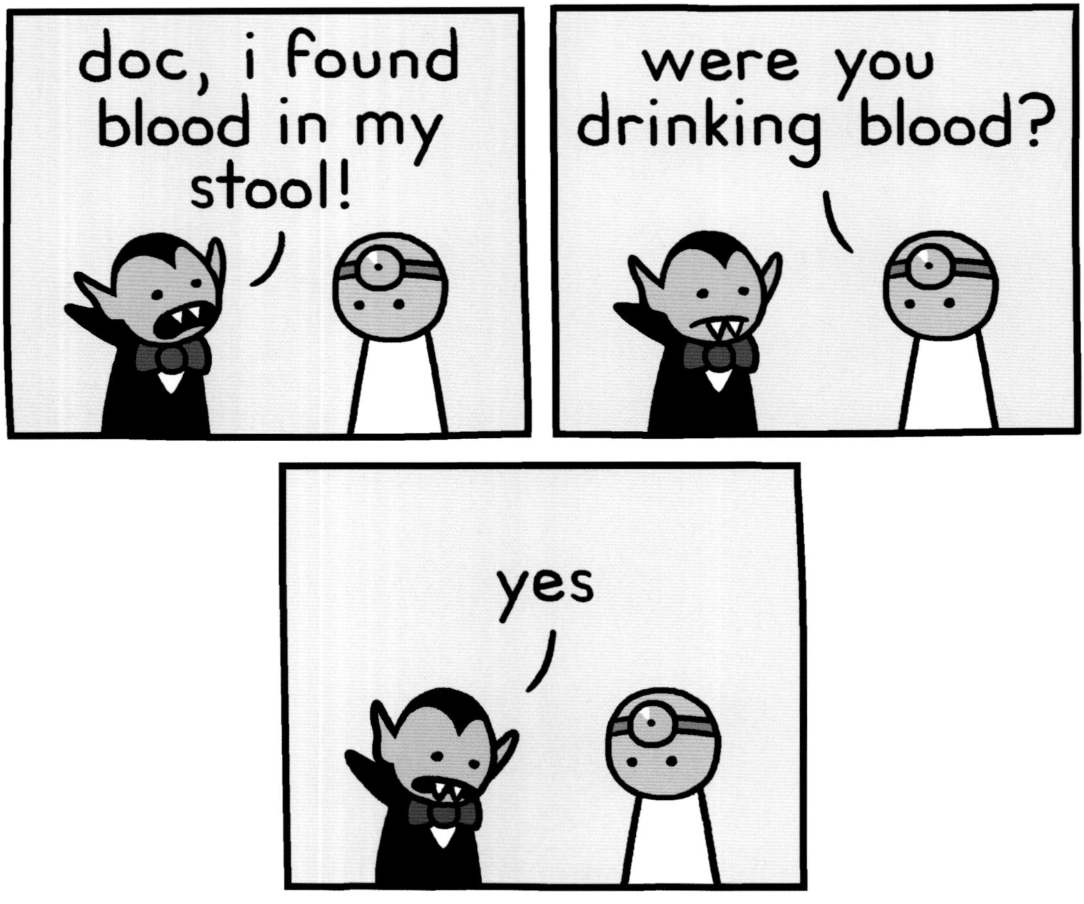
doc, i found blood in my stool!
were you drinking blood?
yes

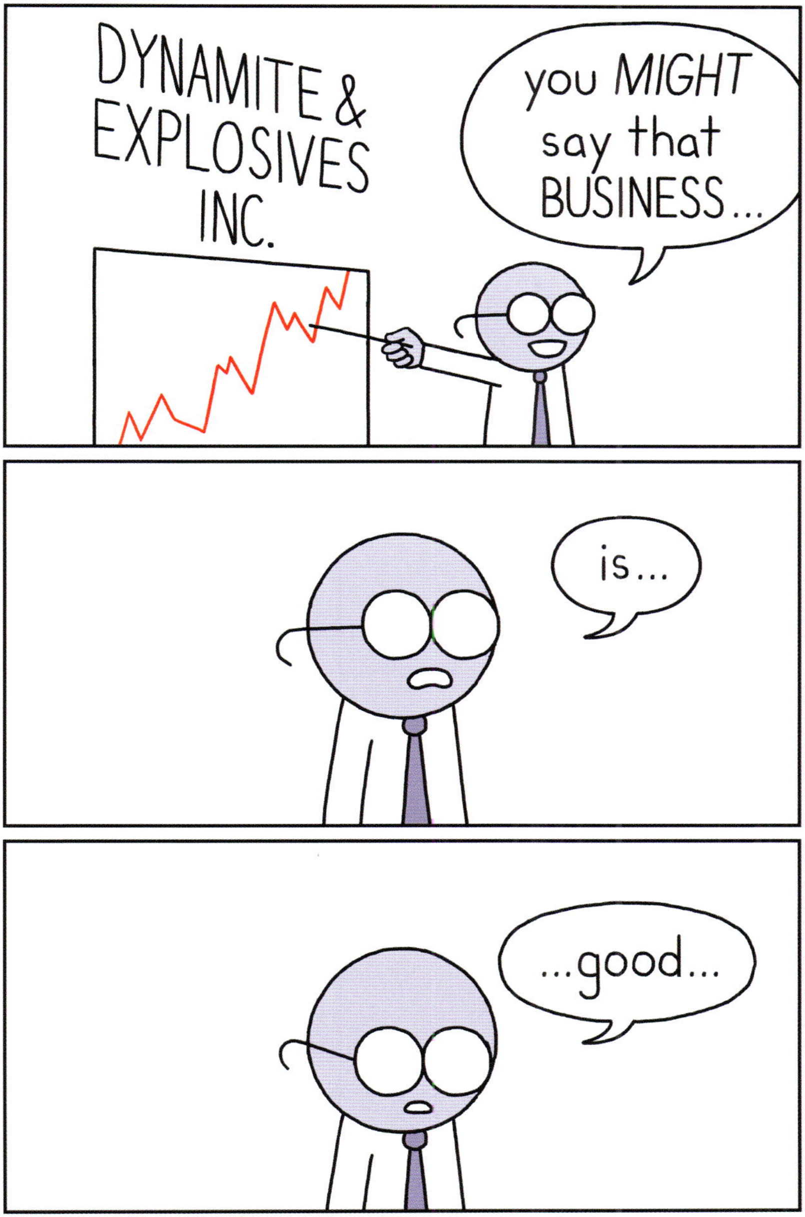
DYNAMITE & EXPLOSIVES INC.
you MIGHT say that BUSINESS...
is...
...good...

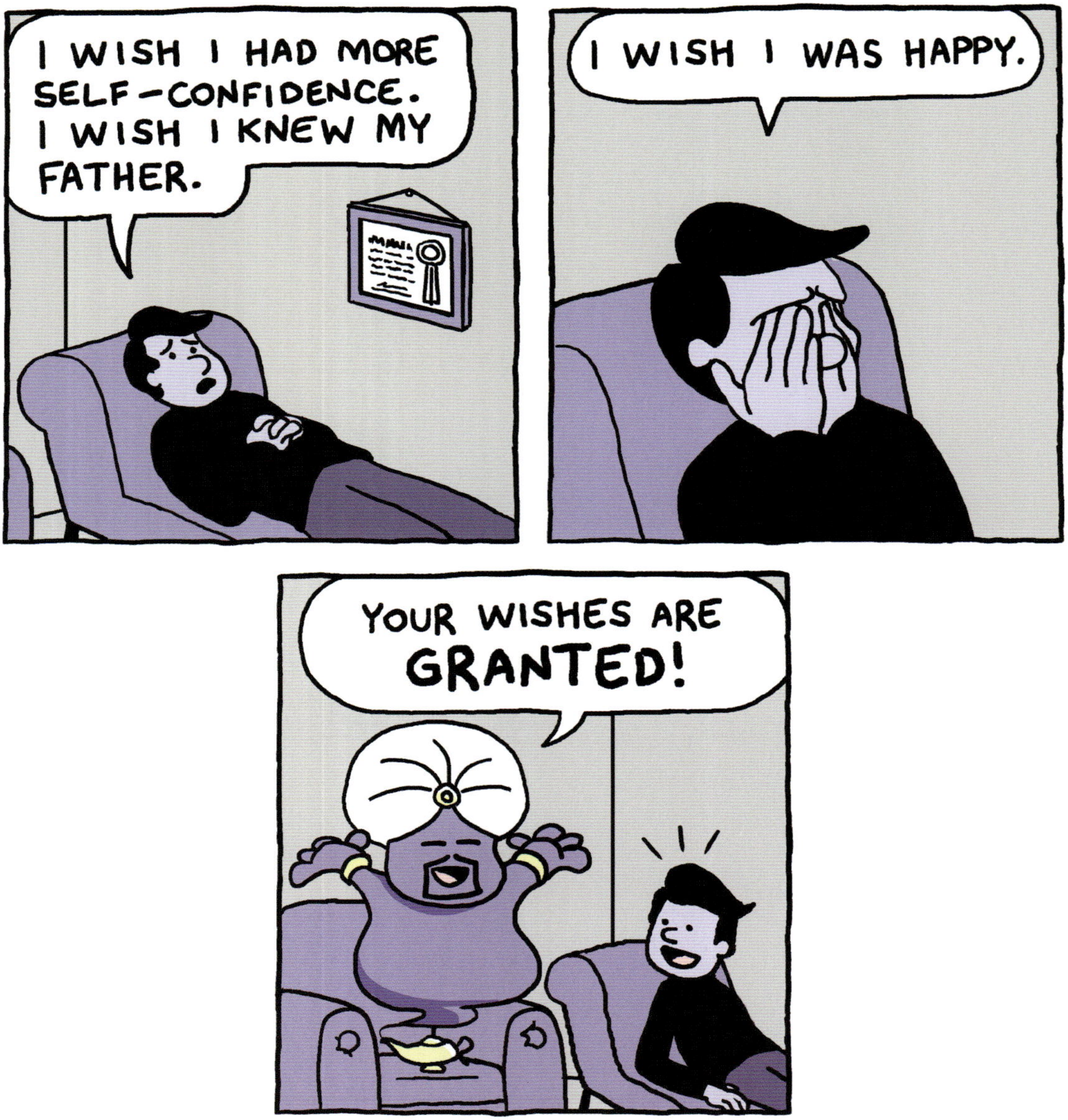
I WISH I HAD MORE SELF-CONFIDENCE. I WISH I KNEW MY FATHER.
I WISH I WAS HAPPY.
YOUR WISHES ARE GRANTED!

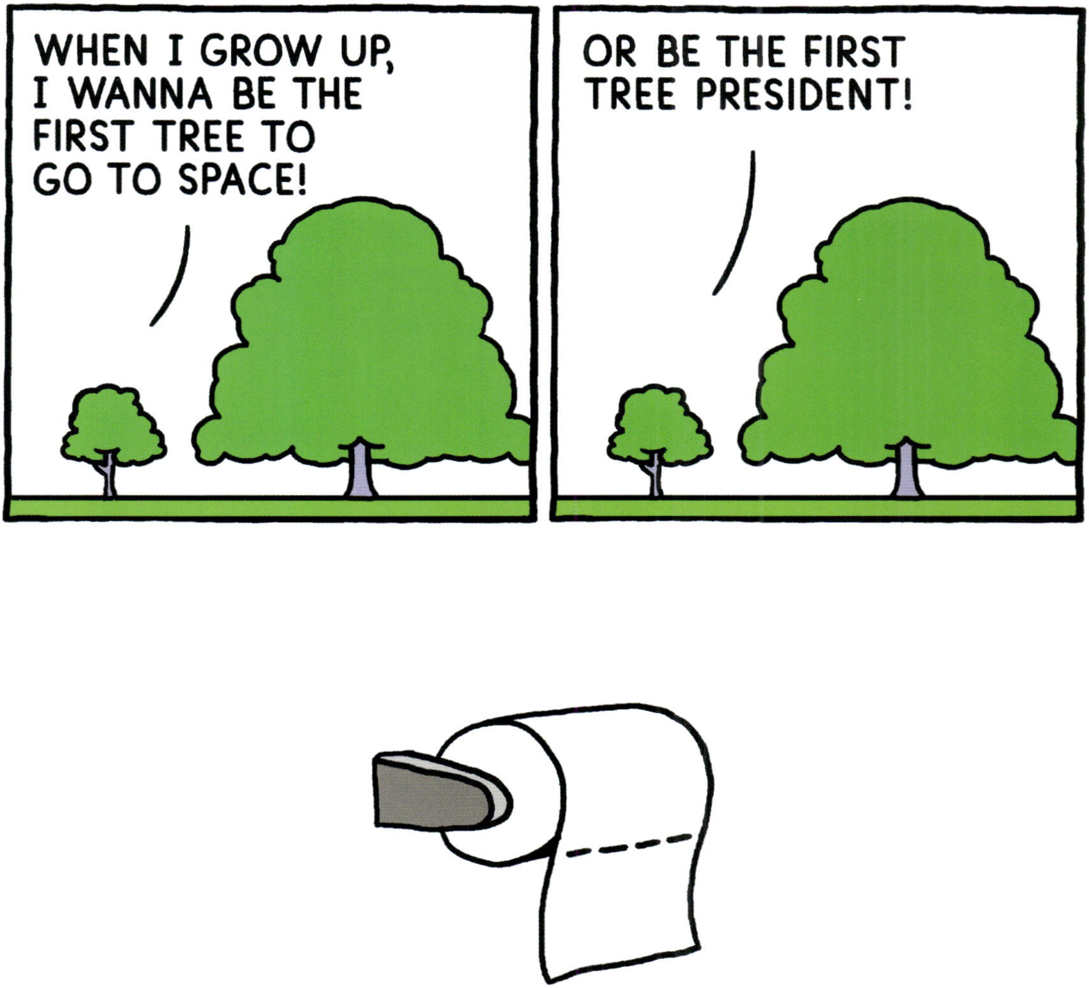
WHEN I GROW UP, I WANNA BE THE FIRST TREE TO GO TO SPACE!
OR BE THE FIRST TREE PRESIDENT!

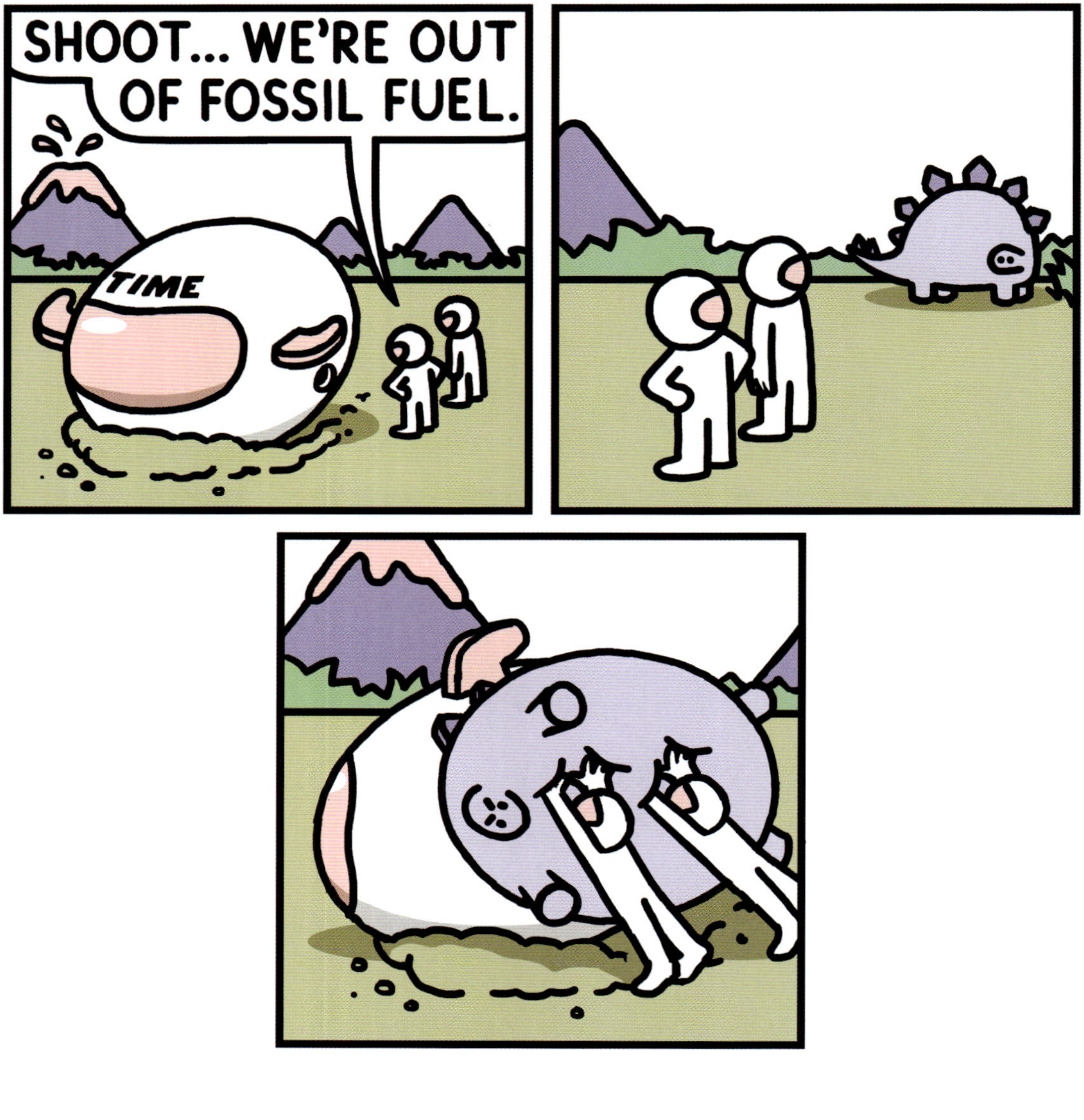
SHOOT... WE'RE OUT OF FOSSIL FUEL.
TIME

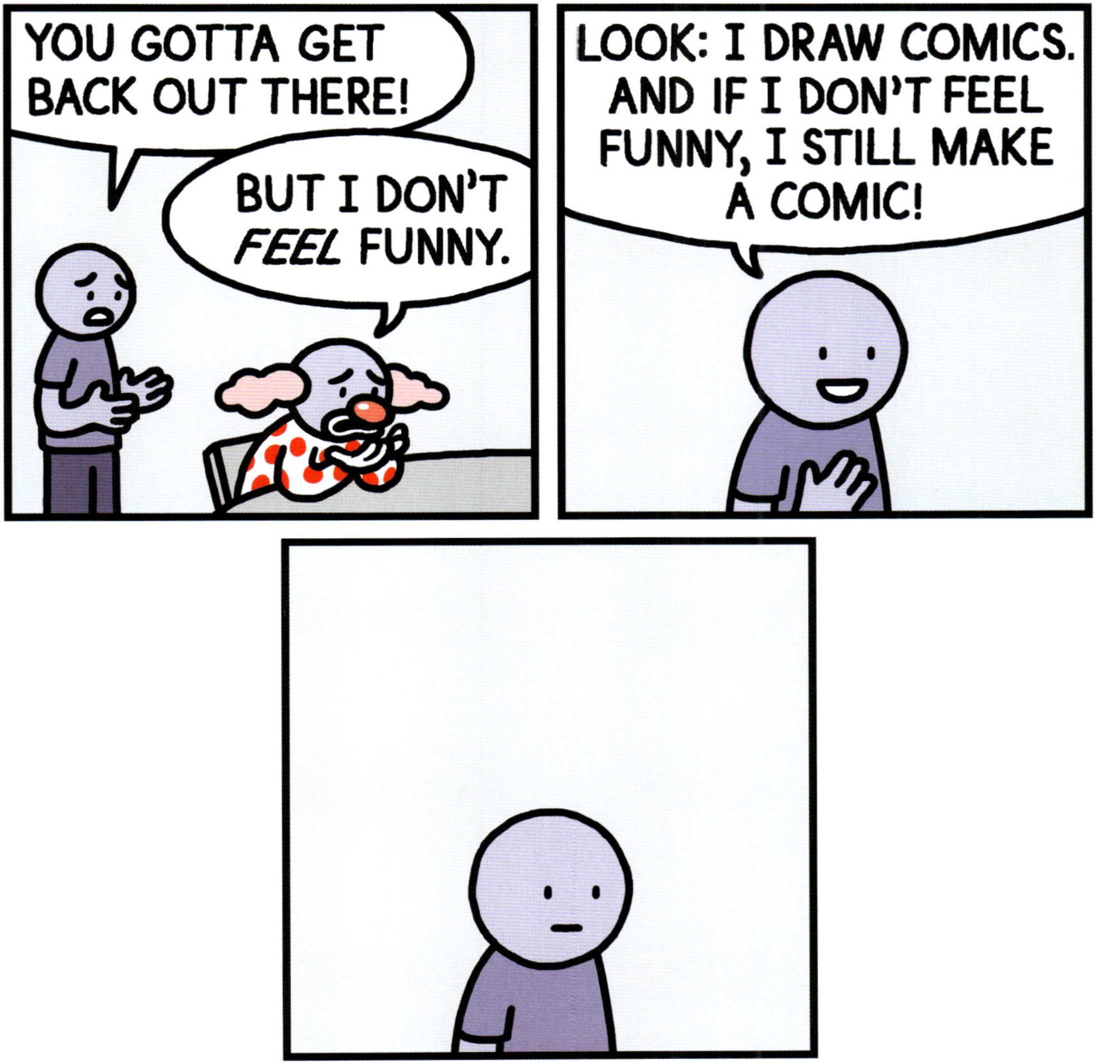
YOU GOTTA GET BACK OUT THERE!
BUT I DON'T *FEEL* FUNNY.
LOOK: I DRAW COMICS. AND IF I DON'T FEEL FUNNY, I STILL MAKE A COMIC!

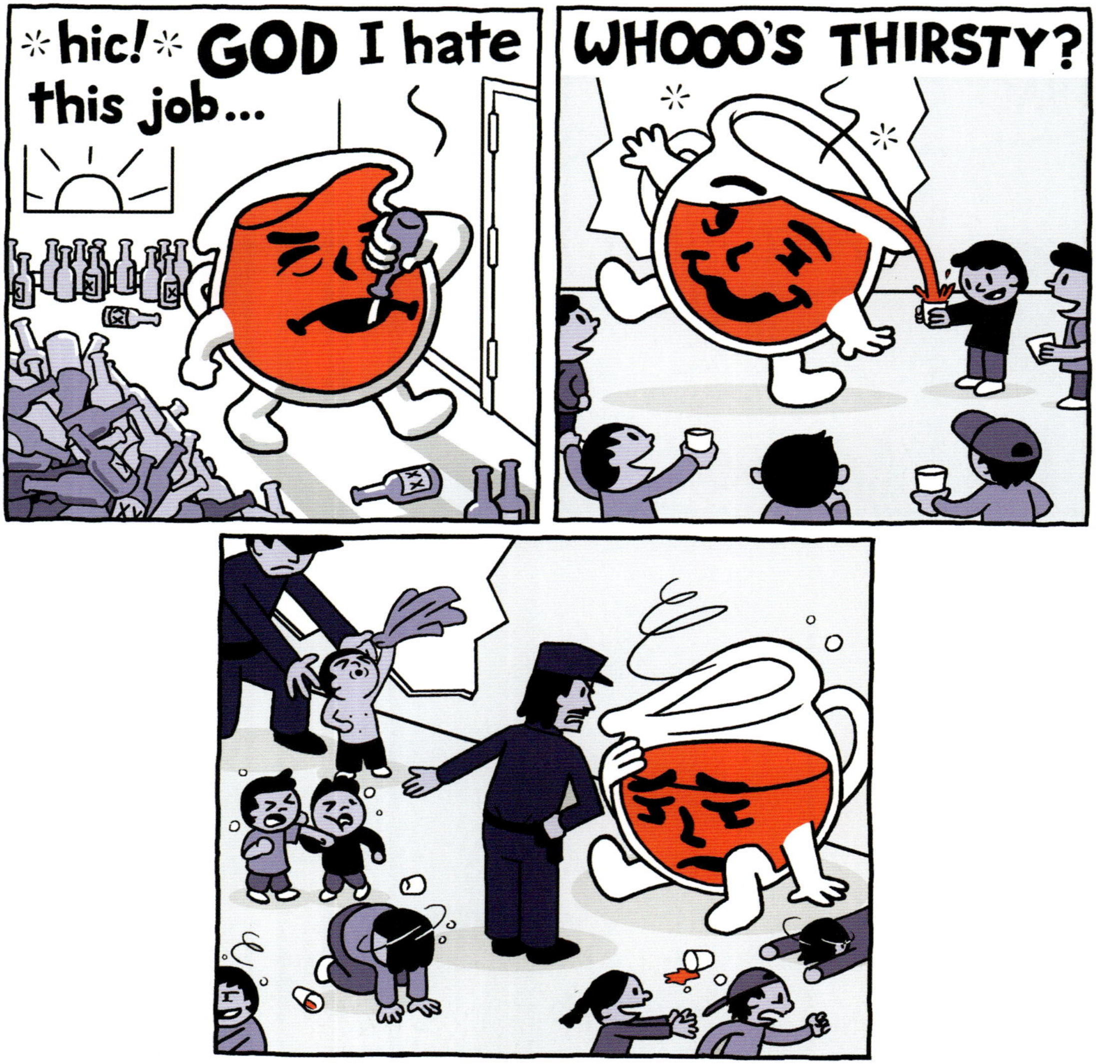
hic! GOD I hate this job...
WHOOO'S THIRSTY?

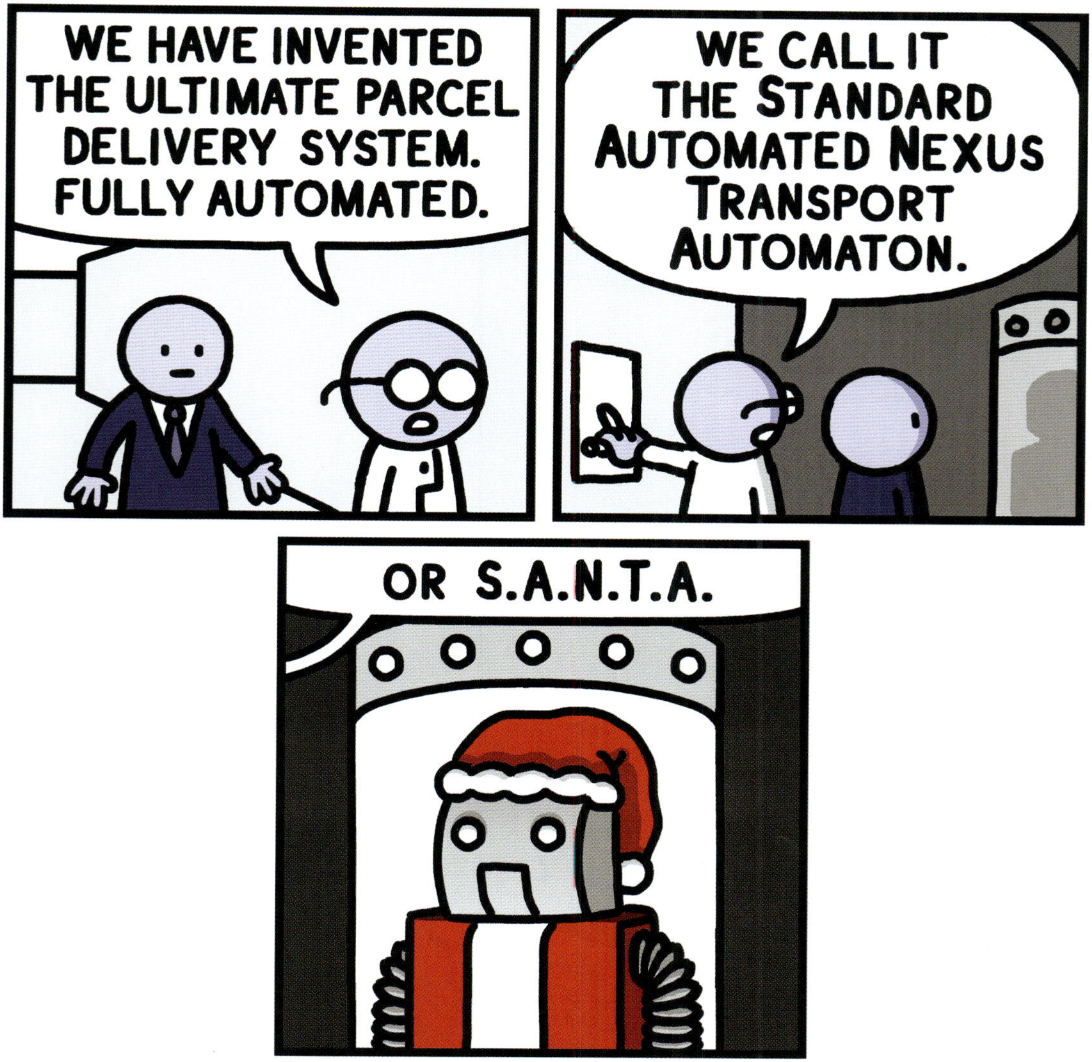
WE HAVE INVENTED THE ULTIMATE PARCEL DELIVERY SYSTEM. FULLY AUTOMATED.
WE CALL IT THE STANDARD AUTOMATED NEXUS TRANSPORT AUTOMATON.
OR S.A.N.T.A.

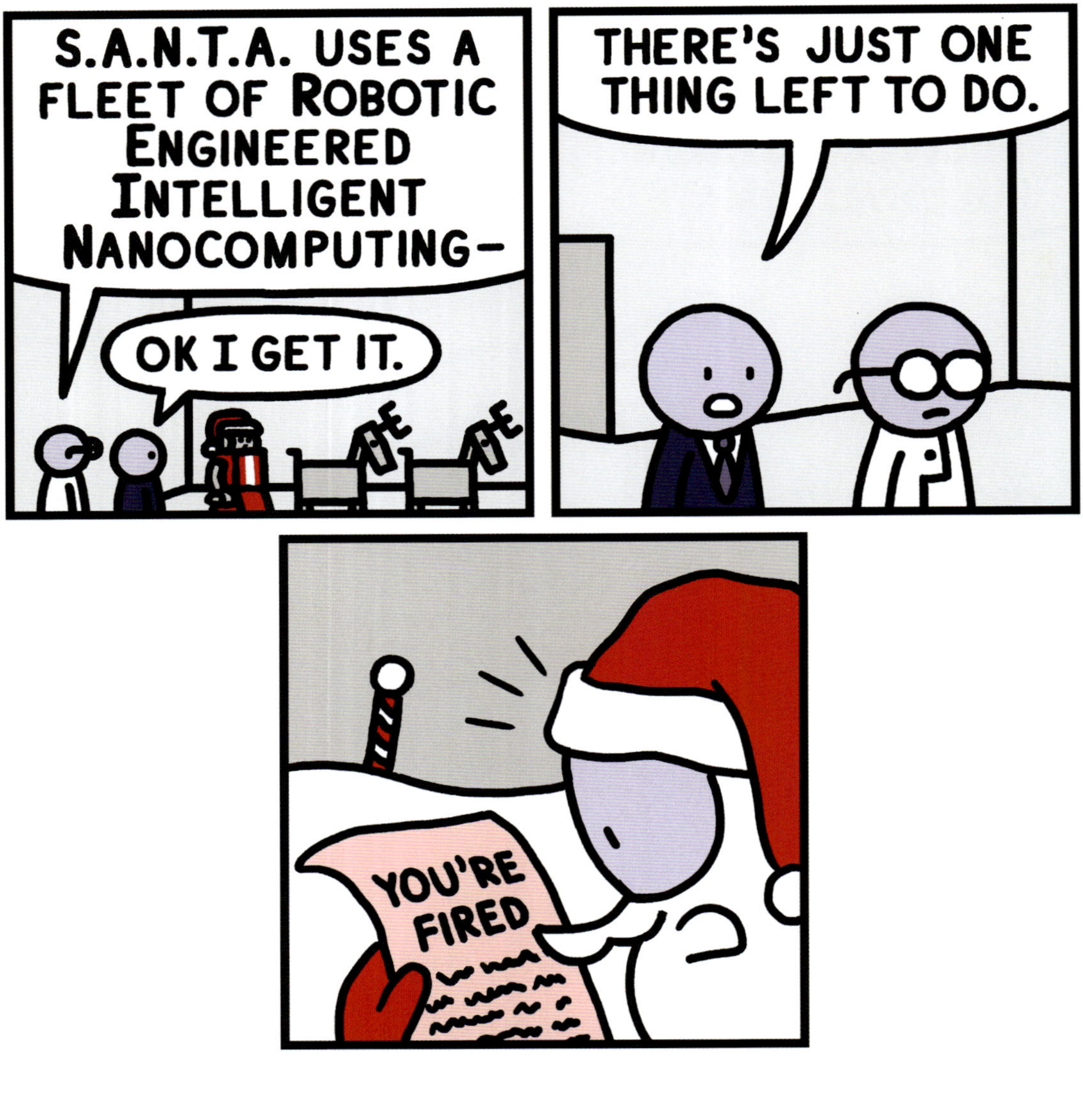
S.A.N.T.A. USES A FLEET OF ROBOTIC ENGINEERED INTELLIGENT NANOCOMPUTING–
OK I GET IT.
THERE'S JUST ONE THING LEFT TO DO.
YOU'RE FIRED

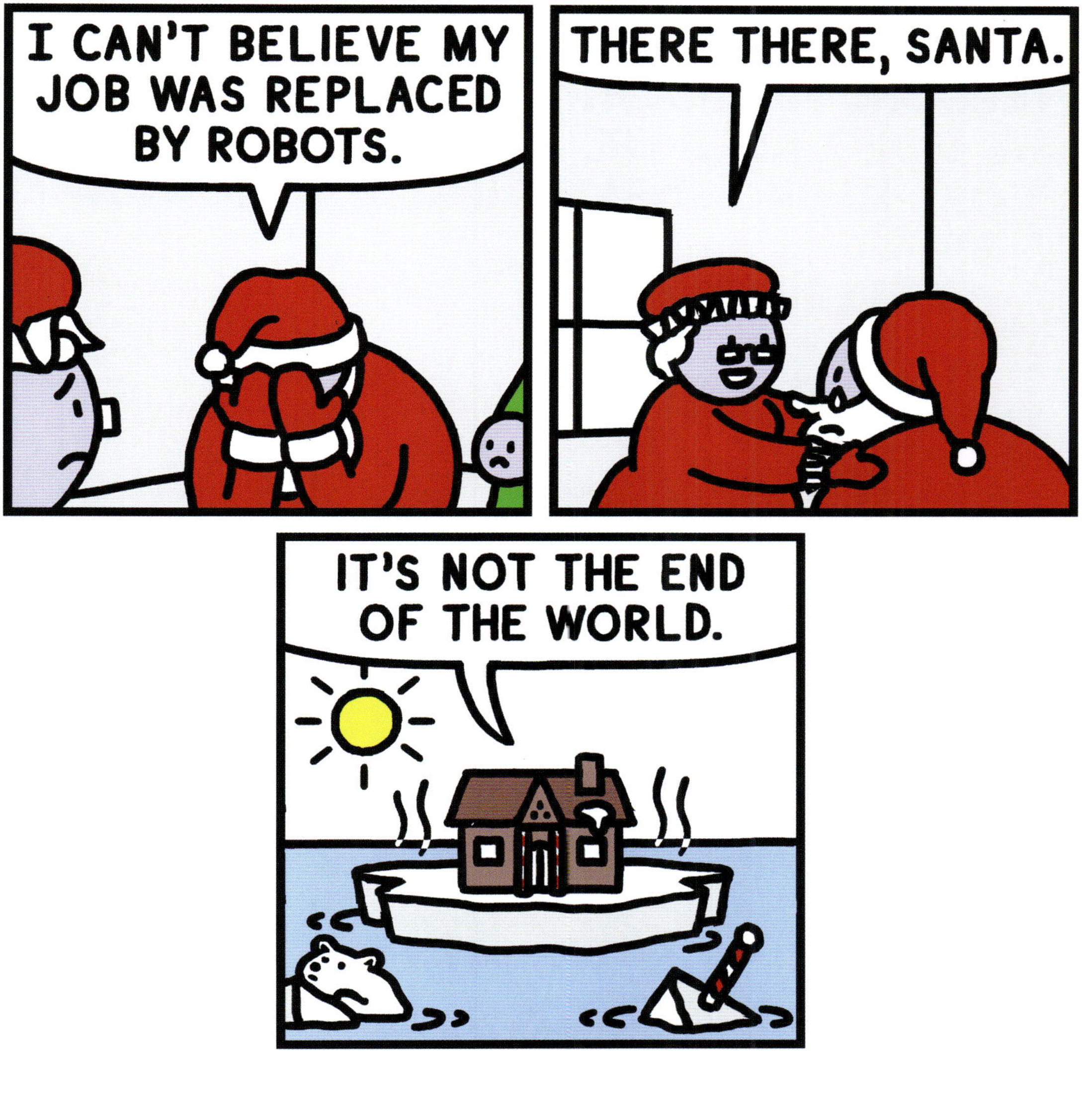
I CAN'T BELIEVE MY JOB WAS REPLACED BY ROBOTS.
THERE THERE, SANTA.
IT'S NOT THE END OF THE WORLD.

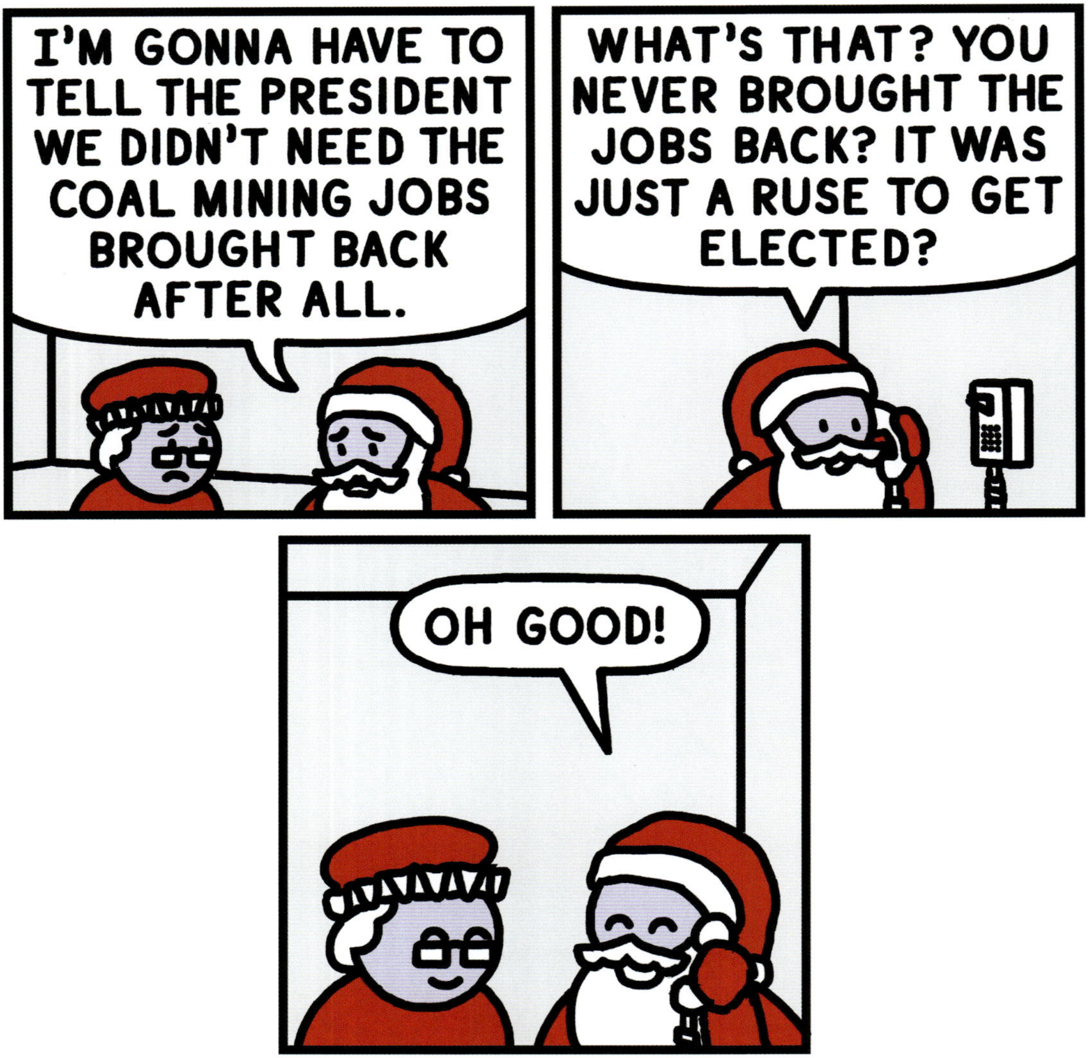
I'M GONNA HAVE TO TELL THE PRESIDENT WE DIDN'T NEED THE COAL MINING JOBS BROUGHT BACK AFTER ALL.
WHAT'S THAT? YOU NEVER BROUGHT THE JOBS BACK? IT WAS JUST A RUSE TO GET ELECTED?
OH GOOD!

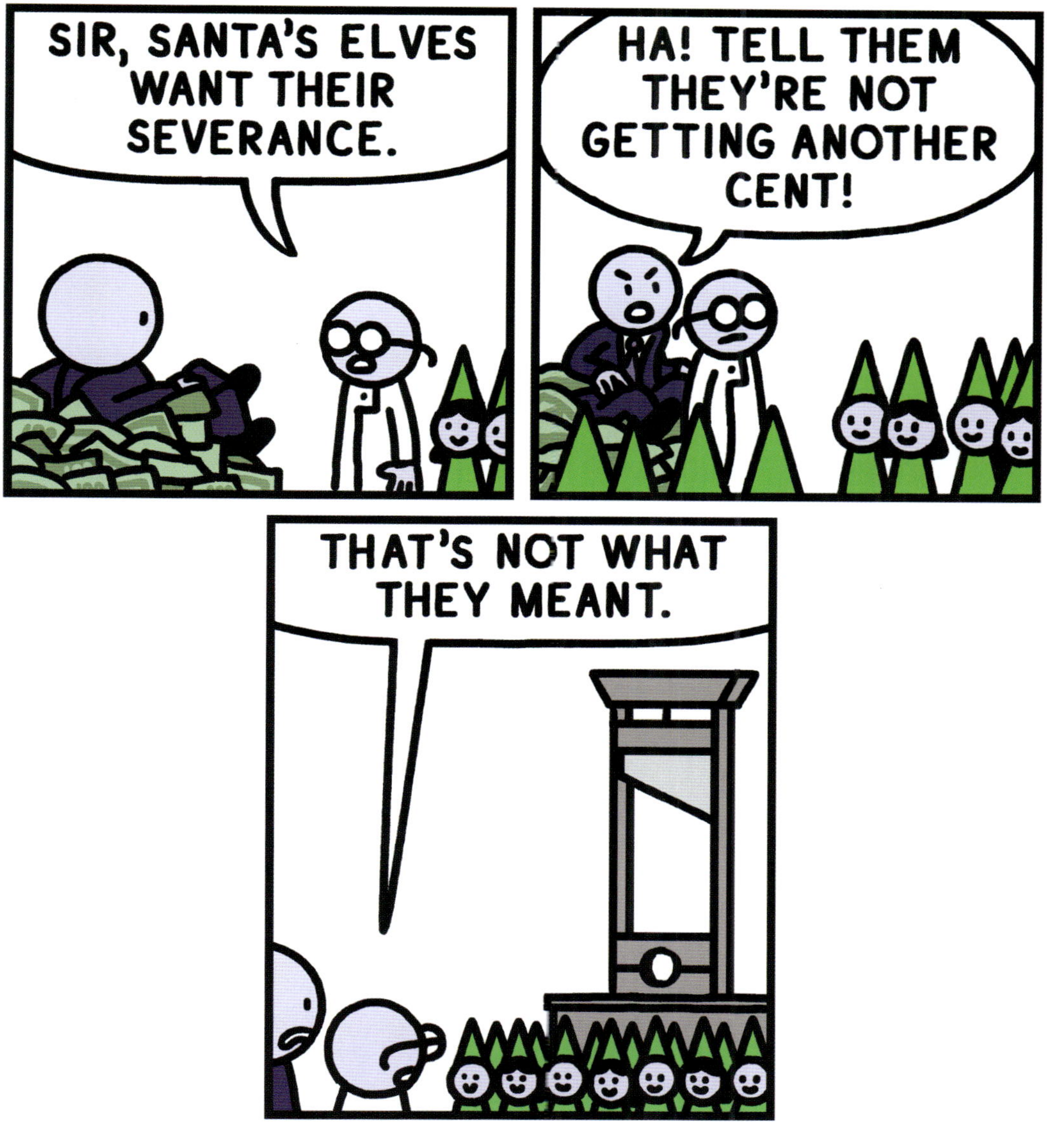
SIR, SANTA'S ELVES WANT THEIR SEVERANCE.
HA! TELL THEM THEY'RE NOT GETTING ANOTHER CENT!
THAT'S NOT WHAT THEY MEANT.

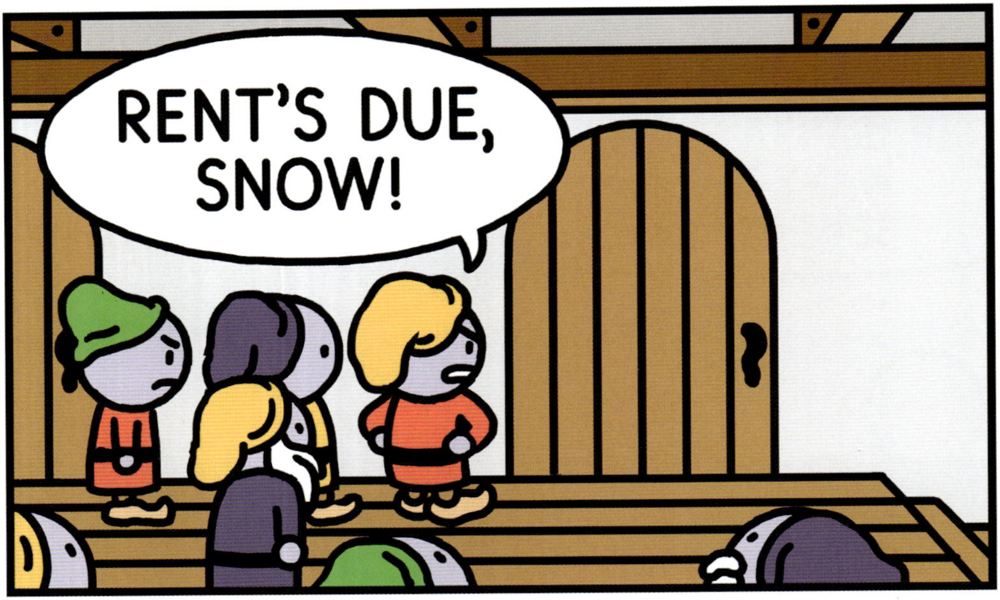
RENT'S DUE, SNOW!

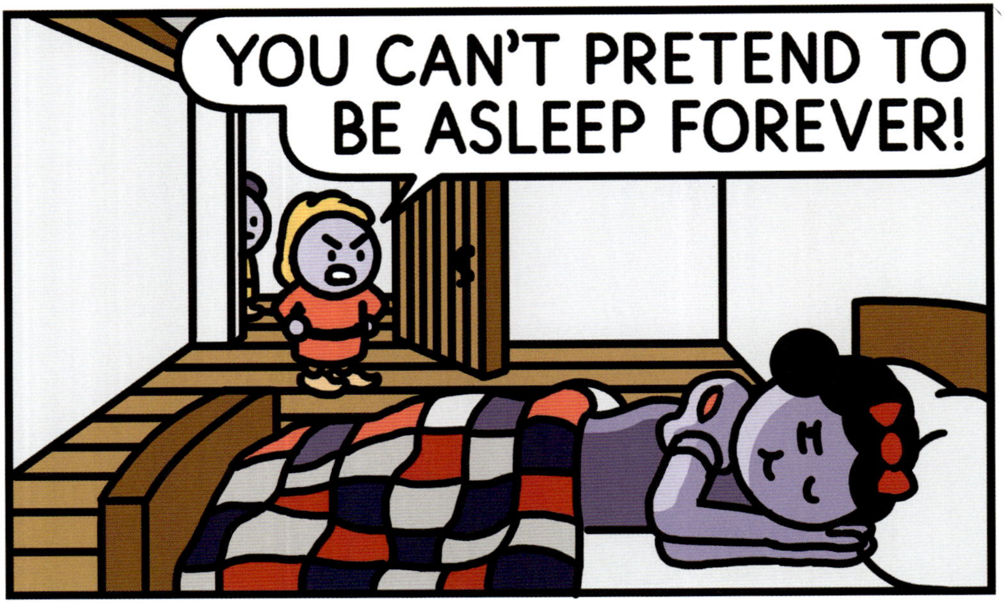
YOU CAN'T PRETEND TO BE ASLEEP FOREVER!

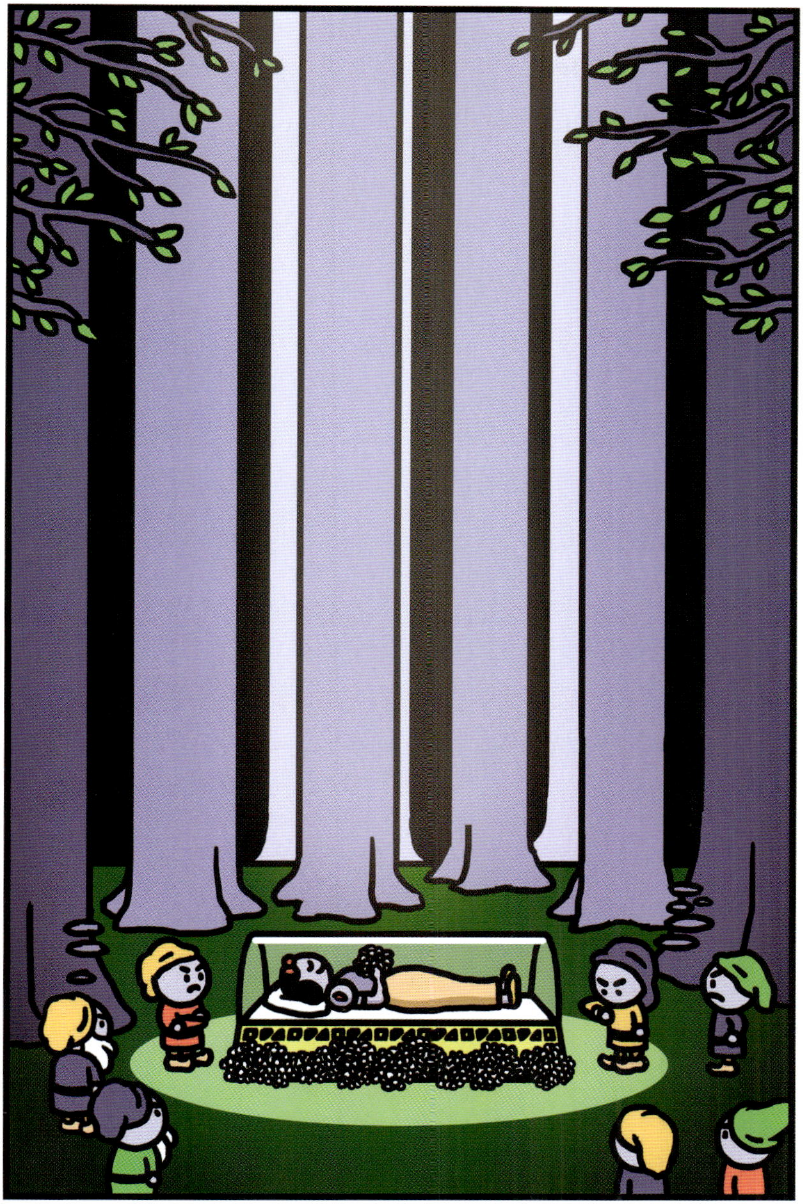

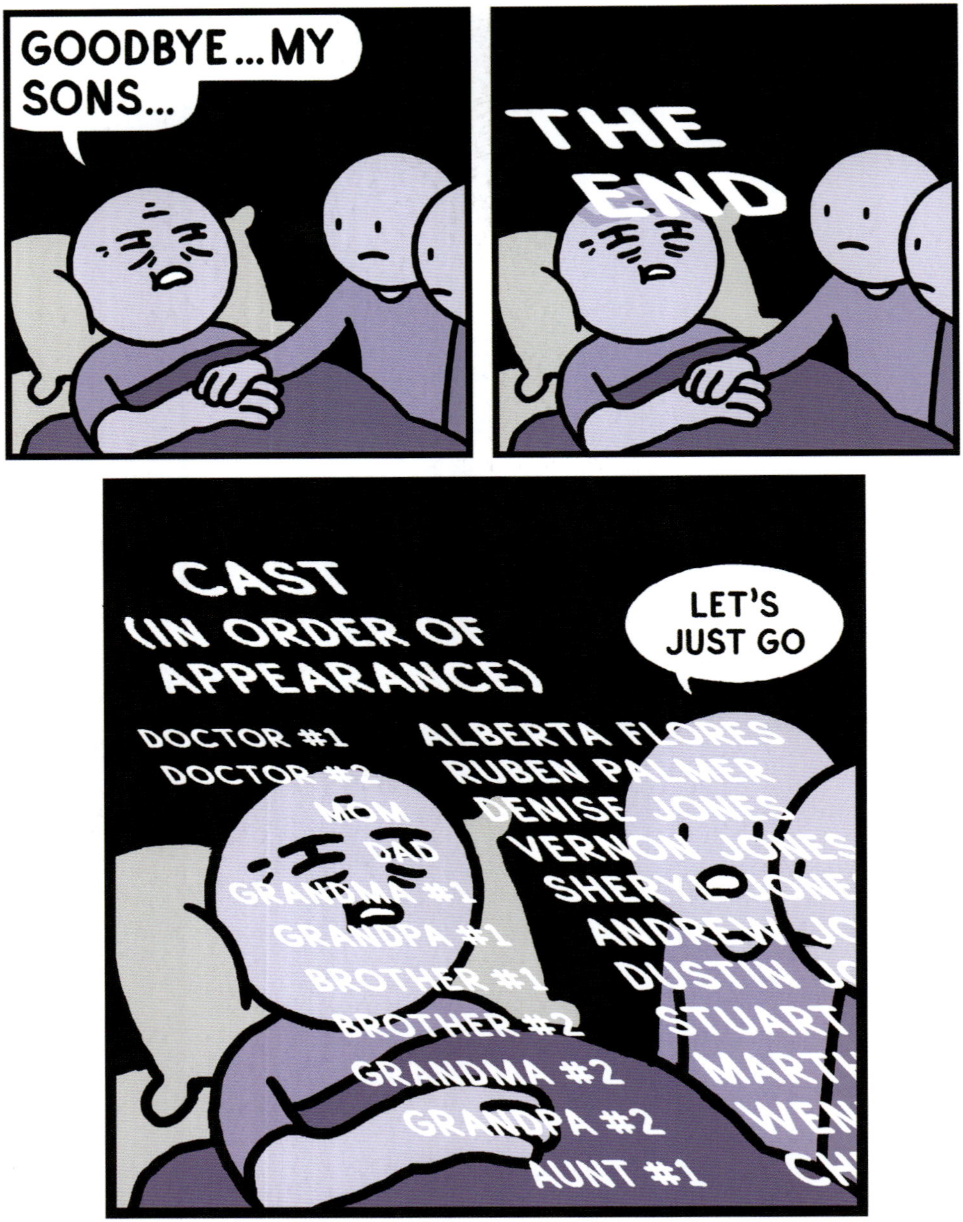
GOODBYE... MY SONS...
THE END
CAST
(IN ORDER OF APPEARANCE)
DOCTOR #1 ALBERTA FLORES
DOCTOR #2 RUBEN PALMER
MOM DENISE JONES
DAD VERNON JONES
GRANDMA #1
GRANDPA #1
BROTHER #1
BROTHER #2 STUART
GRANDMA #2
GRANDPA #2
AUNT #1
LET'S JUST GO